弘扬华夏经典历史文化精髓

中国成语故事

Chinese Idiom Stories

汉英对照 ①

张　羿◎编著

雅　雅◎译

天津出版传媒集团

天津科技翻译出版有限公司

图书在版编目（CIP）数据

中国成语故事.1：汉英对照 / 张羿编著；雅雅译.
天津：天津科技翻译出版有限公司，2025.5 － － ISBN
978-7-5433-4658-1

Ⅰ.H319.4

中国国家版本馆CIP数据核字第2025VV1468号

出　　版：天津科技翻译出版有限公司
出 版 人：方　艳
地　　址：天津市和平区西康路35号
邮政编码：300051
电　　话：022-87894896
传　　真：022-87893237
网　　址：www.tsttpc.com
印　　刷：运河（唐山）印务有限公司
发　　行：全国新华书店
版本记录：710mm × 1000mm　16开本　38印张　500千字
2025年5月第1版　2025年5月第1次印刷
定价：136.00元（全2册）

目录 CONTENTS

目录

CONTENTS

001

一丘之貉

Birds of a feather

出自 《汉书·杨恽传》。

释义 比喻彼此是一路货色，没有什么差别。

汉朝时有一个人叫杨恽，他的父亲当过丞相，母

Yang Yun lived in Han dynasty, whose father was once the prime minister and mother

亲是著名历史学家司马迁的女儿。他从小受到良好的教育，还没到二十岁就成了当时的名人。

杨恽为人正直，经常当面指出别人的缺点和错误，并敢于揭发贪赃枉法的行为。为此招致很多人的嫉恨。

一次，他看到一幅反映古代暴君夏桀、商纣的画，叹息道："皇上要是能看到此画，并从中吸取教训，那我们就可以避免亡国了。"皇帝听到这话，勃然大怒，认为杨恽是在讽刺自己，便命人把他带上大殿质问。杨恽说："我没有讽刺您的意思，只是希望您以史为鉴，不要重蹈覆辙。"皇帝摆摆手，说："看在你以前立过功的份上，这次就饶你一命，以后不许再胡言乱语了。"

was the daughter of Si-ma Qian, who was the famous historian. Yang Yun grew up with a good education and became famous when he was nearly 20 years old.

Yang Yun was too upright to always point out others' shortcomings and mistakes face to face, and he dared to disclose behaviors of corruptions and misuse of laws. Thus he was subjected to hate by many people.

Once he saw a painting reflecting the ancient tyrants Jie of Xia dynasty and Zhou of Shang dynasty and sighed out that we could avoid the state perish if the emperor could see this painting and learn lessons. The emperor believed Yang Yun is satirizing him and burst into anger when heard what he said, and Yang Yun was taken to the palace hall and questioned. Yang Yun said that I have no intention to satirize Your Majesty, I only hope Your Majesty can take history as mirror so that to avoid following the same old disastrous road. The emperor waved his hand and said, "For the sake of your contributions, I can spare your life this time. Don't balderdash nonsense anymore in the future!"

过了几年，匈奴王被手下人杀死。杨恽跟别人说："一个无道的君主不采纳忠言，最后都会落得这般下场。像秦二世信任奸臣，杀害忠良，结果亡了国。如果他能听进去忠臣的意见，恐怕秦朝到现在也不会灭亡。古今的事情，其实是一丘之貉，没什么区别啊！"

Several years later, the king of Xiongnu was killed by his subordinates. Yang Yun said to others, "A ruler of fatuity who doesn't accept the earnest advice will end this way. Such as Hu Hai, the second emperor of Qin dynasty, trusted the treacherous court officials and killed the faithful and upright, and the state perished. I'm afraid the Qin would not perish until now if he could accept the advice of upright court officials. No matter the ancient or the modern dynasties, all the principles are the birds of a feather without differences."

在当时的社会说这种话可是犯忌讳的。后来杨恽的仇家就把这事捅到了皇帝那里，杨恽因此被免了职。

In the ancient time what Yang Yun said was a taboo. The foes informed to the emperor against Yang Yun, and Yang Yun was dismissed therefore.

杨恽失去了官职，心中愤愤不平，有一次给朋友去信，流露出对朝廷的极度不满。后来被人告发，皇帝下令把他处死了。

Yang Yun lost his office and felt aggrieved. A letter he wrote to his friend revealed his extreme dissatisfaction to the current imperial court. Finally Yang Yun was informed against and condemned to forced suicide.

002

一叶障目

A leaf before the eyes

出自 《欧冠子·天则》。

释义 眼前被细小或局部现象所蒙蔽，而看不到事物的全貌。

从前，楚国有个书呆子，家里很穷。有一天，他看

Once upon a time, there was a poor bookworm in Chu State. One day, he read

到一本书上写着，如果得到螳螂捕蝉时用来遮身的那片叶子，就可以把自己的身体隐蔽起来，谁也看不见。于是他想，如果我能得到那片叶子，那该多好呀！我去偷东西别人也看不见了。打这以后，他就整天在树林里转来转去寻找叶子。有一天，他看到一只螳螂隐身在一片树叶下捕蝉,兴奋极了，猛地一下扑上去，摘下那片叶子。可是一不小心，叶子掉在了地上。地上全是落叶，到底哪一片才是能隐身的呢?

a book which says, you could hide yourself if you get the leaf which hiding the mantis when stalking the cicada. Thus he thought it would be great if he could get that leaf. Since then, he began to walk around in the woods to look for that leaf. Finally one day he saw a mantis stalking the cicada under a leaf, he was so excited and jumped over to get that leaf, but unfortunately that leaf dropped to the ground. The leaves were all over the ground, which one was that hiding leaf?

书呆子只好把落叶全都扫起来，带回了家。他把一片树叶挡在自己面前，问他的妻子说："你能看见我吗?"

The bookworm swept the leaves together and took them home. He asked his wife with one leaf before him, "can you see me?"

"能看见。"他妻子回答。

"Yes." His wife said.

"你能看见我吗?"他又举起一片树叶说。

"Can you see me?" He lifted another leaf and asked.

"能看见。"妻子耐心

"Yes." His wife said patiently.

地回答。

他一次次地询问，妻子一次次地回答。到后来他的妻子不耐烦了，随口答道："看不见了！"书呆子一听乐坏了。他拿着树叶来到街上，当着店主的面，随手取了店里的东西就走。店主把他抓住，送到了官府。

He asked his wife again and again, and his wife answered again and again. Finally his wife lost her patience and answered casually "I can't see you!" The bookworm was very excited to hear that. He came out with that leaf and conveniently took away the goods in a store, but the store owner caught him and sent him to the Yamen.

县官觉得很奇怪，居然有人敢在光天化日之下偷东西，便问他是怎么回事。书呆子就把事情的原委一一说了出来，县官听了，不由哈哈大笑，说道："你这真是一叶障目，不见其他啊！"把他放回了家。

The officer in Yamen was very curious that someone was dare to steal goods and asked the reason. After the bookworm explained the officer laugh hardly and said, "You are really hidden by a leaf completely!" Finally the officer released him.

003

一目十行

Read ten lines at a glance

出自 《梁书·简文帝纪》。

释义 读书时可以同时看十行。形容看书非常快。

南朝梁武帝非常爱好文学，他的三儿子萧纲从小聪明过人，四岁开始识字读

Emperor Liang Wu of Southern Dynasties was fascinated in literature. His third son Xiao Gang was much smarter than others when he

书，到六岁时就已经会写文章了。

有一次，梁武帝把萧纲叫来，要他作一篇文章，想考考他。萧纲毫不怯场，不慌不忙提笔就写。不一会儿，就写成了一篇声韵和谐、辞藻华丽的骈文。梁武帝一看，不由喜上眉梢："这孩子真是我们萧家的东阿王！"东阿王是指三国时的文学家曹植，以才思敏捷著称。

随着年龄的增长，萧纲读的书越来越多，阅读的能力也越来越强，他速度惊人，能够"十行俱下"，一次读懂十行的内容，而且过目不忘。

二十八岁那年，萧纲被立为太子。公元549年，萧纲继位，也就是梁简文帝。可惜的是，两年之后，他就被叛军用毒酒害死了。

不过，"一目十行"这个成语流传了下来。

was young, he learned and read at four years old, and write articles at six.

Once Emperor Wu of Liang called in Xiao Gang and required him to write an article. Xiao Gang doesn't flinch at all and leisurely began to write. A few moments later, a parallel prose with prosodic harmony and rhetorical flourishes came out. Emperor Wu of Liang checked and was immediately radiant with joy, he said, "This child is really King Dong'e of our Xiao family!" King Dong'e refers to Cao Zhi, the litterateur of Three Kingdoms Period, who is famous as sharp intellect.

As Xiao Gang grew older, he read more and more books, and his reading abilities became stronger and stronger with surprisingly quick speed. He could read ten lines at a glance, with an extraordinary retentive memory.

At 28 years old, Xiao Gang was established as Prince. In 459 AD, Xiao Gang succeeded to the throne as Emperor Jian Wen of Liang. Unfortunately, after two years, he died due to the poisonous wine by the rebel army.

Nevertheless, the idiom of "read ten lines at a glance" has come down.

004

一字千金

A single word is worth a thousand pieces of gold

出自 《史记·吕不韦列传》。

释义 诗文精妙，价值极高。

战国末期，商人吕不韦通过帮助秦国公子异人

In the late of Warring States Period, the businessman Lu Buwei was established as the

（即秦庄襄王）当上秦王，而被封为丞相。吕不韦效仿当时其他各国的做法，广招文人学士，给予他们优厚的待遇，门下的食客多达三千人。吕不韦为了提高自己的声望，决定编写一本书，于是，他就命令门下这些文人，每个人都把自己的所见所闻和感想写出来。

prime minister after he supported Yi Ren, the prince of Qin State to become the emperor of Qin State. Following the examples of other states, Lu Buwei widely recruited scholars and men of letters with generous treatment, and its size amounts to 3000. In order to enhance his prestige, he decided to write a book, so he called upon these scholars and men of letters to write out their knowledge and thoughts.

等到大家的文章交上来后，五花八门，上到天文地理，下到风土人情，写什么的都有。吕不韦又挑选了几位写作高手，对这些文章进行筛选、归类，综合在一起成书，取名叫《吕氏春秋》。

These articles are of a wide variety, covering astronomy and geography, local customs and practices, and all sorts of other knowledge. Lu Buwei selected several competent writers to filtrate and classify for a comprehensive book, called as *Lu's Spring and Autumn Annals*.

为了慎重起见，吕不韦又让人修改了好几遍，直到确实感到满意为止。然后，吕不韦请人把整本书抄写下来，悬挂在咸阳的城门口，声称如果有谁能改动一字就赏给千金。消息传开后，人们蜂拥前去，最终却没有一

With an abundance of caution, Lu Buwei made this book several times of revisions until he was completely satisfied, then he also made this book copied and suspended on the gateway, and announced that one thousand pieces of gold would be granted for any reasonable revision on a single word. When the news got around, people throng to the gateway, but finally no one

个人能对书上的文字进行丝毫改动。

could revise any words on this book.

《吕氏春秋》一书因此名闻天下，而“一字千金”这个成语也一直流传至今。

Therefore, *Lu's Spring and Autumn Annals* became world-famous, and the idiom of "a single word is worth a thousand pieces of gold" has also come down.

005

一字之师

The teacher who corrects one word

出自 郑谷改僧齐己《早梅》诗。

释义 有些诗文，经人改换一个字后更为完美，往往称改字的人为“一字之师”。

唐朝的时候，有个法名叫齐己的和尚，学识渊

In Tang dynasty, there is a monk whose religious name is Qi Ji. He's a person with profound

博，能诗善文，自号衡岳沙门。齐己虽然才华横溢，但他明白读万卷书不如行万里路，于是他边四处游走边吟诗，一路下来，他的行囊里的纸簿上写了八百多首诗。

and immense learning, and good at poems and articles, self-assumed as Sramana of Hengyue. Although as a talented person, Qi Ji knew that one could learn more by traveling a thousand miles than reading a thousand books, thus he kept composing poems during his traveling, and finally unexpectedly he saved over 800 poems.

当时有个著名的诗人郑谷，经常以文会友，齐己便带着自己写的这些诗，去请郑谷加以指点。其中，有一首齐己很是得意的诗作《早梅》，这样写道：

万木冻欲折，孤根暖独回。
前村深雪里，昨夜数枝开。
风递幽香出，禽窥素艳来。
明年如应律，先发映春台。

There was a famous poet called Zheng Gu, who made lots of friends via literature. Qi Ji went to meet Zheng Gu for directions on his own poems. One poem which Qi Ji was quite proud of, called *Early Plum Blossom*, which says: “The other trees are frozen and easy to be broken, only the root of plum tree can hold the heat underground. In the deep snow in the village, only some branches of plum blossom open. Its fragrance flows with the wind and attracts the bird to see the amazing plum blossom. If the plum blossom can open at the same time next year, we hope it can open in the same place”.

郑谷读完这首诗后，沉思了好大一会儿，然后轻声问齐己：“早梅之‘早’，早在何处？”

Zheng Gu silenced a while after read this poem, and then he asked Qi Ji softly, “The early plum, why it is early?”

齐己回答说：“仅开

Qi Ji answered that only some branches of

‘数枝’。”

郑谷笑了，说道：“‘数枝’并不足以点明‘早’，改成‘一枝’更佳。”

齐已听罢郑谷的这一说法，豁然开朗，连声感谢道：“先生真是我的一字之师啊！”

由此，“一字之师”的佳话，连同齐已和他的“前村深雪里，昨夜一枝开”之诗广为人知，他也因此被后人誉为“晚唐三大诗僧”之一。

plum blossom open.

Zheng Gu smiled and said, “some branches can’t convey the idea of early, it is better to change into one branch.”

After heard what Zheng Gu said, Qi Ji was suddenly enlightened and said with repeated thanks, “You minister is really my teacher of one word!”

Thus, the teacher of one word, along with Qi Ji’s poem “In the deep snow in the village, only one branch of plum blossom open” became popular, and Qi Ji was honored as one of the Three Great Monk Poets in the late Tang dynasty.

006

一衣带水

By a narrow strip of water

出自 《南史·陈后主纪》。

释义 一水之隔，往来方便。

南北朝后期，当时的中国以长江为界分成了两半，长江以北的叫北周，长江以

In the late Northern and Southern Dynasties, the former China was split into two parts by the Changjiang River, with north of

南的叫陈国。后来，北周的丞相杨坚废掉了年仅八岁的周静帝，自己当上了皇帝，建立隋朝。他励精图治，国力一天天地壮大。可陈国的陈后主却沉湎于酒色，不理政事。面对江北虎视眈眈的隋朝，陈后主却并不慌张，因为他觉得自己倚靠浩浩长江作为天险，易守难攻，隋军根本打不过来。

Changjiang called the Northern Zhou and south called Chen Kingdom. Later, YangJian, the prime minister of the Northern Zhou Dynasty, deposed the Emperor Jing of Zhou who was only 8 years old and became emperor himself, so Sui Dynasty was established. He aroused all his efforts to make Sui prosperous. But Emperor Chen Shubao indulged himself in wine and lewdness, and ignored the state affairs. Emperor Chen Shubao was very calm in face of hostile and covetous enemies from North of the Changjiang River, because he thought he bordered on the Changjiang River as natural barrier, which was easy to hold and hard to attack, there was no way for Sui army to attack.

隋文帝早就有心消灭陈国了，他对大臣高颎叹息道：“我身为百姓的父母，却眼睁睁地看着江南的百姓在受苦，我哪里能因为隔了一条衣带那么宽的江水就不去拯救他们呢？”于是，经过七年的精心准备，公元588年，隋文帝杨坚派遣五十万大军，命儿子晋王杨

Emperor Wen of Sui Dynasty premeditated to destroy Chen Kingdom, he sighed to the minister Gao Jiong, “I was like the parents of the common people, how can I give up saving them due to a narrow strip of water which is like a piece of band?” Thus after seven years of meticulous preparation, Emperor Wen of Sui Dynasty dispatched half a million troops to cross the Changjiang River, with his son Yang Guang, the Prince of Jin as commander in

广做统帅，渡过长江，向陈国的都城建康发动猛烈的进攻，很快攻下建康，俘虏了陈后主，灭掉陈国。

现在，人们常用“一衣带水”来比喻两地之间虽有江海阻隔，但在想交往的人心里，它却好像只有一条衣带那样窄。

chief, and made violent attacks on Jiankang, the capital of Chen Kinddom. Finally, he quickly took over the capital and captured the Emperor Chen Shubao, the Chen Dynasty perished.

Nowadays, people always use the idiom of “by a narrow strip of water” as a metaphor, i.e. although there is rivers and seas between, it will only be regarded as a narrow strip of clothes band by people who have strong wish to interact.

007

一身是胆

The whole body is full of courage

出自 《三国志·蜀书·赵云传》注引《云别传》。

释义 形容一个人的胆量大，无所畏惧。

赵云是三国时期蜀国的一员著名战将，名列“五虎上将”之一。

Zhao Yun was a famous warrior of Shu Kingdom during the period of Three Kingdoms, as one of the Five Tiger-like Generals.

当时，蜀国老将黄忠在定军山一战中，杀了曹操部下名将夏侯渊。曹操一气之下，派兵与刘备争抢汉中。曹军在北山下运粮，有几千万袋。黄忠想把这些粮食抢来，于是赵云让他带兵前去。

At that time, an old warrior of Shu Kingdom Huang Zhong killed Xia-hou Yuan, who was a famous general of Cao Cao's subordinates. In a fit of pique, Cao Cao dispatched to battle for Hanzhong against Liu Bei. Cao's troop was transporting tens of millions of packets of rice at the North Mount, and Huang Zhong intended to snatch, so Zhao Yun agreed him to go with troops.

黄忠出发很久，都没返回营地，赵云就带着几十个骑兵出去接应黄忠，遭到了曹军先头部队的袭击，很快，曹军的大部队也赶了过来。赵云奋勇杀敌，冲出阵来，回到了自己营寨。而此时他手下的一名将领受了伤，被困在曹军中间，赵云立刻又回马闯入敌营把他救了出来。曹军随后一直追赶到蜀军营前。

Huang Zhong did not come back to campsite after a long time, so Zhao Yun lead troops to reinforce him, but was attacked by Cao's spearhead, and soon Cao's main troops also arrived. Zhao Yun was so strong against the enemies that he rushed out of the battle formation and come back to his campsite. But one of his generals was hurt and trapped in Cao's troops, so Zhao Yun immediately went back and saved him, and Cao's troops had been following Zhao Yun until the campsite of Shu troops.

赵云回到营内以后，就命令大开营门，收起旗帜，停下战鼓。曹军怀疑赵云营内有伏兵，就向后退去。这时赵云又突然命令大声擂

After back to the campsite, Zhao Yun ordered to widely open the gate and to lower the banners and muffle the drums. Cao's troops doubt that there would be ambush and withdrew. Suddenly Zhao Yun ordered to loudly

鼓，并用箭射杀曹军，曹军害怕，相互践踏，掉入汉水中被淹死的不计其数。

beat the drums and shoot arrows to Cao's troops, Cao's troops were scared to trample each other, and countless people drowned in Han River.

第二天，刘备到赵云营地察看昨天的浴血战场，感叹说："子龙一身是胆啊！"从此蜀军中都称呼赵云为"虎威将军"，而"一身是胆"这个成语，也一直流传到今天。

The next day, Liu Bei inspected the bloodshed battlefield in Zhao Yun's campsite, and sighed, "Zilong is really full of courage!" Hence Shu troops called Zhao Yun as "Tiger-like General", and the idiom of "the whole body is full of courage" had been passed down today.

008

一鸣惊人

Amaze the people with a single brilliant feat

出自 《史记·楚世家》。

释义 平时默默无闻，一旦施展才华，就能做出惊人的业绩。

春秋时期，先后有五个国家称霸中原，他们的国君齐桓公、宋襄公、晋文公、

In the Spring and Autumn Period, five countries successively dominated the central plain, including Duke Huan of Qi, Duke Xiang of Song, Duke Wen

秦穆公和楚庄王，被合称为“春秋五霸”。“一鸣惊人”这个成语故事，就是从其中的楚庄王来的。

of Jin, Duke Mu of Qin and King Zhuang of Chu, who were generally called as “Five Hegemons”. The idiom of amazing the people with a single brilliant feat came down from King Zhuang of Chu.

楚庄王刚当上国君时，另一个大国晋国趁机把几个一向归附楚国的国家又拉了过去，订立盟约。楚国的大臣们很不服气，都向楚庄王建议出兵伐晋。可是楚庄王谁的话也不听，白天打猎，晚上喝酒听音乐，国家大事全不放在心上，而且，他还下了一道命令：谁要是敢再劝谏，就判谁的死罪。

When King Zhuang of Chu became the king initially, another big country Jin took the advantage of this chance and roped in several countries which were always in allegiance with Chu and planned to make a league. The Chu ministers were unconvinced and suggested sending armed forces to suppress Jin. But King Zhuang of Chu didn’t take the advices and indulged in hunting daytime, drinking and enjoying music at night, and put the state affairs aside. Moreover, he ordained that the person who remonstrates will be condemned to die.

三年之后，有个名叫伍举的大臣实在看不过去，决心去见楚庄王。楚庄王正在那里寻欢作乐，见到伍举就问他：“你来干什么？”

Three years later, a minister called Wu Ju couldn’t bear anymore and determined to meet the king. King Zhuang of Chu was indulging in merry-making and asked when he saw Wu Ju, “What are you doing here?”

伍举说：“有人让我猜个谜，我猜不着。大王是个聪明人，想请您猜猜。”

Wu Ju said, “A person gives me a riddle but I cannot guess out, since You King is wise, I’m here to ask for your help.”

楚庄王一听很好奇，就

King Zhuang of Chu was curious and

笑着说："你说出来听听。"

伍举说："在楚国的山上，有一只大鸟，身披五彩羽衣，样子很神气。可是一停三年，不飞也不叫，这是什么鸟？"

楚庄王心里清楚他的用意，便说道："这可不是普通的鸟。这种鸟不飞则已，一飞将要冲天；不鸣则已，一鸣将要惊人。你去吧，我已经明白了。"

打这以后，楚庄王一改往日作风，开始励精图治，操练兵马，把晋国打得大败。楚庄王终于一鸣惊人，成了当时的诸侯国霸主。

smiled to say, "Tell me about it."

Wu Ju said, "There is a huge bird dressed in colorful feather coat, with gorgeous looking. But it keeps still for three years without flying and blaring, what type of bird is it?"

King Zhuang of Chu understood Wu's intention and said, "It is not a plain bird; it keeps still ordinarily but will soar up into the sky once it flies, and it keeps silence ordinarily but will amaze the people once it blares. I understand what you mean, you can go now."

From then on, King Zhuang of Chu changed his tune and began to arouse his efforts to make the country prosperous and drill the troops, and utterly defeated Jin. King Zhuang of Chu finally amazed the world with his brilliant feat and became the current powerful chief of the vassal states.

009

一窍不通

Be utterly ignorant of something

出自 《吕氏春秋·过理》。

释义 人有七窍（眼二、耳二、鼻孔二、口），却没有一窍是贯通的。比喻一点儿也不懂。

商纣王是历史上有名的暴君，他在位后期，非常

King Zhou of Shang dynasty is a notorious tyrant in history. During his reign in the

宠爱妃子妲己，一天到晚跟妲己饮酒作乐，根本不管国家大事，更不管老百姓生活好坏，而且他还听信妲己的话，杀了很多忠臣和无辜的百姓。

latter period, he extremely made a pet of his concubine Su Daji, and had been drinking and making merry all day long, putting aside the state affairs, letting alone the living conditions of the people. He was so bewitched by Su Daji that he killed many loyal officials and innocent civilians.

纣王的叔父比干是个大贤臣，他对纣王的所作所为实在看不下去了，有一天，就很生气地劝纣王说："身为一国之君，你不能一直沉迷在酒色里面，乱杀忠臣和无辜百姓，你应该振作起来，替国家和老百姓做点有用的事情呀！"

The uncle of King Zhou, Bi Gan, who was a great loyal minister. He couldn't bear anymore and one day he said to King Zhou angrily, "As a monarch, you shouldn't indulge yourself in debauchery and casually kill loyal ministers and civilians. You should cheer up and do something useful to the country and civilians!"

比干一连几天极力劝谏纣王，引起了纣王的极大不满，再加上妲己在一旁煽风点火，纣王更是怒火中烧，说："我早就听说圣人的心有七窍，我要把他杀了，取出心来看个究竟！"于是，纣王果真杀了比干，并挖出了他的心。

For days afterward Bi Gan extremely remonstrated and made King Zhou greatly dissatisfied. King Zhou burst into great anger due to Su Daji who had been stirring up troubles and said, "It is early heard that there are seven apertures in a saint's heant, I want to kill him and have a look at his heart!" Hence he killed Bi Gan to dig out his heart.

孔子说起这件事，感叹道："纣王心窍不通，如果通了一窍，那么比干就不会被杀害了！"后来，人们就从这句话中引申出了成语：一窍不通。

When Confucius mentioned this story, he said, "The apertures of King Zhou' heart are blocked, if one aperture is cut-through, then Bi Gan will not be killed!" Afterwards, the idiom of "be utterly ignorant of something" was derived from this sentence.

010

一诺千金

A promise is worth a thousand bars of gold

出自 《史记·季布栾布列传》。

释义 一句许诺就价值千金。比喻说话讲信用。

秦朝末年，楚国有一个叫季布的人，为人侠义，非常讲信用，只要是他答应过

At the end of Qin Dynasty, there was a person called Ji Bu, who was chivalrous and trustworthy. As long as he promised,

的事情，无论有多大困难，都会设法办到。因此受到大家的尊敬。

he will manage to accomplish, regardless of big difficulties, thus he was respected by everybody.

楚汉相争时，季布在项羽的军队中当将领，多次献计打败刘邦。所以当刘邦做了皇帝以后，一想起这事，就愤恨不已，下令通缉季布：凡是抓到季布的人，赏黄金一千两，藏匿他的人则灭门三族。

In the struggle between Chu and Han, Ji Bu was a general in Xiang Yu's troops and always offered advice to defeat Liu Bang. After Liu Bang became emperor, at thought of this, he extremely resented Ji Bu and ordered to catch him. The order says anyone who catches Ji Bu will be rewarded a thousand bars of gold, and anyone who hides him will be condemned to extermination of paternal family, maternal family and subfamily.

季布把头发剃光，化装成奴隶，到鲁国人朱家那里当雇工。朱家明知他是季布，仍然收留了他，而且还到洛阳去找刘邦的老朋友汝阴侯夏侯婴说情。刘邦于是撤销了对季布的通缉令，还封季布做了官。

Ji Bu Shaved his head bald and disguised as a slave, and worked as servant in Zhu Jia of Lu Kingdom. Although fully aware that he was Ji Bu, Zhu Jia still took him in, and went to Luoyang to find Xia-hou Ying for interceding, who was the old friend of Liu Bang. Then Liu Bang withdrew the arrest warrant and offered official posts to Ji Bu.

有一个季布的同乡曹邱生，听说季布做了大官，就马上去见季布。季布不喜欢他的为人，本来不想理会他，可是

One hometown fellow called Cao Qiusheng heard this and immediately went to meet Ji Bu. Ji Bu disliked his moral quality and intended to ignore, but Cao Qiusheng showed a lot of

曹邱生一来，对着季布又是行礼，又是作揖，说："您可能听说过，楚地到处流传着'得黄金千两，不如得季布一诺'这样的话，这个好名声其实是我到处为您宣扬的，可是您为什么不愿见我呢？"季布听后，非常高兴，马上把他作为贵客来招待。

courtesy and made bows, and said, "You may heard a popular saying Ji Bu is worth much more than a thousand bars of gold, actually it is me who propagate around for you, but why you are unwilling to meet me?" Ji Bu was very pleased and treated him as honored guest.

后来，人们就用"一诺千金"来形容一个人很讲信用，说话算数。

Afterwards, people began to use "a promise is worth a thousand bars of gold" to describe a person is trustworthy and keeps his words.

011

一鼓作气

Do something at one fling

出自 《左传·庄公十年》。

释义 要趁着劲头十足时全力以赴，一下子把事情完成。

“一鼓作气”这个成语，来源于春秋时期一个著名的故事：曹刿论战。

The idiom of doing something at one fling derives from a famous story called Cao Gui's debate on battle in the Spring and Autumn Period.

公元前684年，齐国军队攻打鲁国。曹刿拜见鲁庄公，请求跟着一同作战。到了那一天，鲁庄公和曹刿坐着同一辆战车，在长勺和齐军相遇。鲁庄公想要下令击鼓进军。曹刿说："现在不行。"等到齐军三次击鼓之后，曹刿说："可以击鼓进军了。"齐军大败。鲁庄公又要下令追赶齐军。曹刿说："还不行。"说完就下了战车，查看齐军车轮碾出的痕迹，又登上战车，扶着车前横木远望齐军的队形，这才说："可以追击了。"于是追击齐军直到很远。

In 684 BC, Qi's troops attacked Lu, and Cao Gui visited Duke Zhuang of Lu and requested to join. Then that day Duke Zhuang of Lu and Cao Gui took a same chariot and meet Qi's troops at Chang Shao. Duke Zhuang of Lu prepared to beat the drums and attack, Cao Gui said, "It's not a good time." After the Qi's troops beat the drums three times, Cao Gui said, "It's time to beat the drums and attack." The Qi's troops was defeated. Duke Zhuang of Lu just wanted to chase after the army, Cao said, "Don't chase for now." And then Cao Gui got off the chariot and checked the wheel ruts of Qi's troops, and he got on the chariot to overlook the formation of Qi's troops, and finally he said, "Now it's a good time to pursue and attack." So they pursued for a long way after Qi's troops.

打了胜仗后，鲁庄公问他取胜的原因。曹刿回答说："作战，靠的是士气。第一次击鼓能够振作士兵们的士气。第二次击鼓士气开始低落，第三次击鼓士气就耗尽了。他们的士气消失而

After they won the battle, Duke Zhuang of Lu asked Cao the reason, Cao Gui answered, "Winning the battle depends on morale. The morale of soldiers will be cheered up by the first time of beating drums, and weakened by the second time of beating drums, and exhausted by the third time of beating drums. We win the

我军的士气正旺，所以才战胜了他们。我怕他们故意逃走，设有埋伏。后来看到他们的车印杂乱，战旗倒拖，才下令追击。”

battle because our morale is vigorous and the Qi’s is exhausted. At first I was afraid they run away deliberately with ambush, but when I saw their disordered wheel ruts and collapsed banners, I decided to pursue and attack.”

曹刿准确地利用了两军作战的心理，把自己军队的士气提高到最强，把敌军的士气消磨到最弱，这样，利用自己的强势，打击对方的弱势，从而一举战胜了对手。

Cao Gui accurately used warring psychology to strengthen the Lu’s morale to the highest level and weaken the enemies’ morale to the lowest level, that is to say, he won the battle at one fling by his strengths against enemies’ weaknesses.

012

一箭双雕

Kill two hawks with one arrow

出自 《北史·长孙晟传》。

释义 比喻一举两得。

长孙晟是南北朝时期的北周将领。他的女儿嫁给唐太宗李世民，就是长孙皇

Zhangsun Sheng was a general of Northern Zhou during Southern and Northern Dynasties, whose daughter was Empress Zhangsun in

后。儿子长孙无忌，也是唐朝的一代名臣。

marry with Li Shimin, the Taizong of Tang, and whose son was Zhangsun Wuji, a famous minister of Tang Dynasty.

长孙晟智谋过人，武艺超群，十八岁时就当了一名禁卫东宫的武官。那时，北方游牧民族突厥首领摄图，和北周互派使者往来。但傲慢的摄图对北周派来的使者大都瞧不起。

Zhangsun Sheng was surpassingly resourceful with excellent military skills, and became a military officer of Royal Guards for Eastern Palace at his 18 years old. At that time, She Tu, the chief of northern Turkic nomadic people, had friendly intercourse with Northern Zhou by exchange of envoys. But She Tu was arrogant and always looked down on the Northern envoys.

有一次，长孙晟被派去出使突厥。摄图见到长孙晟后，十分欣赏他，竟要求长孙晟留了下来。摄图每次出猎，都要长孙晟陪同。

One time, Zhangsun Sheng was dispatched to Turk as an envoy. She Tu appreciated him a lot and unexpectedly required him to stay in Turk. He required Zhangsun Sheng to accompany during hunting every time.

一天，摄图看见空中有两只大雕盘旋着，正在争夺一块肉。他很有兴致地喊来长孙晟，并叫人拿两支箭递给长孙晟，命令他把两只雕射下来。

One day, She Tu saw two hawks hovering in the sky to fight for a piece of meat, he excitedly shouted Zhangsun Sheng to come, and give him two arrows for shooting the two hawks.

长孙晟接过箭，迅速翻身上马飞驰而去，渐渐地离大雕的位置很近了，只见他

Zhangsun Sheng took over the arrows and got on the horse to pursue. As he got closer and closer, he drew the bow and nocked the arrow,

拉弓搭箭，一箭射去，竟同时射穿了两只大雕的胸膛，大雕一齐落地。长孙晟一箭双雕的高超箭术，博得了在场所有人的连声喝彩。后人便根据这个故事引申出了“一箭双雕”这个成语。

amazingly the single arrow went through the beast of the two hawks, which fell down the ground at the same time. His excellent archery won the repeated cheers from the spectators. Afterwards, the idiom of “kill two hawks with one arrow” derived from this story.

013

九牛一毛

A single hair out of nine ox hides

出自 汉·司马迁《报任少卿书》。

释义 比喻极大数量中微不足道的一点。

汉武帝年间，将军李陵带着部队深入匈奴境内，连败敌军，武帝接到消息，非

During the period of Emperor Wu of Han, the general Li Ling lead the troops to the inner domain of Xiongnu and continuously defeated

常高兴，大臣们也纷纷恭维皇帝英明，善于用人。后来李陵战败投降，武帝非常生气，那些大臣也反过来责骂李陵不忠。

enemies. Emperor Wu was very delighted upon receiving this news, and ministers also compliment on the Emperor's wisdom of selecting talents. Afterwards, when Li Ling was defeated and surrendered, Emperor Wu was very angry and those ministers also blame Li Ling for disloyalty.

这时，武帝看到站在一边不吭一声的司马迁，便问他对此事的意见，司马迁为李陵辩护说，李陵只有五千步兵，却被匈奴八万骑兵围住，打了十几天仗，杀伤了一万多敌人，最后因弹尽粮绝，才没办法假装投降，他的功劳足够弥补他的失败之罪。武帝一怒之下，把司马迁关到牢里。

At this moment, Emperor saw the silent Si-ma Qian and asked for his opinions, Si-ma Qian said in defense of Li Ling, "Li Ling has been fighting for more than ten days and killed over ten thousand enemies, and finally he pretended to surrender due to exhaustion of supplies and ammunition. His contribution is much more enough to make up his sin of failure." Then Emperor Wu put Si-ma Qian in prison in a fury.

司马迁在牢里受尽折磨，而且还遭受了最为耻辱的"宫刑"。司马迁痛苦之余，想到了自杀，但是他转念一想，像自己这种地位低微的人死去，在别人眼中，不过像"九牛亡一毛"，不但得不到同情，而且更会

Si-ma Qian was fully tortured in the prison, even the most humiliating castration. After experienced all the pains, Si-ma Qian once thought of suicide, but on second thought, he realized his suicide would be regarded as a single hair out of nine ox hides because of his humbleness, and it would be mocked instead of pitied. So he decided to endure the humiliating

惹人耻笑。于是决心忍受耻辱，用了整整13年时间，终于完成了一部52万字的辉煌巨著——《史记》。

treat, and spent totally 13 years to accomplish *the Record of History*, a glorious monumental work of 520 000 words.

司马迁曾把他这种思想转变的过程，在信中告诉了他的好友任少卿，后人便据此引申出了“九牛一毛”这个成语。

Si-ma Qian once wrote to his good friend Ren Shaoqing about the process of his changing ideas, so from which the idiom of “a single hair out of nine ox hides” has derived.

014

人面桃花

A female charming face among peach blossoms

出自 唐·崔护《题都城南庄》诗。

释义 指女子的美貌与桃花相辉映，多用于形容男子思念女子的心情。

崔护是唐德宗时期的一位书生，出身于书香门第，平日埋头苦读，很少与人交往。这一年的清明时节，春

Cui Hu was an intellectual during the period of Emperor Dezong of Tang Dynasty, who was born of a literary family, always kept his nose in books and seldom associated with

暖花开，天气晴朗，读了一上午书的崔护放下书本，兴致勃勃地独自步行出城。一路上看不尽的红花绿草，春日山水，不知不觉，他已经走到了很远的郊外。

people. On the Tomb-sweeping day this year, the sky was clear and all flowers bloomed in the warmth of spring, Cui Hu put aside the book which he has read for the whole morning, and walked out of the city alone and in spirits. Embraced by mountains and water in spring, he saw endless red flowers and green grass along the way and unconsciously he had arrived the far outskirts.

这时候，崔护觉得有些腿酸口渴，便寻思着找一处农家歇歇脚，找些水喝。他望见不远处，在一片桃花掩映中露出一角茅屋，于是加快脚步走去。邻近茅屋，就看到眼前一片桃林，桃花缀满枝头，微风吹来，清香袭人。来到茅屋以后，他敲门求水，不一会儿，里面出来了一位非常美丽的少女，为他盛茶倒水。崔护对这位少女一见钟情，一直到离开都是恋恋不舍。

At the moment, Cui Hu felt thirsty with sore legs, and searched a farmhouse for a rest and some water. He saw the top of a thatched cottage among the peach blossoms, and hurried forward. As he got close to the cottage, he saw a grove of peach-trees, with blanches hung with peach blossoms, and the fragrance flew away when a light breeze came. He knocked the door for some a water. After a while, a very beautiful young lady came out and filled a bowl of tea for him. He felt in love at first sight with this lady and was reluctant to leave.

第二年清明节，他又

On the Tomb-sweeping day of next year, Cui Hu went to that cottage again, but the door was found locked without any people. So he wrote a poem on the door, “In the same door of the empty

去到那间茅屋，却看见大门锁着，里面的人已经不知道到哪里去了。于是就提笔在门上写了一首诗：去年今日此门中，人面桃花相映红。人面不知何处去？桃花依旧笑春风。以后，人们便用“人面桃花”来形容女子的美貌，或用来表达爱恋的情思。

cottage last year, the beautiful lady's face and the peach flowers reflected their glow. I'm wondering where the beautiful lady is, but the peach flowers still dancing on the branches." Afterwards, people use "a female charming face among peach flowers" to describe the beauty of female, or to express the emotions of love.

015

入木三分

Penetrating into the trisection of the wood

出自 唐·张怀瓘《书断·王羲之》。

释义 书法写作笔力强劲，也比喻见解深刻。

王羲之是东晋时期著名的书法家，对书法非常着迷，勤学苦练。他曾经在

Wang Xizhi was a famous calligrapher during the East Jin Dynasty, who was fascinated with calligraphy, with diligent study and

池塘边练字，每次写完，就在池塘里清洗笔砚。时间一久，整个池塘的水都变黑了。而且，无论是走在路上，坐在椅子上，他都在揣摩着名家书法的一笔一画，手指还不停地画着字形。时间一久，连自己的衣服都被划破了。

据说王羲之很喜欢鹅，平时常常望着在河里戏水的鹅发呆，后来竟然从鹅的动作中领悟出运笔的原理，这对他的书法技艺提升大有帮助。

正是因为王羲之不停地刻苦练字，天长日久，练得腕力劲足，写出的字笔锋有力。有一次，皇帝要到北郊祭祀，让王羲之把祝词写在一块木板上，再派木匠拿去雕刻。木匠在雕刻时发现，王羲之写的字竟然已经深入木头达三分之多，于是赞叹道：

strenuous training. He used to practice along the pond, and washed the writing brush and ink stone every time after writing, so the whole pond of water turned black after a long time. Moreover, he always figured out every stroke of famous calligraphers no matter during walking or sitting, and gesticulated the character pattern constantly, and after a long time the clothes were broken by himself.

It is said that Wang Xizhi liked goose very much and always stared at the swimming goose in the river, and afterwards he unexpectedly comprehended the principle of wielding the writing brushes, which was a huge help to his calligraphy skills.

Because of his diligent study and strenuous training constantly, after a considerable period of time, his wrist was practiced to be very strong and the characters he wrote were very forceful. Once upon a time, on the sacrificial ceremony in the north outskirts, the emperor asked Wang Xizhi to write the blessing speeches on a piece of wood and then asked a carpenter to sculpture. And the carpenter found that Wang Xizhi's characters were penetrated into the trisection of the wood, and signed with

“右军(指王羲之)的字，真是入木三分啊!”

因此后来人们都说王羲之的字“入木三分”，这虽然是一种夸张的说法，却也说明了他在书法上所下的功夫之深。

praises, “Wang Xizhi’s calligraphy is so forceful to be penetrated into the trisection of the wood!”

Afterwards, people all praise Wang Xizhi’s calligraphy as “penetrating into the trisection of the wood”, although it is a kind of exaggeration, it proves the hard and strenuous work on calligraphy.

016

八仙过海

the Eight Immortals crossing the sea

出自 明·无名氏《八仙过海》。

释义 各自拿出本领或办法，互相竞赛。

《八仙过海》的故事，说的是古时候的八个神仙，分别是铁拐李、张果老、汉

The leading characters of *the Eight Immortals Crossing the Sea* are Iron-Crutch Li, Zhang Guolao, Han Zhongli, Royal Uncle Cao,

钟离、曹国舅、蓝采和、吕洞宾、何仙姑与韩湘子。这八个神仙的外表和性格都各有特色，经常在一起聚会论道，展示自己的独门法术。

Lan Caihe, Lu Dongbin, Immortal Woman He and Han Xiangzi. The eight immortals have their own characteristics in appearance and personalities, who always gathered together for discussion on Daoism and showed off their magic stunts.

一天，这八位神仙一同去参加王母娘娘的蟠桃大会，途经东海。东海浩瀚无边，光靠凡人的力量根本就没有办法穿越它。于是吕洞宾就提议说："不如我们八个人每人都将自己随身所带的一件宝物投进大海，让这些宝物载我们过海。"大家一致同意吕洞宾的意见。

One day, the eight immortals went together to the peach ceremony held by the Empress of Heaven, passing by the East Sea, which is too immense for an ordinary person to cross. So Lu Dongbin suggested, "Let us throw one piece of carry-on treasure into the sea and help ourselves to cross the sea." The other seven immortals all agreed with Lu Dongbin.

铁拐李首先把拐杖投进水里，自己稳稳地站在上面；接下来，韩湘子投下花篮，吕洞宾投下箫，蓝采和投下大拍板，汉钟离投下鼓，张果老投下一个纸驴，曹国舅投下玉笏，何仙姑投下竹篮。他们各自站在自己投放的器物上面，各展神通，乘风破浪，顺利地到达

Firstly, Iron-Crutch Li threw his crutch into the sea, which he steadily stood on. Then Han Xiangzi threw the flower basket, Lu Dongbin threw the bamboo flute, Lan Caihe threw the big clappers, Han Zhongli threw the drum, Zhang Guolao threw a paper donkey, Royal Uncle Cao threw the jade tablet, and Immortal Women He threw the bamboo basket. They stood on their treasures respectively and showed their magic powers, braved winds and waves and finally

了东海对岸。

后来，人们就把这个故事概括成为“八仙过海，各显神通”的谚语，而“八仙过海”也单独被作为成语使用。

arrived at the other side of the East Sea.

Afterwards, people summarize the story as “the Eight Immortals crossing the sea, each one shows his or her special prowess”, the first pant is used as idiom separately.

017

八面威风

An awe-inspiring reputation extending in every direction

出自 元·尚仲贤《单鞭夺槊》。

释义 形容声势气派十足。

元朝末年，各地农民纷纷起义，反抗元朝的统治。日后成为明朝开国皇

By the end of Yuan Dynasty, there were many peasant uprisings against the reign of Yuan Dynasty. Zhu Yuanzhang, the future

帝的朱元璋，也在这时投身郭子兴领导的起义军，郭子兴十分赏识朱元璋的才干，任命他为总兵官。朱元璋带兵攻下安徽和阳，准备乘胜进军集庆（今江苏南京）。

first emperor of Ming Dynasty at that time, also threw himself into the uprising led by Guo Zixing. Guo Zixing appreciated Zhu Yuanzhang's talents very much, and appointed him as chief of soldiers. Zhu Yuanzhang seized Heyang of Anhui, and prepared to march forward Jiqing, the current Nanjing of Jiangsu.

在除夕夜里，朱元璋和大将徐达一起去查探江南元兵的守备情况。二人来到梁山脚下的陈桥洲，等了很久，才看见一个老渔夫驾着一叶扁舟，沿岸逆水而上。二人急忙高呼。老渔夫听见后，把小船停靠到岸边，对他们说："除夕之夜，没有月色，天黑浪险，不好过江。二位不如暂且在小船上过一夜，明天一早再渡河，不知意下如何？"二人答应了。老渔夫于是用鱼肉米酒招待他俩。第二天清晨，老渔夫驾起小船，一边摇桨，一边唱着：

On the eve of Spring Festival, Zhu Yuanzhang and the general Xu Da went to inspect the garrison of Yuan's troops in the south of the Changjiang River. They went to Chenqiaozhou at the foot of Liang Mount and waited. After a long while, an old fisherman rowed a small boat upstream. They hurried to shout out at the fisherman, the old fisherman heard and stopped, and then he berthed along the river, and said, "At the night of Spring Festival eve, there's no moonlight, it is very dangerous to cross the river with black sky and turbulent torrents. How about rest in my small boat tonight and cross the river tomorrow morning?" They agreed, and the old fisherman treated them with fish meat and rice wine. The next morning, the old fisherman rowed the small boat and sang out when he pulled the oars, "Six dragons come to guard the sacred emperor! The senior General

"圣天子六龙护驾！大将军八面威风!"朱元璋心里明白这是祝贺他日后称王的意思，非常高兴。

has an awe-inspiring reputation extending in every direction." Zhu Yuanzhang understood this song was to congratulate him as the future emperor and quite delighted.

朱元璋当了皇帝后，特意派人找到了当年的老渔夫，除了赏赐钱财以外，还把他的渔船漆成朱红色，封号"满江红"。老渔夫此后就驾着"满江红"，免费运载过往行人，风雨无阻，传为佳话。

When Zhu Yuanzhang became the emperor, he specially found the old fisherman, rewarded lots of money and painted the boat as vermilion, and granted the name of the "Red all over the River". Afterwards, the old fisherman rowed the boat of "Red all over the River" to carry passersby for free no matter rain or shine, which is an instructive anecdote.

018

三人成虎

Three people make a tiger

出自《战国策·魏策二》。

释义 谣言经过多人重复述说，就能使人信以为真。

战国时期，魏国有个大臣叫庞恭，深受魏王器重。后来，魏王派他陪太子一起

In the period of Warring States, there was a minister called Pang Gong, who was highly regarded by Emperor Wei. Afterwards, Emperor

去赵国都城邯郸做人质。庞恭担心自己走了以后魏王不再信任他，于是在临行前特地来到王宫里，对魏王说：“大王，如果有人向您禀报，街市上有老虎，您相信吗？”魏王立刻回答说：“我当然不相信。”

庞恭接着问：“如果第二个人也向您禀报，街市上有老虎，您相信不相信？”魏王迟疑了一下说：“我将信将疑。”庞恭紧接着问：“要是第三个人也向您报告说，街市上有老虎，您相信吗？”魏王一边点头，一边说：“我相信了。”

于是，庞恭担忧地说：“街市上本来没有老虎，但如果三个人都说那里有老虎，人们便相信了。如今我陪太子去邯郸，距离比王宫到街市要远得多，而背后议论我的，恐怕也不止三个人。希望大王今后对这些议论加以考察，不要轻

appointed him to accompany prince to Zhao's capital Handan as the hostage. Pang Gong was afraid of loss of trust by Emperor Wei after he left, so he came to meet Emperor Wei and said, "Your Honored Emperor, if someone reported to you that there is a tiger on the street, will you believe?" Emperor answered immediately, "Absolutely not!"

Pang Gong went on asking, "if a second person also report to you that there is a tiger on the street, will you believe?" Emperor Wei hesitated for a moment and answered, "Uncertainly!" Pang Gong followed on and asked, "If a third person also report to you that there is a tiger on the street, will you believe?" Emperor Wei nodded and said, "Completely!"

Then Pang Gong worried and said, "There is no tiger at all originally, if three persons say there is a tiger, the other people will believe. Now I accompany the prince to Handan, which is much further than the distance from the palace to street, and I'm afraid there will be more than three persons to gossip on me. I hope Your Honored Emperor can make some

易相信。”

魏王说：“我明白你的意思，你就放心地陪公子去吧。”

庞恭去了赵国不久，果然有人在魏王面前说他的坏话。魏王开始不信，可后来说庞恭坏话的人越来越多，魏王也就相信了。

在太子结束人质生活回国后，魏王就再也没召见过庞恭，也不再重用他了。

investigation instead of being credulous.”

Emperor said, “I understand what you mean. Please rest assured for accompanying the prince.”

Just as expected, someone gossip on Pang Gong to Emperor after a short while he went to Zhao. Emperor Wei didn’t believe at first, but more and more people gossip on Pang Gong, and finally Emperor believed.

After the prince finished being hostage and came back to Wei, Emperor Wei neither called in Pang Gong again nor regarded him highly.

019

三令五申

Repeated warnings time and again

出自 《史记·孙子吴起列传》。

释义 反复多次地告诫。

孙武是我国春秋时期的一位著名军事家，当时，在吴国大臣伍员的推荐下，孙武带

Sun Wu was a famous militarist of the Spring and Autumn Period. At that time recommended by a Wu's minister Wu Yuan,

着自己写的《孙子兵法》去见吴王阖闾。吴王看后说："你的十三篇兵法，我都看过了，能让人来试试吗？"孙武说可以。吴王又问："用女子来试验可以吗？"孙武也说可以。于是吴王召集了一百八十名宫中美女，请孙武训练。

Sun Wu went to visit the Wu's Emperor He Lu with his book *the Art of War*. Emperor Wu read and said, "I have read the thirteen chapters of your book, can I ask some people to try?" Sun Wu agreed. Emperor Wu asked again, "Can I ask women to try?" Sun Wu agreed. So Emperor called on 180 beauties to be trained by Sun Wu.

孙武把这些女子分为两队，让吴王的两个宠姬各拿着一支长戟，作为队长。孙武向她们反复告诫多遍："我喊前，你们看前面；喊左，看左手；喊右，看右手；喊后，看背后。"然后，击鼓传令："右!"那些女子听到命令竟哈哈大笑，没人照着吩咐去做。孙武说："号令不明，是将领的过错。"于是重新申明号令，击鼓传令："左!"那些女子仍然不听，笑得前仰后合。孙武大声说："号令不明是将领之罪，号令已明而不遵守，是队长之罪！"下

Sun Wu organized the young ladies into two teams and appointed two of the king's favorite concubines as team leaders, with halberds in hand. Sun Wu warned them time and again, "I say 'Front', you look front; I say 'Left', you look at your left hand; I say 'Right', you look at your right hand; I say 'Back', you look back." Then he beat the drums and ordered, "Right!" Those women laughed loudly upon the order, and no one followed. Sun Wu said, "To be unclear of the orders is the fault of General." Then he beat the drums and ordered again, "Left!" Those women didn't follow and laughed themselves into convulsions. Sun Wu said loudly, "To be unclear of the orders is the fault of General, but to disobey orders is the fault of team leaders." So Sun

令将两队队长斩首示众。吴王急忙传令："我已知道将军能用兵了，如果没有这两个宠姬，我吃饭都不香了，将军就不要杀她们了吧！"孙武回复吴王："我既已接受命令为将，将在军中，君王的命令可以有所不听。"便下令斩了两个宠姬。

接下来，孙武重新击鼓传令，队伍中再也没人敢出声，全部按照号令整齐操练。孙武从此受到吴王重用，成就了吴国的霸主地位。

后来，人们便把孙武向女兵再三告诫的做法，引申为"三令五申"这个成语。

Wu ordered to behead the two team leaders and displayed in public. Emperor hurriedly ordered, "I already understand your art of war, I will have no appetite without these two concubines, don't kill them!" Sun Wu replied, "As I take the order to be general, I can ignore the emperor's orders in warfare." Then he ordered to kill Emperor Wu's two favorite concubines.

Then Sun Wu beat the drums and ordered again, nobody dared to make a sound and followed the orders to train. From then on, Sun Wu was regarded highly by Emperor Wu, and Kingdom Wu achieved the position of a powerful country.

Afterwards, the idiom of "repeated warnings time and again" derived from this story.

020

三顾茅庐

Visit the cottage thrice in succession

出自 三国·诸葛亮《出师表》。

释义 诚心诚意，虚心求才。

东汉末年，刘备与曹操作战失败，跑到荆州投奔刘表。为了成就大业，他请当

By the end of Eastern Han Dynasty, Liu Bei was defeated by Cao Cao and went to Liu Biao for shelter in Jingzhou. In order to gain great

时的荆州名士司马徽为他推荐人才。司马徽说："这个地方有'伏龙'和'凤雏'二人，得到其中一人就可以安定天下。"刘备多方打听，得知"伏龙"就是诸葛亮，隐居在襄阳城西二十里的隆中，住着茅草屋，自耕自作，学识过人，是个杰出人才，便专程到隆中去拜访。

achievement, he requested Si-ma Hui to introduce talents for him. Si-ma Hui said, "Here are two reclusive geniuses who are reputed as 'crouching dragon' and 'nestling phoenix', you will unify the whole country as long as you can have one of them." Liu Bei asked many people and knew that 'crouching dragon' is Zhu-Ge Liang, who was a recluse excellent in knowledge and made self-sufficient farming in Longzhong with a distance of 20 li from the west of Xiangyang city, so he paid a special visit to Longzhong.

刘备前后一共去了三次，前两次诸葛亮都避而不见，直到第三次才亲自出来迎接。在茅草屋中，诸葛亮为刘备分析当时的形势，设计如何夺取政权统一天下的策略。刘备非常佩服，就请他出山相助。诸葛亮也被刘备"三顾茅庐"的诚意所打动，答应了刘备的请求。此后，诸葛亮作为刘备的重要谋士，帮助刘备东联孙吴，北伐曹魏，占据荆、益两州，北向中原，建立蜀汉政

Liu Bei visited thrice in succession, for the first twice Zhu-Ge Liang avoided, came out for welcome for the third time. In the cottage, Zhu-Ge Liang analyzed the current situation for Liu Bei and scheme for the future unification all over the country. Liu Bei admired very much and requested him for support. Zhu-Ge Liang was also touched by Liu Bei's sincerity and agreed. From then on, as an important consultant, Zhu-Ge Liang helped Liu Bei to ally with Sun Quan of Wu in the East, attack Cao Cao of Wei in the North, seize Jingzhou and Yizhou, move forward the Central plain, establish

权，形成与东吴、曹魏三国鼎立的局面。

后来，刘备去世，诸葛亮秉承他的遗志，继续出兵伐魏。他在向后主刘禅上的奏表《出师表》中写道："先帝不嫌臣卑微鄙陋，屈尊枉驾，前后三次亲自登门，访臣于草庐之中……"流露出对刘备知遇之恩的念念不忘。

Shu regime, and finally made the situation of three kingdoms.

Then Liu Bei passed away, Zhu-Ge Liang carried on his unfulfilled wishes and continued to attack Wei. In the statement of *the Memorial on Dispatching the Army* to the last Emperor Liu Chan, he wrote, "The late emperor did not detest my lowliness and shallowness, and condescended to visit my cottage thrice in succession...", which exudes that Zhu-Ge Liang kept firmly the gratitude of Liu Bei's appreciation on him.

021

下笔成章

Compose quickly without a draft

出自 《三国志·魏书·陈思王植传》。

释义 一挥笔就写成文章，形容文思敏捷。

曹植是三国时期的著名文学家，曹操的第三个儿子，他的代表作有《洛神

Cao Zhi was a famous writer in the Three Kingdoms period and the third son of Cao Cao. His representative works include “Ode to the

赋》《白马篇》《七哀诗》等，后人将他与父亲曹操、兄长曹丕合称为“三曹”，都名列“建安七子”之中。

Goddess of Luo”, “White Horse”, and “Seven Sorrow Poems”, etc. Later generations called him “Three Cao” together with his father Cao Cao and his brother Cao Pi, and they were all listed among the “Seven Geniuses of Jian ’an Ara”.

曹植从小聪明伶俐，十几岁的时候就能诵读几百篇诗文，而且自己也非常会写文章，所以很多人都称他是个奇才。

Cao Zhi was clever since childhood, reading hundreds of poems as a teenager, and writing so well that many people called him a prodigy.

有一次，曹操看了曹植写的文章后，心里觉得确实写得不错，但却有些怀疑这文章是请人代写的。于是，曹操就把曹植叫到跟前，问道：“你的文章我看过了，写得不错，是不是请别人代你写的呀?”

Once upon a time, Cao Cao read the article written by Cao Zhi and highly appreciated that, but he doubted it was by a ghostwriter. So he called Cao Zhi and asked, “Your article is very good, is it by yourself or a ghostwriter?”

曹植赶忙跪下禀告道：“不是的，我能够言出为文，下笔成章，如果您不相信，可以当面考我，怎么能说我是请别人代写的呢?”

Cao Zhi hurried to kneel down and replied, “I wrote it myself. I have chapter and verse at my tongue’s tip and compose quickly without a draft. You can test on me if you doubt, how can you say it is by a ghostwriter?”

曹操听了禁不住哈哈大笑起来，说：“如果不是那

Cao Cao laughed and said, “That would be great if not.”

就太好了。”

后来，铜雀台建造竣工，曹操就让几个儿子都上去观看，并让他们每人都写出一篇辞赋来，想试一试他们的文采。曹植提起笔就写，一会儿工夫就写好了，曹操看了之后，赞赏不已。这也充分证明了曹植自己说过的：“言出为文，下笔成章。”

Then upon the completion of Bronze Sparrow Terrace, Cao Cao called several sons to have a look, and asked them to write a poem for the test of their literary talents. Cao Zhi immediately began to write and finished in a short while, Cao Cao read and admired constantly. This makes a full proof of what Cao Zhi said "I have chapter and verse at my tongue's tip and compose quickly without a draft."

022

亡羊补牢

Mend the fold after a sheep is lost

出自 《战国策·楚策》。

释义 出了问题以后想法补救，可以防止继续受损失。

战国时期，楚襄王即位后，重用奸臣，政治腐败，国家一天天衰落。大

In the Warring States Period, after the enthronement of King Xiang of Chu, he regarded highly towards the treacherous

臣庄辛非常着急，劝楚襄王不要成天吃喝玩乐，不管国家大事，这样下去就要亡国了。楚襄王听了大怒，骂道："你老糊涂了吧，竟敢这样诅咒楚国。"庄辛见楚襄王听不进去，只好躲到赵国。才过了五个月，秦国果然派兵攻打楚国，攻入楚国都城。楚襄王逃到城阳，这时，他想到庄辛的忠告，非常悔恨，便派人把庄辛迎请回来，说："过去因为我没听你的话，所以才会落到这种地步，现在，你看还有办法挽救吗？"

officials, so the politics corrupted and the country declined. The minister Zhuang Xin worried very much and persuaded King Xiang of Chu not to indulge in drinking and making merry, and told him that the country would be destroyed if he went on ignoring state affairs. King Xiang of Chu burst into a fury and scolded, "You dotard, how dare you make such a curse on Chu?" Then Zhuang Xin fled to Zhao. Just five months later, as expected Qin attacked Chu and seized its capital. King Xiang of Chu thought of the Zhuang Xin's advice when he fled to Chengyang, and regretted very much. He asked people to call back Zhuang Xin and said, "Today I got such a miserable situation because I ignored your advice, do you have any idea to help me recover?"

庄辛诚恳地说：我听说过，看见兔子才想起猎犬，这还不晚；羊跑掉了才补羊圈，也还不迟。现在楚国都城虽被攻陷，但只要振作起来，改正过去的过错，秦国是灭不了楚国的。楚襄王听了，便按照庄辛的话去做，

Zhuang Xin said cordially, "I once hear a saying that it is not late to think of hunting dogs when rabbits appear, and it is not late to mend the fold when the sheep is lost. Although Chu was seized, as long as you cheer up and correct the mistakes, Chu will not be destroyed by Qin. " King Xiang of Chu followed Zhuang Xin's advice and Chu

果真度过了危机。

后来，人们从庄辛所说的话里总结出来“亡羊补牢”这个成语，并且把它演绎成了一个很有意义的寓言故事：

从前有个人，养了许多羊。一天早晨他发现少了一只羊，原来是羊圈破了个大洞，夜里狼钻进来，把羊叼走了。邻居劝他赶快把羊圈修一修，那个人回答说：“羊已经丢了，还修羊圈干什么？”第二天早上，他发现羊又被狼叼走了一只，很后悔自己没有听邻居的劝告，于是赶快堵上窟窿，从此他的羊再也没丢过了。

finally got through the crisis.

Afterwards, an idiom “Mend the fold after a sheep is lost” was derived from what Zhuang Xin said, and interpreted into a meaaingful fable story:

Once upon a time a person raised lots of sheep. One morning, he found a sheep was missing due to a big hole of the fold, through which a wolf got in and carried off the sheep. The neighbors persuaded him to mend the fold, but he said, “It’s no need to mend the fold since the sheep was lost.” The next morning, he found another sheep had been carried off by the wolf, and regretted that he didn’t take the advice of his neighbors, then he immediately mend the fold, and the sheep have never been lost again.

023

千里之行，始于足下

A journey of one thousand miles begins with one step

出自 《道德经》。

释义 事情的成功，是从小到大逐渐积累起来的。

老子姓李名耳，字聃，是春秋时期著名的哲学家、思想家，道家学派的创始

Lao-zi with his family name is Li and name is Er, with the courtesy name Dan, was a famous philosopher, thinker and initiator of

人，关于他的名字有很多有趣的传说。

Taoism in Spring and Autumn Period. There are many interesting stories about his name.

据说老子的母亲有一天正在村头的河边洗衣服，忽见上游飘下一个黄澄澄的李子，他的母亲忙用树枝把李子捞上来，吃了下去，真是香脆可口。不过打那以后，他的母亲就怀了身孕，而且一怀就是八十一年，才生下一个男孩。这个男孩一生下来就是白眉白发白胡子，因此，他的母亲给他取名叫“老子”。老子生下来就会说话，他指着院子中的一棵李子树，对母亲说：“李就是我的姓。”

It is said that one day Lao-zi's mother was washing clothes besides the river, and suddenly saw a yellow plum floating down from upstream, she hurried to pick it up with branches and ate, the plum was really crunchy and delicious. But from then on, she had been pregnant for 81 years, and finally a boy was born. He has with white eyebrows, white hair and white beard, so she called him "Lao-zi". He could speak after birth, and he pointed at a plum tree in the yard and said to his mother "I take Li as my surname."

老子知识渊博，在当时名气很大，孔子在年轻的时候还专门拜访过老子，向他请教周朝的礼仪。他写过一本只有五千字的书，就是著名的《道德经》。书中讲了很多能启发人的道理。其中有一句是这样说的：“合

Lao-zi was famous because of his wide knowledge, and even young Confucius specifically visited him for consulting the etiquette of Zhou Dynasty. He once wrote the famous *Tao Te Ching*, a book of only 5000 words, in which there are lots of inspiring principles. For example, "The tree which fills the arms grew from the tiniest sprout;

抱之木，生于毫末；九层之台，起于累土；千里之行，始于足下。”意思是，合抱的大树是细小的幼苗长成，九层的高台是一筐一筐泥土砌成的，千里远的行程是从脚下开始的。在这里，老子用生动的比喻，说明了事物都是从小到大发展变化的，做任何事情，关键都在第一步。

the tower of nine story rose from a heap of earth; the journey of one thousand miles begins with one step.” Lao-zi used a vivid metaphor to illustrate that the great success is an accumulation of many trivial things, the first step is very important.

024

千钧一发

Hang by a hair

出自 《汉书·枚乘传》。

释义 形容情况万分危急。

汉景帝时期，御史大夫晁错上书《削藩策》，提议削弱诸侯王势力，加

In the reign of Emperor Jing of Han, the imperial censor Chao Cuo submitted a statement called *Strategies of Weakening the*

强中央集权。汉景帝采用晁错的建议，在第二年下诏削夺吴、楚等诸侯王的封地。以吴王刘濞为首的七个诸侯由于不满朝廷削减他们的权力，联兵反叛，史称“七国之乱”。

Vassals, which advised to weaken the power of vassals and strengthen the power centralization. Emperor Jing of Han took the advice of Chao Cuo and issued an edict in the next year to deprive the lands of Wu and Chu's vassals. The seven vassals led by King Liu Bi of Wu were dissatisfied about the weakening and allied to rebel, which is the famous "The Rebellion of the Seven Kingdoms".

起初，吴王刘濞开始想要反叛朝廷，他手下有个郎中官，也是一位著名的文学家，名叫枚乘，他劝阻吴王说：“用一缕头发系上千钧（钧，古代的重量单位，三十斤为一钧）重的东西，上面悬在没有尽头的高处，下边是无底的深渊，即使是再愚蠢的人也知道是极其危险的。反叛朝廷，就如同这种情形一样危险啊！”

At the beginning of Liu Bi's rebellion, an official Mei Cheng, who was also a famous literary figure persuaded him, "A hundredweight hang by a hair is very dangerous, with endless up and bottomless down, even the most stupid person can realize the danger, and rebellion is as dangerous as hanging by a hair!"

枚乘的忠告并没有得到吴王的采纳，他只好离开吴国，去梁国做了梁孝王的门客。后来，吴王纠集其他六个

But Mei Cheng's sincere advice was not taken by the King of Wu, so he left Wu to Liang as a follower of King Xiao of Liang. Then the King of Wu ally with other

诸侯国谋反，结果不到三个月就被平定，自己也被杀身亡。

“千钧一发”这个成语，就是从枚乘原话“其危如一发引千钧”这里来的。

six vassals for rebellion, and finally was suppressed within three months and killed.

The idiom of “hang by a hair” is derived from “Rebellion is as dangerous as hang by a hair”, which is the exact words of Mei Cheng.

025

千虑一得

Even a fool may sometimes have a good idea

出自 《晏子春秋·杂下十八》。

释义 遇到问题要多考虑，才不会犯错。

春秋时期，晏婴在齐国历任三朝国相。他虽然身材矮小，其貌不扬，但为人正

In the Spring and Autumn Period, Yan Ying was successively the prime minster for three emperors in Qi. Although he was short in

直，生活俭朴，在齐国很有威望，深受国君和百姓的尊敬。

stature and unattractive in appearance, he was upright and frugal, and prestigious in Qi, and highly respected by the emperor and common people.

有一天，齐景公派人来看望他。晏婴正在吃饭，就把自己的饭菜分成两份，请来人一起吃。来人很感动，回去就把这事告诉了齐景公。齐景公感叹相国家里竟然如此贫苦，就派人给他送去一千两金子。可是连送了三次，都被晏婴退了回来。

One day Duke Jing of Qi sent a person to visit Yan Ying. Yan Ying was at meals, and divided his food in half and asked the person to eat together. The person was quite moved and reported to Duke Jing of Qi. Duke Jing of Qi sighed at the poverty of a prime minister and sent him a thousand bars of gold, but was rejected by Yan Ying three tines in succession.

于是，齐景公特地召见晏婴，对他说："齐国以前的贤相管仲，为齐桓公称霸诸侯立了大功。桓公赏给他许多封地，管仲没有推辞就接受了。你为什么要拒绝我的赏赐呢？"晏婴说："圣人千虑，必有一失；愚人千虑，必有一得。无论君臣，都要做到清廉，管仲虽然是贤人，但在这件事上的考虑或许欠妥，我虽

Thus Duke Jing of Qi specially call in Yan Ying and said, "The former wise prime minister Guan Zhong made great contribution for the domination of Duke Huan of Qi, and Duke Huan of Qi rewarded him many lands, and Guan Zhong accepted without rejection. Why did you reject my reward? " Yan Ying said, "Even a sage may make a mistake after consideration, and even a fool may make a right choice after consideration. Both emperor and ministers should be free from corruption. Although Guan Zhong is a sage, he made a

然愚笨，这件事处理得可能正确。”

齐景公听了这番话，对晏婴更加敬重了。

mistake in this matter. Although I'm a fool, I made a right choice in this matter. ”

Then Duke Jing of Qi felt more respect for Yan Ying.

026

口若悬河

A rapid talker makes a torrent of words

出自 《晋书·郭象传》。

释义 能说会辩，讲起话来滔滔不绝。

西晋初年，文坛上涌现出许多知名的学者，其中，被称为“竹林七贤”之一的向秀就生活在这个时代。

In the early years of the Western Jin dynasty, many famous scholars emerged in the literary world. Among them, Xiang Xiu, known as one of the “Seven Sages of the Bamboo Grove”, lived in this era.

当时，为《庄子》一书作注的人很多，但是向秀读了这些著作以后，都不大满意，于是自己开始重新注释《庄子》。可惜的是，向秀的这项工作还没有来得及完成，便不幸去世了。有个叫郭象的人，头脑聪明，在当时也小有名气。他发现向秀对《庄子》一书的注释后，便重新整理了一遍，以自己的名义抄写出来，人们争相传阅，而郭象的名声由此越来越大，并且得到了太尉王衍的器重。

At that time, many people wrote annotations for *The Zhuang Zi*, but no one made Xiang Xiu satisfied, so he began to write annotation by himself. Unfortunately he passed away before he completed the annotations. A person called Guo Xiang, who was intelligent and had some fame at the time, he found the Xiang Xiu's annotations and rearranged and finally brought out with his name as the author. This book was quickly circulated among people, and Guo Xiang became more and more famous, and was regarded highly by the official Wang Yan.

一次，郭象与王衍闲聊，他们无所不谈，什么天文地理，诸子百家，郭象都说得头头是道，有声有色。王衍虽是当时一流的学者，口才也很好，但是听了郭象的谈话也禁不住赞叹说：“听郭象说话，就好像看到瀑布之水流泻而下，滔滔不绝。”“口若悬河”的成语便由此而来。

Once, Guo Xiang chat with Wang Yan, they talked about astronomy and geography, different schools of philosophers, and what Guo Xiang said was very clear, logical and impressive. Wang Yan was also a first-class scholar with good eloquence, but he couldn't help to praise, "The way Guo Xiang talks is just like waterfall cascading down unceasingly." Thus from this story the idiom of "a rapid talker makes a torrent of words" derives.

027

口蜜腹剑

A honey tongue and a heart of gall

出自 《资治通鉴》。

释义 说话好听，肚子里却怀着害人的阴谋。

在唐玄宗时期，有个大奸臣叫李林甫，他能书善画，有一些才艺，但为人阴

During the reign of Emperor Xuan Zong of Tang, there was a treacherous minister called Li Linfu, who was good at calligraphy

险狡猾，对皇帝总是想方设法阿谀奉承，取得宠信；对朝中的官员，也经常用甜言蜜语讨得对方的好感，背地里却暗箭伤人。

and painting, but with a sinister heart. He always flattered the emperor by all means for favor and trust, and said sugared words to other official with a stab in their backs.

有一次，他对同事李适之说："华山出产大量黄金，如果能够开采出来，就可以大大增加国家的财富。遗憾的是，皇上还不知道啊。"

Once he said to his fellow official Li Shizhi, "Mount Hua produces tremendous gold, it will be greatly increase the nation's fortune if it can be mined, but it is a pity our emperor doesn't know it."

李适之以为他说的是真话，赶紧跑去建议玄宗开采。玄宗一听很高兴，把李林甫找来商量，李林甫却说："这件事我早知道了。华山是帝王风水集中的地方，怎么可以随便开采呢？别人劝您开采，恐怕是不怀好意。我好几次都想把这件事启奏皇上，只是不敢开口罢了。"玄宗一听，认为他是一位忠君爱国的臣子，反而对李适之很不满意，逐渐疏远了他。

Li Shizhi thought what he said is true and hurried to suggest the Emperor Xuan Zong of Tang to exploit. Emperor Xuan Zong was excited to hear this and called in Li Linfu for discussion, but Li Linfu said, "I knew it already, but Mount Hua is the concentration of the emperor's geomantic omen, how can we exploit it randomly? If someone persuaded you to exploit, I'm afraid he has malicious intentions. By thinking over this matter several times, I'm not dare to tell you this." Then the emperor Xuan Zhong regarded Li Linfu as a loyal and enthusiastic official, and felt badly dissatisfied on Li Shizhi and estranged from him gradually.

李林甫凭借着这套特殊的本事，深得玄宗的宠信，一直做了十九年的高官。然而，时间长了，人们都知道了他的为人，也识破了他阴阳两面的做法。后来，人们每逢谈起李林甫，都说他是一个“口有蜜，腹有剑”的阴险人物。这便是成语“口蜜腹剑”的由来。

Li Linfu won deep favor and trust from the emperor Xuan Zhong by his special skills as this, and held high position for 19 years. Nevertheless, as time went, people all knew his personality, and saw through this double-dealer. Afterwards, as long as people mentioned Li Linfu, they all described him as a person with a honey tongue and a heart of gall. This is how the idiom of “a honey tongue and a heart of gall” comes from.

028

大义灭亲

Sacrifice consanguinity for the sake of righteousness

出自 《左传·隐公四年》。

释义 为了维护正义，对犯罪的亲属不徇私情，使其受到应有的惩罚。

春秋时期，卫庄公有个儿子名叫州吁，是庄公爱妾所生，受到庄公的格外宠

In the Spring and Autumn Period, Duke Zhuang of Wei had a son called Zhou Xu, which was born by his specially favorable

爱，以至于目中无人、骄横自大。当时，卫国大夫石碏的儿子石厚，经常与州吁在一起游玩。石碏多次劝告儿子不要与州吁在一起，他始终不听。

concubine, so that Zhou Xu was supercilious and haughty. At that time, Shi Hou, who was the son of Shi Que' the minister of Wei, always played with Zhou Xu. Shi Que persuaded his son not to play with Zhou Xu for many times, but Shi Hou didn't take his advice.

卫庄公死后，州吁的哥哥卫桓公即位，后来州吁在石厚的帮助下杀兄夺位，石厚因为有功被封为上大夫。州吁让石厚去向石碏求取稳定王位的计策，石碏对他的所作所为非常愤怒，便使了一个计谋，他对儿子说：“只要周天子许可州吁当国君，其他人就一定会服从。陈桓公与周天子关系很好，你到陈国请求陈桓公出面帮助，一定会马到成功。”

After Duke Zhuang of Wei passed away, Zhou Xu's brother became the king, then Zhou Xu killed his brother and usurped the throne by the help of Shi Hou, who was granted as high official. Zhou Xu asked Shi Hou to get some stratagem from Shi Que for throne stabilization. Shi Que was furious about his doings and replied with an ingenious trick, “As long as Emperor Zhou recognized Zhou Xu as the king, the other people will all follow. Duke Huan of Chen has a very good relationship with Emperor Zhou, and he will not hesitate to help if you go to Chen and meet Duke Huan of Chen.”

于是石厚和州吁带上礼物赶往陈国。石碏暗中写信给陈恒公，让他帮助捉拿杀死君王的凶手。石厚和州吁一到陈国就被抓

Thus Shi Hou and Zhou Xu went to Chen with presents. Shi Que wrote a letter in confidence to Duke Huan of Chen and asked him to seize the murderer of the emperor. So Shi Hou and Zhou Xu were seized as soon as

了起来。接着陈桓公派人到卫国去问怎么处置这两人。有的大臣说：“州吁杀兄夺位，罪大恶极，理应处死。但石厚是您的儿子，并且只是从犯，应该从宽处理。”石碏却说：“州吁干的坏事，大多是石厚谋划的。不杀石厚，难以安定民心啊。”就派自己的家臣到陈国去，把石厚杀了。

当时的人赞扬说：“石碏为了国家大义而忍心杀死为非作歹的儿子，真是一个纯正的人。”

they arrived in Chen. Duke Huan of Qi dispatched a person to Wei for the advice of disposition, some ministers said, “Zhou Xu killed his brother and usurped the throne, it is a heinous crime and should be condemned to death, but Shi Hou is your son and merely as an accessory criminal, should be disposed leniently.” But Shi Que said, “The most evil deeds of Zhou Xu are planned by Shi Hou, it will be hard to stabilize the common aspiration of the people if we don’t kill Shi Hou.” Thus he appointed his retainer to go to Chen and killed Shi Hou.

People all spoke highly of Shi Que, “Shi Que is hardhearted to kill his son for his evil doings. Shi Que is really an upright person.”

029

大材小用

A large material for petty use

出自 宋·陆游《送辛幼安殿撰造朝》诗。

释义 比喻用人不当，浪费人才。

辛弃疾是南宋时期著名的爱国词人。金人南侵后，辛弃疾组织了两千多人的队

Xin Qiji was a famous patriotic poet During the Southern Song Dynasty. After Jin's invasion, Xin Qiji organized a troop of

伍在故乡起义，后来又率领队伍投奔耿京组织的农民起义军。不久，起义军接受朝廷任命，与朝廷的军队配合作战，打击南侵的金军。但由于受到投降派的排挤，辛弃疾后来长期闲居，1203年春，才被任命为绍兴府知府兼浙江东路安抚使。这一年，辛弃疾已经六十四岁了。

绍兴西郊有一处地方叫三山，当时著名的爱国诗人陆游就住在那里。辛弃疾到任不久，就去拜访了这位前辈，两人一起议论国家大事。陆游觉得他是一个很有才能的人，希望他在统一国家的事业上取得成功。

第二年春天，南宋皇帝下旨要辛弃疾到京城临安，询问他对北伐金国的意见。辛弃疾把这件事告诉陆游，陆游觉得这是辛弃疾施展自己才能的好机会，为他感到高兴，并且

more than 2000 soldiers for uprising in his hometown, and later he joined in the peasant uprising troops. Soon after, upon the orders of imperial court, the uprising troops coordinated with the imperial troops to attack Jin's troops. Due to the exclusion of capitulators, Xin Qiji stayed at home idle for a long time. Until the spring of 1203, he was appointed as the magistrate of a prefecture of Shaoxing and pacifier of East Road in Zhejiang, and he was already 64 years old then.

In the western suburb of Shaoxing, there is a place called Sanshan, where the current famous patriotic poet Lu You lived. Shortly after Xin Qiji took the office, he went to visit Lu You. They talked about the state affairs, and Lu You thought Xin Qiji was a capable person and hope that he could make successful contribution in the nation unification.

In the spring next year, the Emperor of Southern Song called in Xin Qiji to the capital Lin'an, and consulted him on attacking Jin northward. Hsing Qiji told this matter to Lu You, and Lu You thought it was a good chance for Xin Qiji to display his capabilities and felt

特地写了一首长诗赠给他。诗中写道："你是古代大政治家、军事家管仲和萧何一类的人物，现在做了个浙江东路安抚使，实在是把大的材料用在了小处！"

happy for him, and specially wrote a long poem to him, which said, "You are a great politician of the same kind of militarist Guan Zhong and Xiao He, it is a waste of talents for you to be a pacifier of East Road in Zhejiang, just like a large material for petty use."

辛弃疾到了京城以后，皇帝并没有重用他，只是安排他做了镇江府知府。不久，这位爱国词人就在忧愤中病逝了。

After Xin Qiji moved to capital, he was not regarded highly by the emperor, and he was only arranged as magistrate of a prefecture of Zhenjiang. Soon after, the patriotic poet passed away due to illnesses in the worried and indignant mood.

后来，人们便用"大材小用"这个成语，来比喻才能高，职位低，不能使人才充分发挥作用。

Afterwards, people use the idiom of "a large material for petty use" as a metaphor that someone takes a low post in despite of high capabilities, that means a waste of talents.

030

大逆不道

Commit treason and heresy

出自 《史记·高祖本纪》。

释义 形容罪大恶极。

秦朝末年，陈胜、吴广揭竿起义以后，不少英雄豪杰也都纷纷起兵抗秦。

By the end of Qin Dynasty, after the uprising by Chen Sheng and Wu Guang, many outstanding heroes also joined in the uprisings against Qin.

陈胜、吴广死后，秦国将领章邯趁机采取各个击破的战术，打击起义军。于是，项羽的叔父项梁召集各位起义军领袖，开会推选一位楚王，以便统一领导抗秦的力量。找来找去，找到了楚怀王的一个13岁的孙子，立为楚王，称为楚怀王。当时，包括项羽、刘邦在内，各路反秦军队的将领在表面上服从楚怀王的领导，楚怀王也和大家约好，谁先打进秦都咸阳谁就为王。后来，刘邦率军先进了咸阳，项羽并不甘心，想借楚怀王的命令改变原来的约定，谁知楚怀王给的答复是“依照以前的约定，谁先进关谁做王”，项羽一听火了，就夺了楚怀王的实权，尊他为义帝。后来，又指使人把楚怀王杀掉了。

After Chen Sheng and Wu Guang died, the Qin's general Zhang Han took this chance to attack one by one against the uprising troops. Thus Xiang Liang, who was the uncle of Xiang Yu called up the uprising leaders for a meeting and voted for King Chu, for the purpose of unifying the leadership of the troops against Qin. And finally he selected a 13 years old grandson called him as King Huai of Chu. At that time, all the leaders of the uprising troops including Xiang Yu and Liu Bang seemingly obeyed the leadership of King Huai of Chu, King Huai of Chu also made an agreement with all that the first one invaded into the Qin's capital Xianyang would be the king. Afterwards Liu Bang was the first to invaded into Xianyang, but Xiang Yu was not reconciled and intended to change the original agreement by the orders of King Huai of Chu, but unexpectedly King Huai of Chu replied, “As agreed before, the first one invades Qin's capital will be the king.” Xiang Yu was angry to hear this and deprive the real power of King Huai of Chu and respected him as King Yi. Afterwards, he arranged to kill King Huai of Chu.

不久，刘邦兴兵攻打项羽。有一个被人尊称为董公的老年人对刘邦说，攻打项羽得找个名目，并给刘邦出主意说，可以借义帝被杀这件事做文章。刘邦一听有理，于是就隆重地为义帝发丧，并且派人告诉各路诸侯说："义帝是大家共同拥立的，现在项羽指使人谋杀了义帝，真是大逆不道，我愿意和你们一道去征伐杀害义帝的人。"

Shortly Liu Bang defeated Xiang Yu. An old man who was respected as Duke Dong said to Liu Bang that he should find an excuse to attack Xiang Yu and suggested that he could make a fuss on the matter of killing King Yi. Liu Bang though it reasonable and then sent out an obituary ceremoniously, and announced to the leaders, "King Yi was enthroned commonly by us, now Xiang Yu arranged to kill King Yi, it is really treasonous, now I'd like to go on punitive attack on this person."

刘邦借此赢得人心，后来终于打败项羽，建立汉朝。

Thus Liu Bang won the advocacy of people and defeated Xiang Yu, and established Han Dynasty.

031

大器晚成

Great minds mature slowly

出自 《三国志·魏书》。

释义 成名较晚。

三国时期，曹操手下有一个官员，名叫崔琰，身材高大，仪表堂堂，胡须长

In the period of Three Kingdoms, one of Cao Cao's subordinate called Cui Yan, who was high and tall, and had a noble and dignified appearance,

达四尺，很有威严。有一次匈奴使者来访，曹操觉得自己身材矮小，不够体面，于是让崔琰代替自己坐在王位上，自己则拿着一把刀站在旁边。等待使者拜见之后，曹操派人去询问匈奴使者有何评价，使者说："魏王气度不凡，不过旁边持刀的人，才是真正的英雄。"这个故事是为了衬托曹操，不过也说明崔琰外表出众。

with a four feet long beard which looked very august. Once a Xiongnu envoy visited, since Cao Cao thought he didn't have a high and decent appearance, so he asked Cui Yan to replace him to sit on the throne, and he stood aside with a sabre. When the Xiongnu envoy finished visiting, Cao Cao dispatched to ask for some comments, the envoy said, "King Wei has an impressive appearance, but the person holding the sabre beside is the real hero." This story is intended to highlight Cao Cao, but it also proves that Cui Yan's appearance is outstanding.

后来，曹操想把曹植立为太子，征求大臣们的意见，崔琰反对说："自古以来的规矩都是立长子，怎么能立小儿子呢？这是不可以的啊！"崔琰哥哥的女儿，是曹植的妻子，曹植就是崔琰的侄女婿。崔琰却毫不偏袒，曹操很佩服他的为人正直。

Afterwards, Cao Cao intended to establish Cao Zhi as the crown prince and asked for advice from the ministers, Cui Yan objected, "It is an old rule to make the eldest son as the prince, how can you make the youngest as the prince? It is not a right practice!" The wife of Cao Zhi was the daughter of Cui Yan's brother, so Cao Zhi was the husband of Cui Yan's niece, but Cui Yan showed no favoritism, thus Cao Cao highly admired his uprightness.

崔琰在对人才的识别方面，也有独到之处。他有个堂弟名叫崔林，年轻时没有

Cui Yan also had a unique feature in the discernment of qualified personnel. His cousin Cui Lin had no achievements when he was young

什么成就，亲戚朋友都瞧不起他。但是崔琰对这位堂弟非常器重，经常对别人说："能做大事的人往往要经过长期的磨炼，崔林将来一定会成大器。"后来，崔林果然做了高官。

and was despised by his friends and relatives. But Cui Yan regarded him very much and always said to others, "A greatly-achieved person always endures and accumulates for a long time, and I think Cui Lin will make great achievement in the future." Afterwards, as expected, Cui Lin was appointed as a high-level official.

032

才高八斗

Be of profound learning

出自 宋·佚名《释常谈·八斗之才》。

释义 形容一个人的文采出众。

谢灵运是南北朝时期的一位著名山水诗人，出身名门，聪明好学，从小就受

Xie Lingyun was a famous landscape poet of the Northern and Southern Dynasties, who was highborn, intelligent and studious, and was

到祖父谢玄的器重。谢灵运长大后，继承爵位，身为公侯，却被派到外地做了个小官。他自认为怀才不遇，常常丢下公务不管，四处游山玩水。谢灵运酷爱登山，甚至高达数十丈的险峻岩峰他也敢上，他在登山的时候，经常穿着一双木制的钉鞋，上山取掉前掌的齿钉，下山取掉后掌的齿钉，这样上山下山都格外地省力稳当，这就是著名的“谢公屐”。

regarded highly by his grandfather Xie Xuan. When Xie Lingyun grew up, he succeeded the title of nobility and became a duke, but unexpectedly he was appointed to be a low-level official in other place. He thought his talent was unrecognized and always put aside official affairs to travel around. Xie Lingyun loved climbing mountains very much, and even dared to climb the precipitous and steep mountain of several hundred feet high. He wore a pair of clogs with wooden spikes, and he took off the toothed nails of the half soles upwards and took off the toothed nails of the heels downwards, so it would be stable and labor-saving. This is the famous saying of "Duke Xie's Wooden Clogs".

谢灵运写的山水诗，深受人们的喜爱，他每写出一首新诗，立刻就会被人争相抄录，很快流传开来。宋文帝很赏识他的文学才能，特地将他召回京城任职，并把他的诗作和书法称为“二宝”，常常让他陪同吃饭，写诗作文。

Xie Lingyun's landscape poems were greatly favored by people, as long as a new poem came out, it would be circulated very fast. The Emperor Wen of Song greatly admired his literary talents and specially called him back to capital as official, and called his poems and calligraphy as "Two Treasures", and always asked him to have meals and write poems together.

一直自命不凡的谢灵运受到这种礼遇后，更加高傲自大。有一次，他一边喝酒一边自夸道："魏晋以来，天下的文学之才共有一石（容量单位，一石等于十斗），其中曹植独占八斗，我得一斗，天下其他的人共分一斗。"除了曹植以外，其他人的才华他都不放在眼里。

Since Xie Lingyun was always self-glorying, and became supercilious and arrogant upon receiving such great courtesy. Once he boasted during drinking, "From Wei and Jin Dynasties, the total literary talent is of 10 shares, therein Cao Zhi accounts for 8 shares, and I account for 1 share and other people a share together." He looked down upon all the other people except of Cao Zhi.

"才高八斗"这个成语即由此而来。

Thus the idiom of "be of profound learning" came down.

033

门可罗雀

Birds can be caught by a net at the door

出自 《史记·汲郑列传》。

释义 形容门庭冷落，宾客稀少。

西汉著名的史学家司马迁，曾经为汉武帝手下的两位大臣合写了一篇传记，其中一位是汲黯，另一位是郑庄。这

The famous historiographer Si-ma Qian of Western Han Dynasty once composed a common Biography for the two ministers of Emperor Wu of Han, therein one was Ji An and the other was

两人都位列高官，声名显赫，当时到他们家拜访的人络绎不绝，出出进进，十分热闹，都以能与他们结交为荣。但是由于他们的性格刚正不阿，疾恶如仇，所以后来都被撤职。他们丢了官职，失去权势以后，就再也没人去拜访了。

鉴于二人的遭遇，司马迁在传记中举了一个下邽人翟公的事例，来感叹世态的炎凉。翟公是汉文帝时候的大臣，位高权重，每天来见他的宾客络绎不绝，门前水泄不通。而在他失去官职以后，却门前冷落，甚至都可以张起网来捕捉鸟雀了。过了不久，翟公官复原职，于是，那些宾客又想登门拜访他。翟公感慨万千，就在门上写了几句话："一生一死，乃知交情；一贫一富，乃知交态；一贵一贱，交情乃见。"那些客人望着门上的字，只好红着脸，悻悻地走了。

Zheng Zhuang, both of them were high-level officials and prestigious. At that time a large quantity of visitors came to their houses, it was always bustling and busy at the door. People all regarded it as a pride to associate with them. But due to their uprightness and abhorrence of evil, both of them were removed from the office. No one came to visit them since they lost power.

Based on their experiences, Si-ma Qian made an example of Duke Zhai of Xia Gui in the Biography in order to expose the inconstancy and fecklessness of human relationship. Duke Zhai was a minister for Emperor Wen of Han, and there were endless of visitors because of his high position and enormous power. But no one visited him after he lost power. Shortly afterwards, Duke Zhai recovered his original position, so those people planned to visit him again. Duke Zhai felt various emotions and wrote on the door, "The friendship can be proved by life and death, by poverty and rich, and by nobility and ignobility." Those visitors felt shamed and went off when they saw the words on the door.

034

门庭若市

The courtyard is as crowded as a marketplace

出自 《战国策·齐策一》。

释义 门口和庭院里热闹得像集市一样。形容来的人多。

邹忌是战国时期齐国的相国，身材高大，容貌端庄。一天早晨，他穿好朝

Zou Ji was the prime minister of Qi in the Warring States Period, who was high and tall and decorous in appearance. One day

服，戴好帽子，对着镜子端详一番，然后问妻子说："我和城北徐公比较起来，谁长得英俊。"妻子说："你英俊极了，徐公怎么比得上你呢？"徐公可是齐国出了名的美男子，邹忌听了这话以后将信将疑，于是又去问他的爱妾。爱妾同样回答说："徐公怎能比得上您呢？"第二天，邹忌家中来了一位客人，他又问了客人同样的问题，客人说："徐公哪有您美呢？"过了几天，正巧徐公到邹忌家来拜访，邹忌乘机仔细地打量徐公，发现自己确实没有徐公漂亮。

后来，为了劝说齐王广开言路，鼓励人们进谏，邹忌就给齐王讲了这件事，并且说："我本来不如徐公漂亮，但妻子、爱妾、客人都说我比他漂亮，这是因为妻子偏护我，爱妾畏惧我，客人有事求我，所以他们都恭

morning, he got on the court dress and hat and carefully looked at himself in the mirror and asked his wife, "Between Duke Xu of the north town and me, who is more handsome?" His wife answered, "Certainly you! How can Duke Xu be comparable to you?" Zou Ji doubted his wife's reply because Duke Xu was a well-known handsome man, so he asked his concubine the same question, and his concubine gave the same answer, "How can Duke Xu be comparable to you?" The next day, a guest visited him, he asked the same question, and the guest answered, "How can Duke Xu be comparable to you?" Several days later Duke Xu happened to visit him, so Zou Ji took the chance to observe and found that he himself was indeed less handsome than Duke Xu.

Afterwards, in order to encourage the free airing of views, Zou Ji persuaded King Qi and told this story, "Duke Xu is actually more handsome than me, but my wife, concubine and guest all say I'm more handsome than Duke Xu, because my wife shows partiality of me, and my concubine is afraid of me, and the guest turns to me for

维我。那么大到整个齐国，宫中上下谁不偏护您，满朝文武谁不畏惧你，全国百姓谁不希望得到你的关怀，恭维您的人一定更多，您一定被蒙蔽得非常严重了。大王如能开诚布公地征求意见，一定对国家有益。”

齐王觉得很有道理，立刻下令让众人进谏，并分别给予一定的赏赐。命令一下，前去进谏的人们络绎不绝，朝廷门口每天像市场一样热闹。几个月之后，只有断断续续的人来进谏；一年之后，虽然有想进谏的人，但没什么可说的了。齐国从此一跃成为当时的强国。

help, that is the very reason why they flatter me. And the same for Qi, everyone shows partiality for you, and everyone is afraid of you, and everyone hopes to get your favor. You will be seriously deceived if so many people flatter you. Thus it will be good for our country if you can encourage the free airing of views.”

King Qi thought it reasonable and ordered everyone to give advice with rewards. Upon this order, lots of people frequently went to offer their advice, and it was always bustling at the door of the palace just like the marketplace. After several months, people went to give advice intermittently. After one year, although someone wanted to give advice, nothing else could be reported. From then on, Qi quickly became a powerful country at that time.

035

马首是瞻

Follow a lead

出自 《左传·襄公十四年》。

释义 比喻服从指挥或追随某人。

春秋时期，秦国强大，经常欺负那些弱小的诸侯国，引起众诸侯国的强烈反

In the Spring and Autumn Period, Qin was so powerful and always bullied those weak vassal states, which arouse great

感。公元前559年，晋悼公联合其他诸侯国，组成联军去攻打秦国。

dissatisfaction. In 559 BC Duke Dao of Jin allied with other vassal states to attack Qin.

当时负责指挥诸侯联军的是晋国大将荀偃，他原本估计秦国得知诸侯联军来进攻，肯定会惊慌失措，战争很容易取胜。没想到联军内部人心不齐，士气低落，秦军一点也不怕，还在泾河的上游下毒，毒死了不少联军的士兵。

The current commander was the general Xun Yan of Jin, he had estimated that Qin's troops would be panic upon their attack and it would be easy to win the battle. But unexpectedly, his troops were of different minds with low morale, and Qin's troops were not afraid at all and even poisoned the upstream of the Jing River, thus many soldiers of his troops died.

看到这种情况，荀偃想早点发动进攻，就发布命令说："明天早上鸡一叫，我们就准备出发，各支部队都要拆掉土灶，填平水井，以便布阵。作战时，大家都看着我的马头来行动，我指向哪里，大家就奔向哪里。"

In this case, Xun Yan decided to make an early attack and ordered, "As soon as the cock crows tomorrow morning, we'll prepare to start off. All the troops should take down the earthen stoves, and fill the water wells, for the convenience of embattling. When in battle, everyone should refer to the direction of my horse head, you should attack where I direct."

荀偃手下的将领听了他的话，觉得他太专横了，都非常反感。其中有个将领说："晋国从来就没有下过这种命令。你要向西去打秦

The military officers all disliked Xun Yan's arbitrariness and one offer said, "There is no such order in Jin, if you want to attack Qin westwards, go by yourself, and my horse head for east, I will go back to my country."

国，那你自己去吧，我的马头可要向东，回到我们晋国去。”其他诸侯国的将领看到晋国的将领带兵回国，也纷纷撤退，联军不战自乱，荀偃眼看无法挽回，仰天长叹道：“既然下的命令不能执行，就不会有取胜的希望。”只好下令将全军撤了回去。

The other officers also withdrew, thus the allied troops became disordered without even going into battle. Xun Yan understood he could not turn it back, and looked up to heaven and sigh heavily, “Since the orders can’t be implemented, there will be no hope for winning the battle.” Then he ordered the whole troops to withdraw.

036

不入虎穴，焉得虎子

Nothing ventured, nothing gained

出自 《后汉书·班超传》。

释义 不亲历艰险就不能取得成功。

东汉时，班超被派去出使西域，他带了三十六名勇士，首先来到鄯善国。国王

In the period of Eastern Han Dynasty, Ban Chao was dispatched to the Western Regions as an envoy with 36 warriors. He

开始对他们很尊敬，招待也很周到，但过了几天忽然变得冷淡起来。原来是北方匈奴的使者也来到这里，国王的态度摇摆不定，不知道该服从哪一方。

arrived in Kingdom of Shan Shan first, the king offered respectful treatment to him at beginning but turned indifferent several days later. It turned out that the Xiongnu envoys also arrived, and the king was undecided to submit which side.

班超得到消息后，把三十六名勇士集合起来喝酒。喝得畅快的时候，他对大家说："如果国王逮捕我们，把我们送给匈奴使者，那我们的尸骨都会被豺狼吃掉。现在情况危急，不进入老虎洞穴，就不能捉到虎崽。我们何不趁着黑夜，放火攻击匈奴派来的人。他们不知道我们有多少人，一定非常惊慌，这样就可以把他们全部消灭。"

Upon this news, Ban Chao gathered the 36 warriors for pleasant drinking, and said, "If the king seized us and hand us over to the Xiongnu envoys, then our skeletons will be eaten by jackals and wolves. Now in such a critical moment, you can't catch tiger cubs without entering the tiger's lair. Why not set fire and attack the Xiongnu envoys at night? They will be very panic due to unawareness of our quantity of warriors, thus we can kill them all."

大家都同意了。当天夜里正刮着大风，班超带领勇士们悄悄来到匈奴使者住的地方，顺着风向烧起火来，匈奴人惊慌失措，乱成一团。班超亲手杀死三个敌

All agreed, and Ban Chao stealthily lead warriors to set fire on the residence of the Xiongnu envoys. The fire started down the wind, and the Xiongnu envoys were panic and disordered. Ban Chao himself killed three enemies, and the warriors

人，勇士们杀了匈奴使者和随从三十多人，还有一百多人被烧死。

killed more than thirty Xiongnu envoys and followers, and over one hundred people were burned to death.

第二天，班超去见鄯善国王，并把匈奴使者的头颅给他看。国王十分害怕，终于决定投靠汉朝，并把自己的儿子送到汉朝去做了人质。

The next day, Ban Chao went to visit King Shan Shan and showed him the skulls of the Xiongnu envoys. The king was scared and decided to submit to Han Dynasty, and sent his son as a hostage.

037

不可救药

Too seriously ill to be cured by medicine

出自 《诗经·大雅·板》。

释义 已经到了无法挽救的地步。

周厉王暴虐无道，老百姓都在外面公开议论他的过失。大臣召公劝谏说：“人

King Li of Zhou was brutal and immoral, and common people all talked about his mistakes. A minister Shao Gong persuaded

民忍受不了您的命令了！”厉王非常生气，从卫国找来一个巫师，让他来监视那些议论的人，发现以后就来报告，立即杀掉。这样一来，议论的人大大减少了。到后来，厉王的统治越发严苛，老百姓没有谁再敢开口说话，路上相见也只能互递眼色示意而已。

厉王见到这种情景，非常高兴，告诉召公说：“我能消除人们对我的诽谤了，他们都不敢说话了。”召公说：“堵住人们的嘴，要比堵住水流的后果更严重。所以，治水的人要开通河道，使水流通畅，治理民众的人，也应该让他们畅所欲言。如果堵住他们的嘴，那能维持多久呢？”厉王不听劝阻。

眼看周王朝政权摇摇欲坠，忠心耿耿的老臣凡伯极力劝谏厉王施行德政，挽救国家于危亡之际，结果却

him, “People can’t stand your orders!” King Li was very angry and appointed a wizard to keep watch on those people talking about him, and kill immediately. Thus the quantity of those people decreased greatly. Afterwards, King Li’s governing means was more and more severe, and no one dared to speak out and only signaled with eyes when meeting on the street.

King Li was very happy to see this status and told Shao Gong, “I eliminated people’s defamation towards me, and no one dare to say bad things about me.” Shao Gong said, “The result of muzzling people’s mouth will be more serious than plugging up water, and in order to regulate rivers, it is a good idea to unclog water, and the same way to govern people, you should let them speak out freely. How long the country will last if you muzzle people’s mouth? ” King Li didn’t take him dissuasion.

In witness of Zhou’s toppling, a loyal old minister Fan Bo spared no efforts to persuade King Li to carry out benevolent rule in order to save the country, but was framed by treacherous

受到奸臣的诬陷，使厉王对凡伯十分厌烦。凡伯非常愤慨，写了一首诗，后来收入《诗经》。诗中抨击奸臣说：“作恶多端，不可救药！”

果然不出凡伯所料，公元前842年，平民和奴隶们拿起武器，冲进王宫，厉王仓皇逃走，凄凉地度过了14年后病死。

court officials, thus King Li became so sick of Fan Bo. Fan Bo was indignant and wrote a poem which was collected into *the Book of Songs*, which lashed out at the treacherous court officials, “All kinds of evil doings and be irretrievable!”

As expected by Fan Bo, in 842 BC, the civilians and slaves took up arms and burst in the palace, and King Li run away in panic and died of illness after 14 years of bleak life.

038

不求甚解

Read without thorough understanding

出自 晋·陶潜《五柳先生传》。

释义 读书只求懂得大概，不加深入了解。

陶渊明又名潜，是我国最早的田园诗人。他九岁的时候父亲去世，孤儿寡母，

Tao Yuanming, with alternate name as Qian, was the earliest pastoral poet in china, whose father passed away at his nine years old,

在外祖父家里生活。

陶渊明长大后，叔父介绍他任彭泽县令，到任八十一天就辞官回乡，还因此写了一首《归去来兮辞》，表明自己不与世俗同流合污的志向。回到故乡后，陶渊明一面耕田，一面读书写诗，虽然收入微薄，仅够维持一家老小的生活，但他仍然过得十分逍遥自在。

大概在二十八岁那年，陶渊明为自己写了一篇文章，取名《五柳先生传》。文章中这样写道："五柳先生不知道是什么地方的人，也不清楚他的姓名和字。因为住宅旁边有五棵柳树，就以此为号。五柳先生安闲沉静，很少说话，也不羡慕荣华富贵。五柳先生喜欢读书，但只求领会要旨，不在一字一句的解释上过分深究，每当读书有所领悟的时

he and his mother lived with his grandfather.

After Tao Yuanming grew up, his uncle recommended him to be the county magistrate of Pengze, but he quit and returned home after eighty-one days, and wrote a poet of *Homeward Bound I Go* expressing his ambition of not collaborating in worldly evil. When at hometown, Tao Yuanming did farming on one hand and did reading on the other hand, although with humble income supporting the whole family of the old and young, he had a leisurely and carefree life.

At his eighty-two years old, he wrote an artide for himself and called it as *the Biography of Mr. Five Willows*, saying, "It is unknown where Mr. Five Willows comes from, and his name and alternate name, just because there are five willows besides the residence, so Five Willows is taken as his alternate name. This Mr. Five Willows takes a leisurely and peaceful life, and he neither talks much nor envies the wealth and rank. Mr. Five Willows likes reading and only aims at comprehending the main idea instead of thorough interpretation of each sentence,

候，就会高兴得忘了吃饭。五柳先生非常喜欢喝酒，但因为家里穷，不能经常喝到酒。亲戚朋友知道他这种情况，经常叫他来一起喝酒。他每次都会喝个尽兴。简陋的房间里空空荡荡，破旧得都无法遮挡风和太阳，粗布短衣打着补丁，盛饭的竹篮子经常是空的，而他却能安然自得，这样过完自己的一生。”

and he will be so happy and forget to have meals. Mr. Five Willows likes drinking very much, but seldom drinks due to his poverty. His relatives and friends always invite him for drinking by understanding his situation, and he will drink to his satisfaction. In his barely furnished room which is too shabby to shelter from wind and sunlight, he wears coarse short clothes with many patches, and his bamboo rice basket is always empty, nevertheless he lives a life of peace and contentment.”

“不求甚解”的成语就是从这篇文章中引申而来的。

The idiom of “read without thorough understanding” derives from this article.

039

不学无术

Have neither learning nor skill

出自 《汉书·霍光传》。

释义 读书很少，学识浅薄。

汉武帝在位的时候，大将军霍光深受信任，是朝廷里举足轻重的大臣。武帝临

In the reign of Emperor Wu of Han, the senior general Huo Guang was deeply trusted as an important minister. Emperor Wu resigned his

死前，把小儿子刘弗陵（昭帝）托付给霍光辅佐。昭帝去世后，霍光又拥立刘询做皇帝，就是汉宣帝。

youngest son Liu Fuling (Emperor of Zhao) to Huo Guang for support. After Emperor Zhao passed away, Huo Guang enthroned Liu Xun as Emperor Xuan.

宣帝即位以后，立许妃做皇后。霍光的妻子霍显贪图富贵，想把自己的小女儿成君嫁给刘询做皇后，就乘许皇后患病的机会，买通女医下毒害死了许皇后。后来事情败露，女医被逮捕入狱。霍光起先对这件事情一点也不知情，等到这时霍显才告诉了他。霍光非常害怕，指责妻子不该做这种事情。他想去告发，但又不忍心妻子被治罪，思前想后，最终还是把事情隐瞒了下来。

After Liu Xun ascended the throne, he made Imperial Concubine Hsu his as the Empress. Huo Guang's wife Huo Xian covert wealth and honor, and intended to marry her youngest daughter Cheng Jun to Liu Xun as the Empress, so she bought over the woman physician to kill the Empress Xu by taking advantage of her illness. When this matter was uncovered, the woman physician was arrested to prison. Huo Guang knew nothing about this matter until Huo Xian told him. Huo Guang was very scared and blamed his wife for such evil doing. He intended to inform against his wife, but he thought that his wife would be convicted, after considering over and over again, he finally decided to hide the truth.

霍光去世后，有人向宣帝告发这件事情，宣帝派人去调查处理。霍光的妻子听说了，与家人和亲信商量对策，决定召集族人策划谋反，不想走漏了风声，宣

After Huo Guang passed away, someone had informed emperor this matter, and Emperor Xuan appointed people for investigation. When Huo Guang's wife heard this, she discussed with the family members and trust followers and decided to conspire against the emperor with her kinsmen. But

帝派兵将霍家包围，满门抄斩。

unexpectedly someone leaked out the information, and she was besieged by the imperial troops, and finally was condemned to extermination of the whole family.

霍光前后掌握朝政大权四十多年，为西汉王朝立下大功，却因为一时糊涂，导致全家被杀。因此，班固在《汉书·霍光传》中说他“不学无术，暗于大理”，批评霍光因为读书少，见识短浅，不明大局，结果落得一个如此的下场。

During the over forty years of Huo Guang's authority, he made great contributions to the Western Han Dynasty, but due to a thoughtless decision, his whole family was killed. Thus in *the History of Han Dynasty, the Biography of Huo Guang*, Ban Gu described him as “little learning and lack of overall consciousness”, and criticized that because Huo Guang had little learning and no overall consciousness, so he got such a miserable ending.

040

不耻下问

Be modest enough to consult one's inferiors

出自 《论语·公冶长》。

释义 虚心向别人请教。

春秋时期，卫国有个大夫叫孔圉，聪明好学，为人谦虚。在他去世后，卫国国

In the Spring and Autumn Period, there was an official Kong Yu in Wei, he was smart, diligent and modest. After he passed away,

君为了让后代的人都能学习和发扬他好学的精神，因此特别赐给他一个“文公”的谥号。后人就尊称他为孔文子。

the emperor of Wei specially granted him a posthumous title as Duke Wen for encouraging people to carry forward his studious spirit, and the later generations respectfully called him as Kong Wenzi.

在孔圉活着的时候，曾经发生过这样一件事：卫国的太叔疾娶了宋国子朝的女儿。子朝因故逃亡后，孔圉让太叔疾把妻子休掉，而把自己的女儿嫁给了他。后来，太叔疾又与前妻的妹妹私通，孔圉大怒，就把自己的女儿强行夺回来，又嫁给了太叔疾的弟弟。

There was a story when Kong Yu was alive that Taishu Ji married Zi Chao's daughter of Song, after Zi Chao fled due to some reason, Kong Yu asked Taishu Ji to replace Zi Chao's daughter with his own daughter. Afterwards, Taishu Ji had affairs with his ex-wife's younger sister, and due to fury, Kong Yu forcibly took back his daughter and married to Taishu Ji's younger brother.

孔子的弟子子贡认为，作为一个臣子，孔圉以下犯上，并且随意地将女儿嫁来嫁去，都是不符合礼的行为，所以对他被授予“文公”这一谥号不太理解，于是就去问孔子：“孔圉的学问和才华虽然很高，但是比他更杰出的人还有很多，凭什么赐给他‘文公’的谥号？”

The Confucius' disciple Zi Gong believed that Kong Yu offend his superiors and married his daughter randomly, which was incompatible with the traditional ethical codes, so Zi Gong doubted about the posthumous tile of Duke Wen and asked Confucius, "Although Kong Yu had great learning, there are many people who are more excellent than him, what made him deserve for the posthumous title of Duke Wen?"

孔子听了，微笑着说：“孔圉非常勤奋好学，就算对方地位或学问不如他，他都会谦虚地请教，一点都不因此感到羞耻，所以赐给他这个谥号并不会不恰当。”

Confucius smiled and answered, “Kong Yu was very diligent and intelligent, and he always modestly consult his inferiors and felt no shame at all, so he deserved this posthumous.”

听过孔子的解释，子贡终于服气了。

Zi Gong was finally convinced by Confucius’s explanation.

041

不越雷池

Remain within bounds

出自 晋·庾亮《报温峤书》。

释义 做事不敢超越一定的界限。

庾亮是东晋时期的大臣，他的妹妹是晋成帝的母亲。晋成帝即位的时候只有

Yu Liang was a minister of Eastern Jin Dynasty, whose younger sister was the mother of Emperor Cheng of Jin. Emperor Cheng

五岁，庾亮凭借着外戚的身份，掌握中央大权，凡是朝廷大事，都要听取他的意见。

ascended the throne at his five years old, and Yu Liang took hold of the central power by the status of the royal ralative, and the emperor had to take his advice about state affairs.

庾亮掌权后，开始大肆排除异己，将领司马宗心生不满，起兵反叛，不久战败被杀。他的党羽卞阐投奔到历阳将领苏峻那里。庾亮命苏峻交出卞阐，苏峻却包庇不给。因此，庾亮让皇帝下诏召苏峻到都城建康，想趁机解除对方的兵权。

When Yu Liang was in power, he began to discriminate against those who hold different views recklessly, which triggered Si-ma Zong's discontent, thus Si-ma Zong raised troops for rebellion, but was shortly defeated and killed. His adherent Bian Chan went to the general Su Jun of Li Yang for shelter. Yu Liang ordered Su Jun to turn in Bian Chan, but Su Jun harbored Bian Chan and didn't agree. Thus Yu Liang requested the emperor to issue an imperial decree to call Su Jun into the capital Jian Kang, and intended to get rid of his military power by this chance.

苏峻知道庾亮的用意，多次推辞不来，又怕朝廷怪罪自己不听命令，于是以讨伐庾亮的名义起兵，发动叛乱。消息传到驻守在雷池（在今安徽望江县城东南10公里处）附近的温峤都督那里，他立刻给庾亮去信，

Su Jun saw through Yu Liang's intention and declined many times, but he was afraid to be blamed by the imperial palace for disobedience, so he raised troops for rebellion in the name of suppressing Yu Liang. This news spread to Wen Qiao who garrisoned Lei Chi, a place located 10 kilometers southeastward the Wang Jiang County of the current Anhui.

想发兵去保卫都城。庾亮不同意，给温峤回了一封信，说：“我担忧西边的陶侃远远大于担忧历阳的苏峻，请你千万不要越过雷池一步。”陶侃是当时一个有名的将领，手握重兵，因此也受到庾亮的怀疑。

由于庾亮拒绝援军前来，苏峻率领叛军一路长驱直入，攻入都城建康，挟持了小皇帝，庾亮狼狈出逃才免于一死。

Wen Qiao immediately wrote to Yu Liang for sending troops to defend Wei's capital, Yu Liang didn't agree and replied in a letter, "I fear Tao Kan in the west much more than Su Jun of Liyang, please just remain in bounds." Tao Kan was a famous general in hold of millions of troops, and was suspected by Yu Liang.

Because Yu Liang refused the reinforcements, Su Jun drove straight into the capital of Jian Kang and seized the young emperor, and Yu Liang fled helter-skelter and escaped being killed.

042

专心致志

Devote oneself to something wholeheartedly and exclusively

出自 《孟子·告子上》。

释义 做事情时一心一意，聚精会神。

战国时期，齐宣王想聘请孟子做官，孟子不愿辅佐他，推辞而去。有人问孟子

In the Warring States Period, the Emperor Xuan of Qi intended to hire Mencius, but Mencius was not willing to assist him and

为什么不愿意到齐国做官，孟子便给大家讲了这样一个小故事：

declined, someone asked him the reason, and Mencius told a little story as following.

弈秋是当时最会下棋的人。有一次，弈秋收了两个学生，为他们两人同时上课。他一心想使这两个学生尽快掌握要领，把自己的棋艺教给他们，就非常仔细地给他们讲解。

At that time Yi Qiu was the best in playing chess, once he took two students and gave lessons to them together. He hoped these two students could grasp the essentials quickly, so he passed on know-how to them very carefully.

其中一个学生听讲非常认真，一心一意地注意弈秋的讲解和分析，对旁边的事全都不加理会。而另一个学生，看上去他也坐在那里，好像在听讲，实际上却心不在焉。他的脑子里总想着天上会有大雁飞过来，自己要怎样拿弓箭去射它，想着烤肉的味道会有多么鲜美。因为他总是胡思乱想，老师的讲解一点也没听进去。

One of the students listened very carefully to Yi Qiu's interpretation and analysis and paid no attention to other things. While another student seemed to absent-minded, he thought of the wild geese in the sky and how to shoot it and how delicious of roasted geese would be, so he listened nothing of the teacher's interpretation and analysis.

学了一段时间，弈秋让两个学生对下一局，看看他们究竟学得怎么样。起先，

After a period of time, Yi Qiu asked them to play chess for a test. At first, that absent-minded student could barely handle it,

那个开小差的学生还能勉强应付，可渐渐地就显出差距来，最后只有招架之功，没有还手之力了。

but the gap of their skills gradually showed up, and finally he was only able for defense instead of attack.

讲完故事后，孟子接着说："你们认为这是他的聪明才智不如前一个人吗？不是这样的，只是因为他不够专心致志罢了。齐王也是这样，他不能认真地专心听取我的意见，所以我才不愿辅佐他，辞别他离开齐国的。"

Then Mencius explained, "You must think the intelligence of the absent-minded student is inferior to another student, but actually it only because he didn't devote himself wholeheartedly and exclusively. Similarly, the Emperor of Qi didn't listen to my advice carefully, so I'm not willing to assist him, that's the reason I left Qi."

043

为虎作伥

Play the jackal to the tiger

出自 《太平广记》。

释义 帮助坏人作恶。

唐朝有个隐士马拯，听说衡山祝融峰上住着一个伏虎长老，便带着一个童仆上

In Tang Dynasty, a recluse Ma Zheng heard a tiger-subduing elder lived at Zhurong summit of Hengshan Mountain in Hunan, so he

山去拜访。

他们登上祝融峰，来到一座寺庙，看见一位须发皆白的老和尚。老和尚非常热情地挽留他们吃饭，刚巧厨房里的油和盐用完了。马拯就叫童仆下山去买，老和尚陪着他走出寺门。马拯一个人站在寺边观赏山景。这时，从山下又来了一个叫马沼的隐士，告诉马拯说，他在半山腰看见一只猛虎在吃人。马拯听了他的详细描述，惊叫道："那个被吃的是我的童仆！"马沼又说："奇怪的是，那猛虎吃了人后，忽然变成了一个须发皆白的老和尚。"不一会儿，老和尚回来了，马沼凑到马拯耳边悄悄地说："正是这个老和尚。"

两人决心要除掉这只吃人的老虎，于是就谎称后院一口井里传出怪声，把老和尚骗到井边。当老和尚凑到

went to visit with a houseboy.

They ascended to Zhurong summit and saw an old monk of white hair and beard. The old monk showed kind hospitality and asked them to stay for dinner, but the oil and salt were just used out, so Ma Zheng asked houseboy to go downhill and buy. The old monk accompanied him to walk out of the temple, and Ma Zheng was enjoying the mountain landscape by himself. At the moment another recluse Ma Zhao came and told Ma Zheng that he saw a fierce tiger was eating a man, and by his detailed description Ma Zheng screamed out, "That was my houseboy!" Ma Zhao went on, "But it is strange that tiger turned into an old monk of white hair and beard." After a while, the old monk came back and Ma Zhao whispered to Ma Zheng, "That is just the old monk."

These two persons decided to kill this man-eating tiger, and they lied there was strange noise from a well in the backyard, and asked the old monk to have a look besides the

井口看时，马沼用力把他推了下去。老和尚一落水，立刻现出老虎的原形。两人赶紧搬来大石头扔到井里，把老虎砸死了。

well. As soon as the old monk moved besides the well, Ma Zhao push him into the well forcefully, and the old monk turned into a tiger, and they threw huge stones into the well and killed the tiger.

除掉老虎后，两人下山，临时住在猎人搭建在树上的窝棚里过夜。半夜里，树下突然传来一片嘈杂声，他们惊醒过来一看，居然有几十个人哭着要替老虎报仇。猎人解释说：“这些都是被老虎吃掉的人，变成了伥鬼。”马拯听完，骂道：“你们这些伥鬼，死在老虎口里，竟然还要为它痛哭报仇！”

Then they went downhill and stayed overnight in a temporary shack on the tree by a hunter. At midnight, there was noisy under the tree, they waked up and saw scores of people crying to revenge for the tiger. The hunter explained, “Those people were eaten by the tiger and turned into ghosts leeched on to the tiger.” Then Ma Zheng scolded, “You ghosts were eaten by the tiger, but you even cry to revenge for the tiger!”

“为虎作伥”的成语即源出于此。

Afterwards the idiom of “play the jackal to the tiger” derives.

044

井底之蛙

A frog in a well

出自 《庄子·秋水》。

释义 比喻见识短浅，却又妄自尊大。

在一口浅井里，住着一只青蛙。有一天，青蛙在井边看到了一只从海里来的大

A frog lived in a shallow well, one day a sea turtle went by, and the frog boasted, "I live a happy life in the well, I can jump

龟，它就对海龟自夸说："你看，我住在这里是多么快乐啊。有时高兴了，就在井栏边跳跃一会儿；疲倦了，就回到井里，找个洞隙睡上一会儿。或者只留出头和嘴巴，安安静静地把全身泡在水里；或者在软绵绵的泥浆里散散步，也非常舒适。看看那些鱼虾，谁也比不上我。我就是这个井里的主人，无拘无束，你为什么不到井里来游赏一下呢！"

besides the well when I'm happy, go back to the well for a sleep when I'm tired, or just keep my head and mouth out, soak myself in the water quietly, or take a walk in the soft mud, which is also very comfortable. Look at those fish and shrimp, I'm superior to all of them. I'm the owner of this well without any constraint, why not come and enjoy the well?"

海龟听了青蛙的话，想进到井里去看看。但它的左脚还没有整个伸进去，右脚就已经被井壁卡住了。它连忙后退了两步，对青蛙说："你看到过大海吗？海的广大，哪止千里；海的深度，又哪止千丈。古时候，十年有九年发大水，海里的水并不见涨了多少；后来，八年里有七年大旱，海里的水也不见浅了多少。大海不像

The sea turtle wanted to jump into the well to have a look, but its right front foot was trapped in the borehole well when the left front foot prepared to get in, it hurriedly withdrew and said, "Did you have a look at the sea? The sea is more one thousand kilometers wider and deeper, and it neither increases due to frequent floods nor decreases due to great drought. Unlike this shallow well, the sea will not be affected at all by flood and drought, and it will be really free in the sea!"

这口浅井，它丝毫不会受到旱涝的影响。住在那样的大海里，才是真正的自由自在呢！”

青蛙听了海龟的一番话，吃惊得两眼圆睁着，呆在那里，再没有话可说了。

The frog surprised with wide-open eyes, and stupefied with nothing more to say.

045

从容不迫

Take it leisurely

出自 《庄子·秋水》。

释义 不慌不忙，沉着镇静。

战国的时候，宋国有两位大哲学家庄子和惠子，他们是非常要好的朋友。一

In the Warring States Period, there were two great philosophers called Zhuang Zi and Hui Zi, they were very good friends. On a fine

天，风和日丽，庄子和惠子两人兴致勃勃地来到河边散步。两人边走边聊，非常愉快，不知不觉就走到一座桥上，顿时被眼前清澈河水中的鱼儿吸引住了。

and warm day, Zhuang Zi and Hui Zi happily chat and walked beside the river in high spirits, and they were attracted by the fish swimming in the clear river when they got to a bridge.

两人出神地在桥上观赏了很久，庄子忽然脱口而出："看啊，这水里的鱼儿是多么从容自在啊，它们看起来是多么快乐呀！"

They were lost in thought on the bridge for a long time, Zhuang Zi blurt out suddenly, "Look, how leisurely and happy those fish are!"

惠子是个喜欢辩论的人，他一听，立即表示反对："你又不是鱼，怎么知道鱼儿现在很快乐呢?"

Hui Zi was an eloquent person and objected, "You are not the fish, how can you know they are happy now?"

庄子反驳道："你又不是我，又怎么能断定我不知道它们现在很快乐呢?"

Zhuang Zi objected, "You are not me, how can you judge that I don't know they are happy now?"

惠子回答道："照你所说，我不是你，当然不能知道你是喜还是忧。同样，你不是鱼，当然也不知道鱼儿是快乐还是不快乐。"

Hui Zi answered, "According to what you say, because I'm not you, so I don't know you're happy or not. Similarly, you are not a fish, certainly you don't know the fish are happy or not."

庄子不慌不忙地说："我完全是从自己的感受中

Zhuang Zi said without hurry, "I know it from my own feelings, because we are happy

体会到的。咱们二人站在这桥上观赏鱼儿，悠闲自在，心里好不快乐。再看看这鱼儿，它们在水中自由自在地嬉戏，从容不迫地观望着我俩，当然也应该感到十分的快乐啊。”

when we appreciate the fish leisurely, and the fish freely swim and play in the water and leisurely look on us, so they should also feel very lappy.”

046

凤毛麟角

Precious and rare as the phoenix feather and unicorn horns

出自 《南齐书》。

释义 比喻珍贵、稀少的人或事物。

南北朝时期的著名文学家谢灵运，有个孙子叫谢超宗，聪明好学，一手文章写

The famous litterateur Xie Lingyun of Southern and Northern Dynasty had a grand son called Xie Chaozong, who was smart and

得非常漂亮。

谢超宗曾经在宋孝武帝的儿子新安王刘子鸾手下做官，王府中的重要文书，都是出自他的手笔，受到很多人的推崇。新安王的母亲殷淑仪去世的时候，谢超宗为她写了一篇悼念的文章，孝武帝读了以后，对他的才华大加称赞。说：“谢超宗确实有些凤毛，真是谢灵运复生啊!”

当时，右卫将军刘道隆也在旁边，听到了孝武帝的这番话。于是，他专程到谢超宗家登门拜访，对他说：“刚才听皇上说你有凤毛，我想见识一下，开开眼界。”刘道隆不知道谢超宗的父亲名凤，他这样一口一声吵着要看“凤毛”，触犯了谢超宗的家讳。所以谢超宗一听，来不及穿鞋就急忙躲到室内。刘道隆不明白怎么回事，还傻傻地等在那

studious and good at writing poems and essays.

Xie Chaozong was once the official subordinate to Liu Ziluan (the King Xin An), who was the son of Emperor Xiao Wu of Song, and Xie Chaozong was responsible for writing important documents and praised highly and widely. When the mother of King Xin An passed away, Xie Chaozong wrote a mourning article for her and was highly praised by the Emperor Xiao Wu, “There are really some phoenix feather on Xie Chaozong just like the resurrection of Xie Lingyun!”

At that moment, the right-guard general Liu Daolong heard what the emperor said, so he paid a special visit to Xie Chaozong and said, “According to what the emperor said, there are some phoenix feather on you, would you please let me have a look and broaden my vision?” Liu Daolong didn’t know the name of his father was “phoenix” and insisted on seeing the phoenix feather, who offended his father’s name, so Xie Chaozong hurriedly hid in the room even without wearing shoes. Liu Daolong didn’t understand and waited there foolishly because he thought Xie Chaozong

里，以为谢超宗进去是为他找凤毛去了，结果等到天黑也不见谢超宗出来，只好悻悻地走了。

was finding out the phoenix feather for him, and finally he didn’t see Xie Chaozong until dark and went away bitterly.

凤凰和麒麟，都是传说中的珍禽异兽。而凤凰身上的羽毛、麒麟头上的犄角，也是极其珍贵之物，因此也被人用来比喻才华出众的人或不寻常的事物。

The phoenix and kylin refer to the precious fowls and rare animals in the legendary, and it is also extremely precious for phoenix feather and kylin horns, so people use them to describe the outstanding and unusual people or things.

047

分道扬镳

Take separate ways

出自 《北史·魏诸宗室·河间公齐传》。

释义 因志趣或目标不同而各走各的路。

北魏孝文帝时期，有一个人叫元志，饱读诗书，才华出众，孝文帝很赏识他，

In the reign of Emperor Xiao Wen of the Northern Wei, there was a well-educated person called Yuan Zhi, who was highly appreciated

任命他为洛阳令。年纪轻轻的元志手中权势大了以后，渐渐生出骄气，对朝廷中其他一些达官贵族，往往不放在眼里。

by Emperor Xiao Wen and was appointed as the county magistrate of Luoyang. This young guy became arrogant when his power became stronger, so he always looked down upon the high ranking officials and aristocrats.

一天，元志外出，恰巧碰到一个叫李彪的官员乘坐马车从对面飞驰而来。这个李彪任职御史中尉，官位比元志高出许多。按理说，官位小的应该先让官位高的人过去，可元志偏偏不让，两个人因此僵持不下。李彪当众责问元志为何不让路，元志说："我是都城洛阳的长官，你不过是洛阳户籍中的一员，哪有长官给辖下住户让路的？"

One day, Yuan Zhi went out and came across the official Li Biao's galloping carriage. Li Biao held the position of Palace commandant of censors, which was much higher than Yuan Zhi. In this case, the lower official should make way for the higher official, but Yuan Zhi didn't, so they were in a deadlock. Li Biao blamed Yuan Zhi in public for not making way for him, Yuan answered, "I'm the county magistrate of Luoyang, but you are only one of the residents of Luoyang, what's the reason that an official makes way for a resident?"

两人互不相让，最后没办法，只好来到孝文帝那里评理。孝文帝听了他们的话，觉得他们各有各的道理，于是便笑着说："我觉得你们各有各的道理，那为何不分道扬镳，各走各的，不就可以了吗？"

They neither give way to the other, and finally they went to Emperor Xiao Wen for argument. Emperor Xiao Wen thought each had his own reason and smiled to say "Since each of you has your own reason, why not take separate ways?"

两人听后连连点头。于是，他们就把经常通行的道路进行了丈量，各取一半，从此各走各的道。此后，“分道扬镳”一语便逐渐流行开了。

Then they nodded repeatedly in approval, and measured the road for two parts and took each way from then on. Afterwards, the idiom of "take separate ways" became popular.

048

天衣无缝

A seamless heavenly robe

出自 前蜀·牛峤《灵怪录·郭翰》。

释义 比喻事物周密完善，找不出什么毛病。

唐朝的时候，有个人叫郭翰，一天晚上，因夏天炎热，他就借着月色躺在庭院的长椅上乘凉。忽然，有一股清

In Tang Dynasty, there was a person called Guo Han, one night in the heat of summer, he lied on the bench in the yard and enjoyed the cool. Suddenly, a cool breeze

风袭来，风中带着香气，而且越来越浓。郭翰觉得很奇怪，仰视空中，只见天上一朵白云向他飘来。等到白云飘近，他定睛一看，却是个穿着白衣的年轻女子。

blew with fragrance, and fragrance became more and more strong. Guo Han felt curious and lifted up to the sky and saw a white cloud flew to him, and then he took a closer look and found that was a young lady with white robe.

郭翰连忙起身，作揖拜见，说："没有料到尊贵的仙人突然降临，希望您赐教。"那位女子微微一笑，对郭翰说："我是天上的织女。"

Guo Han hurried to get up and bowed, "It is unexpected for your noble fair to suddenly descend, please give me some enlightenment!" That lady smiled and said, "I'm the Weaving Girl from heaven."

织女身上的衣服非常漂亮，郭翰禁不住上上下下地仔细打量。看着看着，他发现这衣服全身都没有针线缝制的痕迹，觉得纳闷，就向织女请教。织女说："我穿的是天衣。本来就不是用针线缝成的。"郭翰听了，不由得连声赞叹："真是天衣无缝呀！"

The robe worn by the Weaving Girl was very beautiful, and Guo Han couldn't help to look at it up and down carefully. Suddenly he found there was no trace of the needle sewing, he felt curious and asked for the reason, and the Weaving Girl answered, "What I wear is a heavenly robe, which is unnecessary to be sewed by needlework."Guo Han couldn't help to praise repeatedly and said, "It is really a seamless heavenly robe!"

成语"天衣无缝"就是从这个故事来的。

Thus the idiom of "a seamless heavenly robe" derives.

049

天花乱坠

Flowers cascading from the sky randomly

出自 《心地观经·序品》。

释义 说话巧妙动听，但往往不着边际。

两晋南北朝时期，佛教开始在中原盛行。南朝梁武帝萧衍带头求神拜

In the Jin and northern and southern dynasties, the Buddhism prevailed in Central Plains. The Emperor Wu of Liang in Southern

佛，在全国修建了很多寺庙。公元527年，梁武帝第一次到同泰寺舍身出家，当了三天住持。他不近女色，不吃荤食，还要求全国效仿。后来，他又多次脱下帝袍，换上僧衣，出家讲解经书。每次都是大臣们捐出大量的钱财，才把皇帝赎回来。

Dynasty called Xiao Yan took lead for praying to Buddha and built up many temples nationwide. In 527 AD, for the first time the Emperor Wu of Liang was tonsured as a monk in Tongtai Temple, and took the office as the Buddhist abbot for three days. He didn't get close to women, didn't eat meat, and he also required the whole country to follow his example. Afterwards, for many times, he took off imperial robe and took on monk dress, and he was keen on interpretation the Buddhist scriptures. Each time the ministers had to donate a lot of money for the redemption of the emperor.

云光法师是梁武帝的好朋友，听云光法师讲诵佛经是梁武帝生活中一件重要的事情。云光法师讲诵经书，有时候会从早上一直讲到晚上，梁武帝也听得非常认真，以至于废寝忘食。据说有一次，因为云光法师讲说佛经绘声绘色，竟然感动了上天，天上的香花从空中纷纷落

The Master Yun Guang was a good friend of the Emperor Wu of Liang. For the Emperor Wu, it was an important thing to listen to the interpretation of Buddhist scriptures by Master Yun Guang. Sometimes the interpretation by Master Yun Guang would last from morning until night, and the Emperor Wu of Liang listened very carefully and even forgot sleep and meals. Once a time, because of the vivid interpretation of Master Yun Guang, the Heaven was moved and a large quantity of fragrant

下。梁武帝看着飞舞的鲜花，大为感叹，说：“想不到佛法竟然如此奇妙！”

从此，梁武帝更加沉迷于佛教，不理朝中政事，导致后期的政绩大大下降。

flowers showered down. The Emperor Wu of Liang was amazed by the flying flowers and praised “How marvelous the Buddha dharma is!”

From then on, the Emperor Wu of Liang was more indulged in Buddhism, and due to his ignorance of state affairs, his political achievements decreased greatly in his later reign.

050

天经地义

The God's Truth

出自 《左传·昭公二十五年》。

释义 指绝对正确，不能改变的道理。

东周时期，周景王去世后，按照惯例，由他的正夫人所生的儿子姬敬

In the Eastern Zhou Dynasty, the Emperor Jing of Zhou passed away, and according to usual practice, his son Ji Jing (the Emperor Jing

（即周敬王）继位。但是，周景王生前曾与一些大臣提过，打算立非正夫人所生的长子姬朝为王位继承人。这样一来，在周敬王继位后，王子姬朝和他的拥护者便起兵反对，周王室内部发生了激烈的王位之争。

of Zhou) born by his first wife would ascend the throne. But when the Emperor Jing of Zhou was alive, he once suggested some ministers for making Ji Chao as the successor, who was born by his concubine. Thus after the Emperor Jing of Zhou ascended the throne, the prince Ji Chao and his supporters arose for rebellion, and a fierce struggle for the throne broke out inside the royal family of Zhou.

在这种情况下，晋顷公召集各诸侯国的代表会盟，商量如何能够使王室安宁下来。参加会议的有晋国的赵鞅、郑国的游吉等人。

In this case, the Duke Qing of Jin called on the representatives of vassal states for alliance and discussed how to pacify the royal family, therein Zhao Yang of Jin, You Ji of Zheng and other people joined in the meeting.

会上，赵鞅向游吉请教什么叫"礼"。游吉回答说："我国的子产大夫在世时曾经说过，礼就是天之经，地之义，也就是老天制定的原则，大地施行的正理！它是百姓行动的依据，不能改变，也不容怀疑。"

During the meeting, Zhao Yang consulted You Ji for the meaning of "propriety", You Ji answered, "When our senior official Zi Chan was alive, he once said that the propriety is the principles of the heaven and earth, which is the God's truth and should be carried out! It is the basis for the civilians' behaviors, and it is unalterable and unquestionable."

赵鞅对游吉的回答很满意，其他诸侯国的代表听了，也大多表示有理。于

Zhao Yang was satisfied at You Ji's answer, and the representatives of other vassal states also agreed. Thus Zhao Yang suggested

是，赵鞅提出各诸侯国应全力支持周敬王，为他提供军队和粮草，帮助他巩固王室。

whole-heartedly support to the Emperor Jing of Zhou for troops and army provisions in order to help him to consolidate his royal power.

后来，在晋国的领导下，各诸侯国军队帮助周敬王赶跑姬朝，结束了周王室的王位之争。

Afterwards, under the leadership of Jin, the troops of vassal states helped the Emperor Jing of Zhou to drive away Ji Chao and finished the struggle of Zhou's throne.

051

天罗地网

Plots in the heaven and traps in the earth

出自 元·李寿卿《伍员吹箫》。

释义 包围得非常严密，无处可逃。

春秋时期，楚平王的手下有个很会溜须拍马的人，叫费无极。有一次，

In the Spring and Autumn Period, there was a person called Fei Wuji as the subordinate of the Emperor Ping of Chu, who was good at flattering.

他奉命到秦国去给太子建迎接新娘，见新娘非常美丽，便怂恿平王留作自己的妃子。昏庸好色的平王居然同意了。

Once he was appointed to Qin for welcoming bride for the prince, since the bride was very beautiful, so he instigated the Emperor Ping to keep her as concubine, and unexpectedly the fatuous and lecherous Emperor Ping even agreed.

太子建的老师伍奢，是个正直的大臣。费无极害怕他将来帮助太子惩罚自己，便怂恿平王杀了伍奢及其长子。然后，又派人去杀害太子建。

Wu She was the teacher of the Prince Jian and he was a righteous minister. Fei Wuji was afraid that Wu She would help the prince to punish him, so he instigated the Emperor Ping to kill Wu She and his eldest son, and then he dispatched to kill the prince Jian.

太子建得到风声，连夜逃到伍奢的二儿子伍员那里，告诉了他父兄被杀的情况，并说费无极已派他的儿子费得雄赶来这里，想骗伍员回去，然后杀掉。

This news leaked to the Prince Jian, so he fled to Wu Yun, the second son of Wu She, overnight and told him the truth that his father and brother were killed by Fei Wuji, who dispatched his son Fei Dexiong to cheat Wu Yuan to come back and kill him then.

过了几天，费得雄果然到来，他见了伍员后，谎称平王因伍员屡立战功，要重加赏赐，请伍员立刻启程回朝，接受赏赐。

Several days later, Fei Dexiong arrived as expected, and he lied to Wu Yun that the Emperor Ping would grant him heavy reward for his may victories, and he required Wu Yuan to set out immediately.

伍员故意问："我已半年未曾回朝，不知我的父亲兄长是否安康？"费得雄装

Wu Yun asked intentionally, "I have not come back for half year, how are my father and brother?" Fei Dexiong answered in a feigned

模作样地说："你们家门兴旺，有哪家比得上!"伍员勃然大怒，一把抓住费得雄的衣襟，痛斥道："如果不是太子建来到这里说明内情，道破你们这些奸人的谎言，我险些被你骗进天罗地网!"

manner, "Your family is so prosperous and no others can compare with you!" Wu Yun was furious and seized the clothes of Fei Dexiong and scolded, "If the Prince Jian didn't come to tell me the truth and exposed your lies, I will almost be deceived into the plots in the heaven and traps in the earth!"

于是，伍员把费得雄痛打一顿，弃官而走。后来他来到吴国，当了吴国的大夫，促使吴国战胜楚国，为父兄报了仇。

Thus Wu Yun gave Fei Dexiong a sound thrashing and discarded the office, then he went to Kingdom Wu as an official, and due to his contribution, Wu defeated Chu, and he made revenge for his father and brother.

052

开卷有益

Reading enriches the mind

出自 宋·王辟之《渑水燕谈录》。

释义 多读书就会有收获。

北宋初年，宋太宗命人编纂了一部规模宏大的分类百科全书《太平御览》，这部书收集摘录了一千六百多种古籍的重要内容，分别归纳

At the beginning of Northern Song Dynasty, the Emperor Tai Zong appointed people to compile a grand-scale classified encyclopedia called *Taiping Imperial Encyclopedia*, including over 1600 ancient

为五十五个种类，共一千卷，是一部很有价值的参考书。

books, totally 55 varieties and 1000 chapters, which was a very valuable reference book.

对于这部巨著的编辑工作，宋太宗非常重视，规定自己每天至少要看两三卷，预计一年内全部看完。有的时候因为公务繁忙来不及阅读，改天一定补上。曾经有人觉得皇帝每天要处理那么多国家大事，还要花费时间看这么一部大书，太过劳累了，就劝告太宗少看些，也不必每天都看，以免过度疲劳，影响身体健康。太宗说："只要打开书本，总会有益处的，况且我并不觉得劳累。"

The Emperor Tai Zong attached great importance to the compiling of this monumental work, and he at least read two to three chapters each day and prepared to finish reading within one year. Sometimes he missed reading due to business and would catch up on another day. Some people thought it would be too tired for an emperor to deal with so many state affairs and read such a monumental work, so persuaded the Emperor Tai Zong to read less or read every few days in order to avoid burnout and affect his health. But the Emperor Tai Zong said, "Reading enriches the mind, and moreover I don't feel tired at all."

当时的大臣们见皇帝如此勤奋读书，也纷纷效仿，所以当时读书的风气很盛，连平常不喜欢读书的宰相赵普，也孜孜不倦地阅读《论语》，享有"半部《论语》治天下"的美誉。

Those ministers began to imitate since they saw the emperor was so diligent in reading, so rcading was very popular at that time, and even the Prime Minister Zhao Pu also read *The Analects of Confucius* diligently although he disliked reading before, so he enjoyed the good reputation of "ruling with half of the analects".

053

手不释卷

Always with a book in one's hand

出自 《三国志·吴书·吕蒙传》。

释义 书不离手。形容勤奋好学。

吕蒙是三国时期的吴国大将，勇敢善战。有一次，他带领三万士兵，乘

Lu Meng was a great general in the Period of Three Kingdoms, who was brave and resourceful in battle. Once he led 30 000 soldiers to attack

坐八十多只船袭击荆州。水手一律穿着白衣，大批精兵埋伏在船舱里，一路前行，来到当阳江边。岸上守卫的汉兵盘问他们是干什么的，吕蒙假称是商船，请求靠岸避风，汉兵信以为真。到了夜间，吕蒙带兵突然发动袭击，打败关羽，夺取荆州，立下了大功。

Jingzhou by taking over 80 boats. The sailors wore white clothes in uniform, and a large quantity of picked troops ambushed inside the boat. When they arrived beside the edge of Dang Yang, the guard soldiers of Han interrogated them, and Lu Meng pretended to be business boats and requested to sock shelter. The guard soldiers of Han believed. At night, Lu Meng suddenly launched an attack, then he defeated Guan Yu and seized Jingzhou as vital contribution.

吕蒙虽然作战勇猛，平时却不喜欢读书。孙权劝他学习史书与兵法，吕蒙总是推托说军队事多没有时间学习。孙权对他说："我并不是要你去研究学问，只是要你翻阅一些古书，从中得到一些启发罢了。"吕蒙问道："可是我不知道应该去读哪些书？"孙权听了，微笑着说："你可以先读一些像《孙子》《六韬》之类的兵法，再读些《左传》《史记》等史书，这些对于你以

Although Lu Meng was brave in the battle, he disliked reading, so Sun Quan persuaded him to read history and military tactic, but Lu Meng always declined and said he had no time to read. Sun Quan said, "I don't ask you to study, just advice you to learn through some ancient books and get some enlightenments." Lu Meng asked, "But which books I should read?" Sun Quan smiled and said, "Firstly you can read some military tactic such as *Sun-Zi* and *Six Arts of War*, and then you can read some historical books such as *Zuo's Biography* and *the Records of History*, which will be good

后带兵打仗很有好处。”接下来，孙权又说：“从前汉光武帝在行军作战的紧张关头，手里还总是拿着一本书不肯放下来，你为什么就没有时间呢？”

for your future battle.” Sun Quan went on, “Formerly in the critical moment of battle, the Emperor Guang Wu of Han always held a book in his hand, why you don’t have no time to read?”

吕蒙听了孙权的话，回去便开始读书学习，并坚持不懈，最终成为一代名将。

Lu Meng took the advice of Sun Quan and began to read diligently and unremittingly, and finally became a famous general.

054

无价之宝

A priceless treasure

出自 《尹文子·大道上》。

释义 比喻极其珍贵的东西。

战国时期，魏国有一位农夫在田里锄草，挖出了一块一尺多长的玉石。他不知道这

In the Warring States Period, a farmer dug out a foot length of jade stone during weeding, since he had no idea of what it was,

到底是什么东西，便拿着玉石来到邻居的家里请教。

he brought the jade stone and went to his neighbor for help.

邻居告诉农夫说：“这块石头很不吉利，放在家中会招灾惹祸，你不如把它放回原处，自己回家过太平日子。”农夫非常相信邻居的话，便将玉石重新放回地里。邻居悄悄跟在后面，等农夫走后，偷偷地把玉石拿回了自己家中。

His neighbor told the farmer, “This jade stone is ominous, taking it home will invite troubles and disasters, you’d better put it in the original place, and you can continue your peaceful life.” The farmer absolutely believed in what his neighbor said and placed the jade stone in its original place, and his neighbor quietly followed him and furtively took it back home.

夜里，那块玉石大放异彩，照得满屋光华四射。邻居的妻子忙对丈夫说：“这样的宝贝放在我们这样的家里，如果让强盗们知道了，为了得到它，还不把我们全家都杀了！”

At night, the jade stone showed unusually brilliant lights and enlightened the whole house. The wife of the neighbor said, “The robbers will kill us if they know we have such a priceless treasure!”

邻居便问妻子怎么处理。妻子说：“你去把这块玉石献给国君，国君看到有人献宝一定十分高兴，他肯定会奖赏你，这样你不就发财了吗!”

The neighbor asked his wife how to deal with it, his wife said, “You present this jade stone to the emperor, and the emperor will be very happy and certainly reward you, then you can make a fortune!”

邻居觉得有道理，于

The neighbor thought it right and brought

是带上玉石，直接向王宫赶去。魏王听说有人来献宝，让人把他带进宫里，并且找来玉工鉴定。玉工对魏王说："大王，这块玉石是无价之宝，用五座城池也换不来啊。"魏王非常高兴，命人重重地赏赐了献宝的人。

the jade stone to the palace, and the Emperor Wei asked a jade worker for authentication。The jade worker said, "Your Honor, this jade stone is a priceless treasure and worth more than five cities." The Emperor Wei was very happy and granted the neighbor heavy reward.

055

日下无双

Unique and unparalleled in the world

出自 《东观汉记·黄香传》。

释义 比喻才能出众，无人能比。

《三字经》里有这么一句话，“香九龄，能温席”，讲的是我国汉代“黄

“The age of nine, Xiang warms bed” is a famous sentence in *the Three-Character Classic*, says the story of Huang Xiang warming bed for

香温席”的故事。

his father when he was nine.

黄香是江夏安陆（今湖北云梦）人，小时候家中生活很艰苦。在他九岁时，母亲就去世了。黄香非常悲伤。他天生就非常孝敬父母，在母亲生病期间，黄香一直不离左右，守护在母亲的病床前，母亲去世后，他对父亲更加关心照顾。冬夜里，天气特别寒冷。为了让父亲少挨冷受冻，他每次读完书，便悄悄走进父亲的房里，给他铺好被子，然后脱了衣服，钻到里面用自己的体温温暖被窝，之后才招呼父亲睡下。街坊邻居都夸奖黄香是个孝敬的孩子。

Huang Xiang was born in a poor family in Anlu of Jiangxia (the current Mengyun of Hubei), and his mother passed away at his nine years old. He showed great filial respect to his parents, when his mother was ill in bed, he kept on taking care of her, and when his mother passed away, he showed more concerns to his father. In the cold night, in order to make his father ensure less cold, he got into his father’s room quietly after reading, spread the quilt, undressed himself and got into the quilt to warm the bed with his temperature, then he asked his father to lie down when the bed was warm. The neighbors all praised Huang Xiang as a filial child.

黄香从小聪慧过人，博览群书，十二岁的时候便精通经史，会写文章，得到了当地官员的赏识，之后又被送到京城洛阳。皇帝特别下诏，让黄香到宫廷中贮藏档案、典籍的东观，自由阅览

Since Huang Xiang was outstandingly excellent as a child, due to extensive reading, he was proficient in interpreting history and writing articles at the age of twelve, so he was highly praised and sent to the capital Luoyang by the local officials. The emperor made a special decree to allow Huang Xiang to freely

官藏的典籍，并且对众人称赞他是“日下（指京城）无双江夏黄童”。

read the ancient books in Dongguan, which was the imperial library, and praised him as “the unparalleled Huang Xiang in capital”.

黄香后来做了地方官，果然不负众望，为当地老百姓做了不少好事。

Afterwards, Huang Xiang took the office as the magistrate, and as expected, he made great contribution to the local civilians.

056

毛遂自荐

Volunteer to do something

出自 《史记·平原君虞卿列传》。

释义 自告奋勇去做某事。

战国时，秦军在长平大胜赵军，坑杀赵国40万降兵后，主将白起领兵乘胜追

In the Warring States Period, Qin's troops defeated Zhao in Changping. After 400 000 capitulated soldiers were buried, the main general

击，包围了赵国都城邯郸。大敌当前，赵国形势万分危急，赵王命平原君赵胜前去楚国寻求援助。

Bai Qi followed up a victory with hot pursuit and encircled Handan, the capital of Zhao. At this critical moment, the Emperor Zhao ordered Duke Ping Yuan to seek help from Chu.

平原君把门客召集起来，想从中挑选20个人陪他一起去。精挑细选之后，还差一个人。这时，有一个叫毛遂的人走上前来，向平原君自我推荐说："我听说先生将要到楚国去签订盟约，现在还少一个人，希望先生就用我凑足人数出发吧！"

Duke Ping Yuan called on his followers and intended to pick up 20 persons for accompany. Although after careful selection, he still needed one more person. Then a person named Mao Sui came along and recommended himself, "I heard you will go to Chu for agreement and there's still a gap of one person, please take me to meet the number!"

平原君说："先生来到我的门下有几年了？"

Duke Ping Yuan asked, "How many year have you been my follower?"

毛遂说："三年了。"

Mao Sui replied, "Three years."

平原君说："贤能的人活在世上，好比锥子处在囊中，尖梢会立刻显现出来。现在，你在我的门下已有三年，人们对你没有称道的话，这是因为你没有什么才能的缘故。就请你留下吧。"

Duke Ping Yuan said, "A competent person is just like an awl in the bag, its point will immediately shows up, but now you have been my follower for three years, if people don't praise you, it is because you are not competent, so please stay here."

毛遂说："我不过是今天才请求进到囊中罢了。如

Mao Sui said, "I just request to be in the bag until today, if I was in the bag earlier, I

果我早就处在囊中的话，就会像稻穗的尖芒那样，整个都会挺露出来，不单单是露出一点尖梢而已。”

should stick out as the whole awn of rice ears would instead of mere tip.”

平原君于是决定让毛遂一道前往楚国。到楚国以后，平原君与楚王谈判半天没有成效，毛遂手拿宝剑走上宫殿，陈述利害关系，说得楚王心悦诚服，答应马上出兵。没过几天，楚、魏等国联合出兵救援赵国，秦军撤退。平原君回到赵国后，从此便把毛遂作为贵宾招待。

Thus Duke Ping Yuan decided to take Mao Sui together to Chu. When the negotiation between Duke Ping Yuan and the Emperor Chu seemed to be ineffective, Mao Sui went into the palace and made a statement of advantages and disadvantages, and the Emperor Wei was sincerely convinced and agreed to dispatch troops. After several days, Chu, Wei and other states dispatched troops in alliance to help Zhao and defeat Qin. When Duke Ping Yuan came back to Zhao, he began to treat Mao Sui as a distinguished guest.

057

水滴石穿

Constant dripping water wears through a stone

出自 宋·罗大经《鹤林玉露》。

释义 只要目标专一，持之以恒，再艰难的事情也能办成。

宋朝时，有个叫张乖崖的人，在崇阳县担任县令。当时，崇阳县社会风气很

In Song Dynasty, there was a person called Zhang Guaiya as the county magistrate of Chongyang. The social morality of Chongyang

差，盗窃成风，甚至连县衙的钱库也经常发生失窃的事件。张乖崖决心要好好刹一刹这股歪风。

was bad, many people stole things, and even the coffer of the county government was stolen frequently, so Zhang Guaiya decided to exterminate such bad social morality.

有一天，他在衙门周围巡视，看到一个管理县里钱库的小吏，慌慌张张地从钱库中走出来，张乖崖想到钱库经常失窃，判断库吏可能是监守自盗。便让人对库吏进行搜查。结果，在库吏的头巾里搜到一枚铜钱。

One day, he made an inspection around the county government and saw a petty official walking out of the coffer in a flurry, and in consideration of the recent frequent pilferage of the coffer, he judged it was an inside job. So he ordered to search on this coffer official, and finally found a copper coin in his kerchief.

张乖崖把库吏押回大堂审讯，问他一共从钱库偷了多少钱，库吏不承认另外偷过钱，张乖崖便下令拷打。库吏不服，争辩说:“偷了一枚铜钱有什么了不起，你竟这样拷打我？”

Zhang Guaiya escorted this coffer official to tribunal for interrogation, and asked how much money he had stolen, but the coffer official, refused and contested, “It is not a big deal to steal one copper coin, why you interrogate me in this way?”

张乖崖十分愤怒，他拿起朱笔，宣判说：“一日一钱，千日千钱，绳锯木断，水滴石穿。”意思是说，一天偷盗一枚铜钱，一千天就偷了一千枚铜钱。用绳子不

Zhang Guaiya was furious and pronounced his judgment with a cinnabar brush in hand, “One coin for each day, a thousand coins for a thousand days; a constant friction by ropes will cut off the wood, and the constant dripping water can wear through a stone.”

停地锯木头，木头就会被锯断；水滴不停地滴，也能把石头滴穿。

判决完毕，张乖崖下令把库吏押到刑场，斩首示众。从此以后，崇阳县的社会风气大大好转。

After the pronouncement, Zhang Guaiya ordered to escort the coffer official to execution. ground and cut off his head in public. From then on, the social morality of Chongyang had improved greatly.

058

车水马龙

Incessant stream of carriages and horses

出自 《后汉书·明德马皇后纪》。

释义 形容车马往来的热闹场景。

东汉名将马援的小女儿马氏，由于父母早逝，在年纪很小的时候就开始操办

Miss Ma was the youngest daughter of Ma Yuan who was a famous general in the Eastern Han Dynasty. Due to the early death

家中的事情，把家务料理得井然有序，亲朋们都称赞她能干。十三岁那年，马氏被选进宫里。光武帝去世后，汉明帝即位，马氏被封为皇后。

of her parents, Miss Ma began to make orderly arrangement for family affairs at an early age, and was highly praised by relative and friends. She was selected to the imperial palace at her 13 years old and ennobled as the Empress when the Emperor Guang Wu passed away and the Emperor Ming of Han ascended the throne.

马氏当了皇后以后，生活仍然非常俭朴，经常穿着粗布衣服，裙子也不镶边。后宫内的嫔妃们都对她非常尊敬。

Although as the Empress, she still lived a thrifty and simple life, and wore coarse clothes, none frilly skirts. She was greatly respected by the concubines of the imperial harem.

明帝死后，马氏的儿子即位，这就是汉章帝。马皇后被尊为皇太后。不久，章帝根据一些大臣的建议，打算对皇太后的弟兄封爵。马太后遵照光武帝有关后妃家族不得封侯的规定，明确反对这样做。第二年夏天，发生了大旱灾。一些大臣又上奏说，今年所以大旱，是因为去年不封外戚的缘故。他们再次要求分封马太后的舅父。马太后还是不同意，并

After the Emperor Ming passed away, her son ascended the throne as the Emperor Zhang of Han, and she was honored as the Empress Dowager. Soon after, the Emperor Zhang intended to confer the brothers of the Empress Dowager according to suggestions of some ministers. But the Empress Dowager Ma refused definitely according to the regulations of the Emperor Guang Wu that the empress' family shouldn't be conferred. Heavy drought happened in summer of the following year, and some ministers said it because family members of the Empress Dowager were not conferred, so

且为此专门发了诏书，诏书上这样说道："前几天我路过娘家门前，看见从外面到舅舅家拜见请安的，车如流水，马如游龙，往来不绝。我当时竭力控制自己，没有责备他们。他们只知道自己享乐，根本不为国家忧愁，我怎么能同意给他们加官晋爵呢？"

they suggested conferring the maternal uncle of the Empress Dowager. But the Empress Dowager Ma refused again and made a special decree saying, "Several days before, I passed by my maternal house and saw the visiting carriages were like an endless stream of water and horses like swimming dragon, with people streaming in and out. At that moment, I held myself not to blame them, because what they cared are only selfish pleasure instead of state affairs, who can I agree to confer them?"

后来，人们便把其中的"车如流水，马如游龙"一句总结成了成语：车水马龙。

Afterwards, people summarize the idiom of "incessant stream of carriages and horses" out of the sentence that "the visiting carriages were like an endless stream of water and horses like swimming dragon".

059

长风破浪

Ride the wind and cleave the waves

出自 《宋书·宗悫传》。

释义 比喻志向远大，不怕困难，奋勇前进。

南北朝时期，有个叫宗悫的人，从小就不爱读书，却一味喜欢舞刀弄

In the Southern and Northern Dynasty, there was a person called Zong Que, who disliked reading as a child but only liked

枪，练拳习武，年纪不大，武艺就十分高强。宗悫的叔父担心他不走正道，就询问他的志向是什么，宗悫大声回答说：“愿乘长风破万里浪！”

brandishing weapons and practicing boxing and martial arts. Although as a young man, he excelled in martial arts. His uncle worried that he would deviate from the right track and asked his ambition, and Zong Que replied loudly, “I'd like to ride the strong winds and cleave the ten thousand miles of waves!”

宗悫的哥哥结婚时，家里宾客盈门，非常热闹。有十来个盗贼也乘机冒充客人，混了进来。正在大家喝酒道贺的时候，这伙盗贼潜入宗家的库房里抢劫起来。有个家人去库房拿东西，发现了盗贼，大声惊叫着跑到客厅。一时间，客厅里的人都被惊呆了，不知如何是好。只有宗悫镇定自若，拔出佩剑，直奔库房。盗贼一见来了人，挥舞着刀枪恐吓宗悫，宗悫面无惧色，举剑直刺盗贼，盗贼见势不妙，丢下手中的财物，脱身逃跑了。宾客们见盗贼被赶走，纷纷称赞宗悫机敏勇敢，少

On the marriage ceremony of Zong Que's elder brother, it was very bustling to have lots of visitors, by this chance a dozen robbers pretended to be guests and mixed in. When people showed congratulations by drinking, those robbers sneaked into the storeroom and began to loot. At that time a family member happened to take something in the storeroom, he screamed out and run to the reception room when he found the robbers. For a moment, all the people in the reception room were too stunned to do anything. Only Zong Que was perfectly calm and collected, he pulled out the sword and rushed into the storeroom. The robber brandished knives and tried to intimidate him, but Zong Que was not afraid at all, he lifted the sword and stabbed at the robbers. The robbers understood the situation was

年有为。

unfavorable and run away, and the visitors all praise Zong Que for his smartness and bravery at such a young age.

几年以后，林邑国侵扰边境，皇帝派交州刺史檀和之前去讨伐，宗悫自告奋勇请求参战，被皇帝任命为振武将军。林邑国放出象群出战，士兵们无法抵抗。紧急关头，宗悫做了几头假狮子，摆在大象前，把大象吓跑了。于是宗悫带头，攻下了林邑。

Several years later, the kingdom Linyi invaded and harassed Song's territorial boundaries, so the emperor dispatched the Jiaozhou provincial official Tan Hezhi to suppress, while Zong Que volunteered to join the battle and was appointed as the General Zheng Wu. The kingdom Linyi let out herds of elephants in the battle, which make the soldiers unable to fight back. At the critical moment, Zong Que made several fake lions and scared away the elephants, then Zong Que lead the troops to attack and occupy Linyi.

就这样，宗悫为国家打了不少胜仗，立下许多战功，被封为洮阳侯，实现了他少年时的志向。

In this way, Zong Que won many battles and made lots of battle achievements.Finally, he was conferred as Duke Taoyang, with his juvenile ambitions realized.

060

风声鹤唳

The sound of the wind and the cry of the crane

出自 《晋书·谢玄传》。

释义 形容人在惊慌时疑神疑鬼。

公元383年，前秦皇帝苻坚率领九十万大军，南下攻打东晋。东晋皇帝派谢石

In 383 AD, the former Qin emperor Fu Jian led 900 000 troops to attack the Eastern Jin southward. Xie Shi was appointed as the senior

为大将，谢玄为先锋，带领八万精兵迎战。苻坚把兵力集结在寿阳（今安徽寿县）东面的淝水边，想等后续大军到齐，再向晋军发动进攻。

general and Xie Xuan as the pioneer, they took lead of 80 000 picked troops against the enemies. Fu Jian assembled the troops besides Feishui of Shouyang (the current Shou County of Anhui) and planned to launch attack when the reinforcement troops arrived.

谢玄派人到秦营，对他们说："你们在淝水边安营扎寨，显然是为了持久作战，而不能速战速决。如果你们稍向后退，让我军渡过淝水，一决胜负，不是更好吗？"秦军将领们都认为要坚守淝水，不让晋军过河。等后续大军抵达，就可彻底击溃晋军，因此劝苻坚拒绝晋军的建议。但是苻坚求胜心切，不同意将领们的意见，说："我军只要稍稍后退，等晋军一半过河，一半还在渡河的时候，用精锐的骑兵冲杀上去，我军肯定能大获全胜！"

Xie Xuan dispatched people to Qin's camp and said, "The purpose that you pitched the camp besides Feishui is obviously for a long-term battle instead of a quick-fix battle, if you could draw back slightly to let us cross Feishui, than we could have a showdown, wouldn't it be better?" The generals of Qin troops believed that they should hold fast to Feishui and stop Jin troops to cross the river, and when the reinforcement troops arrived, they could annihilate the enemies, thus they persuaded Fu Jian to refuse the suggestions of Jin troops. But Fu Jian was eager to win, he disagreed the advice of the generals and said, "We could make slight withdrawal and wait until Jin troops cross over half of the river, then our picked troops will rush ahead and attack, thus we can gain a complete victory!"

于是，秦军决定后退，

So, Qin troops decided to draw back, but

可是苻坚万万没有料到，士兵们一接到后退的命令，都以为前方打了败仗，慌忙向后溃逃。谢玄见敌军溃退，马上指挥部下快速渡河杀敌。秦军一片混乱，自相践踏而死的不计其数。那些侥幸逃脱的士兵，在路上听到呼呼的风声和鹤的鸣叫声，都以为晋军又追来了，于是不顾白天黑夜，拼命地奔逃。就这样，晋军以少胜多，取得了淝水之战的大捷。

unlike what Fu Jian had expected, when the soldiers received the order to withdraw, all of them thought that the frontline failed the battle, so they fled in panic. Then Xie Xuan ordered the soldiers to quickly cross the river and attack. Qin troops were in utter confusion and countless soldiers trampled each other down to death. When those soldiers who narrowly escaped heard the sound of wind and the cry of the crane, they even believed that Jin troops caught up again, and then they fled desperately regardless of day or night. Finally, Jin troops defeated the enemies with a force inferior in number and gained a complete victory in the Feishui Battle.

061

东山再起

Bob up like a cork

出自 《晋书·谢安传》。

释义 失势之后重新得势。

谢安，字安石，是东晋时期的著名政治家和军事家，他在少年时就很聪

Xie An, with the alternate name as Anshi, was the famous politician and militarist in the Eastern Jin Dynasty. When in the boyhood, he was

明，不仅学识很高，而且擅长书法，写得一手好字。谢安年轻时不愿做官，任著作郎不久便以有病为借口辞官回家。隐居在浙江会稽的东山，经常与王羲之、许询等人一起游山玩水，写诗作文。朝廷知道他很有才干，征召他做吏部侍郎，也被他拒绝了。后来，征西大将军桓温邀请谢安做司马，在迫不得已的情况下，谢安只好答应，这时，他已经四十多岁了。

clever, knowledgeable and good at calligraphy. When Xie An was young, he disdained to be a court official and quit for home by the excuse of illness soon after he took the office as the assistant official historian. He lived in seclusion in the Eastern Kuaiji Mount of Zhejiang, and always traveled and exchanged poems with Wang Xizhi and Xu Xun. In consideration of his competence, the imperial court called him up to be the official assistant minister, but was declined by Xie An. Afterwards, the Subduing-the-west General Huan Wen invited Xie An to be the minister of war, and Xie An was compelled to agree. At that time, he was forty years old.

在谢安将要出发的那天，朝廷的官员们都前来送行。这时，御史中丞高崧对他开玩笑说："你过去高卧东山，多次违背朝廷旨意，人们常常议论说，谢安石不肯出山做官，将怎样面对江东百姓；那么，现在江东百姓将怎样面对出山做官的谢安石呢！"谢安听了这

All the court officials came to see him off when he was about to start off, at this moment the assistant minister of justice Gao Song said in joke, "In the past, you lived in seclusion in the Eastern Kuaiji Mount in violation of the imperial orders and refused to take the office times again, so people all discussed how Xie Anshi would face the civilians of the Eastern Kuaiji Mount; and now, how the civilians of the Eastern Kuaiji Mount would face Xie Anshi when he leaves the Mount and takes the office! " Xie An felt very

话，感到很惭愧。

谢安到了桓温那里，两个人交谈了一整天，非常投机。桓温死后，谢安接替桓温掌握了东晋的军政大权。在前秦与东晋的淝水之战中，他派侄子谢玄和弟弟谢石担任将领，带兵迎敌，打败了苻坚的百万大军。

"东山再起"这个成语，就是从高菘说的话中总结而来的。

ashamed by hearing this.

After Xie An met Huan Wen, they chatted happily whole day long. After Huan Wen passed away, Xie An replaced him and took over the military power of the Eastern Jin. In Feishui Battle between the former Qin and the Eastern Jin, Xie An appointed his nephew Xie Xuan and younger brother Xie Shi as the generals, and they led troops and finally defeated millions of troops of Fu Jian.

Thus the idiom of "bob up like a cork" is summarized from what Gao Song said.

062

东施效颦

An ugly woman trying to imitate a famous beauty knitting her brows

出自 《庄子·天运》。

释义 盲目模仿，适得其反。

春秋时期，越国有一位美女名叫西施，是传说中的

In the Spring and Autumn Period, there was a beauty called Xi Shi in the kingdom

中国古代四大美女之一。她无论是举手投足，还是音容笑貌，都十分招人喜爱；她走到哪里，哪里就有很多人向她行注目礼。

of Yue, who was one of the legendary Four Beauties. People all liked her gestures and expressions, her voice and countenance, and people always stared at her wherever she went.

西施一直患有心痛的毛病。有一天，她从乡间走过，这时心痛病又犯了，于是便手捂胸口，双眉皱起，自然流露出一种娇媚柔弱的女性之美，旁边的人无不睁大眼睛注视着。

Xi Shi always had the problem of heartache. One day, she had an attack of heartache when she passed through the country path, with her hands covering the chest and her eyebrows wrinkling, which reveals a kind of delicate feminine charms, and people around all focused on her with widely opened eyes.

乡里有一个叫东施的女子，相貌很丑，却一天到晚做着美女的梦。这一天，她看到西施捂着胸口、皱着双眉的样子，觉得特别的美。回去以后，她也学着西施的样子，手捂胸口、紧皱眉头，在街上走来走去。结果，人们看见她走过来，马上远远地躲开，简直像见了瘟神一样。

There was an ugly woman called Dong Shi, who dreamed to be a beauty all day long. This day, she saw Xi Shi covering the chest and wrinkling her eyebrows and thought it was very beautiful. So she began to imitate Xi Shi to cover the chest and wrinkle the eyebrows when walking through the street, but people all kept far away from her as if she was the God of Plague.

东施只知道西施皱眉的样子很美，却不知道她为什

Dong Shi only knew it was beautiful when Xi Shi wrinkled her eyebrows, but didn’t know

么美，而去简单模仿她的样子，结果反而受到了人们的讥笑。

why she was beautiful, so she was ridiculed by people when she imitated Xi Shi in a simple way.

063

东窗事发

One's criminal conspiracy is unmasked

出自 元·刘一清《钱塘遗事》。

释义 形容阴谋败露。

南宋初期，金国大举进攻中原，在国家危难之际，岳飞率领岳家军对金兵进行

At the beginning of Southern Song Dynasty, the Kingdom of Jin launched a massive attack on the central plain. At the

了顽强的抵抗，接连打了好几次胜仗。可是奸臣秦桧却在宋高宗面前竭力宣扬议和的好处，宋高宗同意了。岳飞多次上书，请求取消和议抗击金兵，因此得罪了秦桧。

critical moment of national crisis, Yue Fei led Yue's troops to put up a stiff resistance, and gained several battles. But the treacherous court official Qin Hui endeavored to advocate the benefits of peace negotiation to the Emperor Gao Zong of Song, and finally the emperor agreed. Yue Fei submited letters to the emperor many times asking for canceling peace negotiation and insisting on fighting, which offended Qin Hui.

秦桧一心想着把岳飞除掉，可是岳飞威望很高，手中又有兵权，他一时难以下手。有一天，秦桧坐在东窗下，正为这事发愁，夫人王氏走进来，对他说："这有何难，你找几个罪名安在岳飞头上不就行了？"秦桧说："罪名不难找，难找的是告发岳飞的人啊。"王氏想了想，说："我听说岳飞手下的都统王贵，在一次战斗中胆小怕死，岳飞想把他斩首示众，后经众将求情，岳飞才免他一死。他肯定怀

Qin Hui set his mind on killing Yue Fei, but it was difficult to find a chance due to Yue Fei's high prestige and military power. One day, Qin Hui was worrying about this matter when he sat under the east window, his wife Wang walked in and said, "It is actually quite easy, you can place several accusations on Yue Fei." Qin Hui said, "It's not difficult to find accusations, but it is difficult to find an informer." His wife Wang thought it over and said, "It is heard that the commander-in-chief Wang Gui was nearly beheaded due to his cowardice in a battle, and was spared because the general pleaded for him, so he must hold grudge against Yue Fei, why not

恨在心，你何不找他告发呢？”秦桧一听，大喜道：“夫人高见！”

you persuade him to be the informer?” Qin Hui was excited to hear that and said, “How brilliant my wife is!”

结果，秦桧终于把岳飞陷害而死。后来，秦桧因病去世，他死后七天，王氏请来道士做法事。道士痛恨秦桧杀害忠良，就对王氏说：“我看见了大人，阎王小鬼正在拷问他，大人对我说，麻烦你告诉我的夫人，东窗事发了。”

Finally, Yue Fei was framed up to death by Qin Hui. Afterwards, seven days after Qin Hui died due to illness, his wife Wong asked a Taoist to perform a religious rite. The Taoist hated Qin Hui’s behavior to kill the upright Yue Fei, and said to Wang, “I saw the Hades and goblins are torturing him during interrogation, and he asked me to tell you that the criminal conspiracy you discussed under the east window was exposed.”

064

乐不思蜀

Indulge in pleasure and forget home and duty

出自 《三国志·蜀书·后主传》。

释义 形容乐而忘返或乐而忘本。

三国时期，蜀国的刘备因病去世，儿子刘禅继位，被称为后主。刘禅昏

In the period of Three Kingdoms, Liu Bei of Shu died due to illness, and his son Liu Shan ascended the throne as the emperor. Liu

庸无能，只知道玩乐，而且由于丞相诸葛亮等人先后去世，蜀国国势日趋衰弱。魏国大将邓艾率军攻打到蜀国都城成都，刘禅投降，当了俘虏。魏帝命刘禅迁到魏国都城洛阳居住，封他为安乐公。刘禅衣食无忧，在异国他乡仍然过着享乐的生活。

Shan was stupid and incompetent and indulged himself in pleasure, and moreover Zhu-ge Liang and other ministers passed away one after another, the national power of Shu became more and more weak. The Wei's general Deng Ai led troops to attack the capital of Shu, and Liu Shan surrendered and became captive. The Wei's emperor ordered Liu Shan to stay in the capital Luoyang and conferred him as the Duke Pleasure, thus Liu Shan still led a pleasurable life without worrying about food or clothing in foreign country.

一天，大将军司马昭请刘禅饮酒。席间，特地让美女为他表演蜀地歌舞，在场的蜀汉旧臣看了，都十分难过，只有刘禅看得津津有味，一点也没有亡国之恨。司马昭故意问刘禅说：“你思念蜀地吗?”刘禅回答道：“这里很快乐，我不思念蜀地。”过了一会儿，刘禅起身上厕所，他的旧部下郤正跟着出来，暗地里对他说：“今后大将军再问您是否还

One day, the great general Si-ma Zhao invited Liu Shan for drinking, and he specially arranged beauties to sing and dance for him, all the former ministers of Shu were very sad, only Liu Shan enjoyed very much, without any hatred of national subjugation. Si-ma Zhao specially asked Liu Shan, “Do you miss Shu?” Liu Shan answered, “There's so much pleasure here, I don't miss Shu at all.” After a while, Liu Shan got up and went to the toilet, his former subordinate Xi Zheng followed up and privately said to him, “Next time when the great general asks you the

思念蜀地，您应该哭着说，我没有一天不思念。这样，您还有希望回到蜀地去。”

第二天，司马昭又召见刘禅，对他说：“你真的不思念蜀地吗？”刘禅便捶胸顿足地说：“祖上的坟墓都在蜀地，我无时无刻不在思念啊。”却没有流下半滴眼泪。司马昭笑着问：“这是郤正教你说的吧？”刘禅睁大双眼道：“正是，您是怎么知道的呢？”司马昭不由得哈哈大笑，私下对人说：“一个人竟糊涂到这等程度，真是不可思议。即使诸葛亮还活着，也不能保住蜀国的江山啊。”

same question, you should cry and say that you're always missing Shu. In this way, it is hopeful for you to be back to Shu."

Next day, Si-ma Zhao called in Liu Shan again and asked, "You really don't miss Shu at all?" Liu Shan thumped his chest and stamped his feet, "The graves of my ancestors are all in Shu, I have been missing Shu all day long." But Liu Shan didn't shed any tears, so Si-ma Zhao smiled and asked, "Is that Xi Zheng taught you?" Liu Shan answered with eyes widely opened, "Exactly, how do you know that?" Si-ma Zhao couldn't help to laugh and said to others in private, "It is really unbelievable that a person can be so muddleheaded. Zhu-ge Liang shall not preserve Shu even if he is alive."

065

令行禁止

Strict enforcement of orders and prohibitions

出自 《逸周书·文传》。

释义 法令严明，执行认真。

商朝末年，纣王残暴无道，不得人心。与此同时，西周的诸侯姬昌却勤于政

By the end of Shang Dynasty, the King Zhou was thuggish and unpopular. In the meantime, Ji Chang, the vassal of the Western

务，广招贤才，施行仁政，大力发展农业生产，使得西周的疆土日益扩大，百姓安居乐业，许多诸侯都拥戴姬昌。

Zhou diligently worked on government affairs, widely recruited capable people, implemented benevolent governance, and particularly developed agriculture, which made Zhou an expanded territory and the civilians a peaceful life, thus many vassals all supported him.

面对越来越强大的西周，纣王心里十分不安，生怕威胁到自己的统治，就找了个借口，把姬昌召来，并把他囚禁在羑里。

As the Western Zhou grew stronger and stronger, the King Zhou was very upset and afraid that his governance would be threatened, so he called in Ji Chang by an excuse and shut him up in Youli.

为了解救姬昌，西周的臣子们想尽办法，最后有一个叫散宜生的人，抓住纣王贪财好色的爱好，找到一个有莘氏的美女，以及骊戎宝马和许多奇珍异宝，通过纣王的宠臣费仲献给纣王。纣王一见到美女和宝物，心花怒放，当即就把姬昌释放出狱。

In order to save Ji Chang, the ministers of the Western Zhou tried many methods, and finally there was a person called San Yisheng, who found that the King Zhou was fond of money and beauty, so he dedicated a beauty of You Shen and picked Lirong horses and priceless treasures to King Zhou via his favored minister Fei Zhong, King Zhou was immediately excited upon receiving the beauty and treasures, and released Ji Chang at once.

姬昌回到西周以后，便筹划起讨伐商朝的事宜，由于日夜操劳，加上年老体弱，积劳成疾。姬昌在临死

After Ji Chang came back to the Western Zhou, he began to make plans for attacking Shang, but due to his indefatigable work and feebleness in old age, he fell sick. Before

之前，把儿子姬发叫来，对他说："我一生最大的愿望就是消灭商纣振兴国家，你如果能够做到有令即行，禁行即止，那才是真正建立王朝事业的开端。我希望你能够实现我的愿望。"

姬发发愤图强，立志要灭掉商朝，两年以后，他率领诸侯起兵伐纣，纣王最终自杀。

death, he called in his son Ji Fa and said, "My biggest wish is to eliminate the King Zhou of Shang and vitalize our country. If you can insist on strict enforcement of orders and prohibitions, it will be a real beginning of establishing dynasty. I hope you could make my wish come true."

Afterwards, Ji Fa devoted himself to make the country strong and was determined to eliminate Shang. Two year later, he led vassals to attack Zhou, and finally, the King Zhou committed suicide.

066

以卵击石

Throw straws against the wind

出自 《墨子·贵义》。

释义 比喻不自量力，自取灭亡。

墨子是墨家学派的创始人，也是战国时期著名的思想家。他创立墨家学说，在

Mo Zi was the initiator of Mohism and a famous philosopher in the Warring States Period. The Mohism he initiated had a great

先秦时期影响很大，与儒家并称“显学”。

influence in the former Qin dynasty, it was jointly named as “Practice Theory” with Confucianism.

有一年，墨子前往北方的齐国，在途中遇见算命先生，他对墨子说：“您不能往北走了，今天天帝在北边杀黑龙，你的皮肤很黑，去北方是不吉利的。”

One year, Mo Zi went to Qi in the north and met a fortune-teller, who said to him, “You’d better not go northward, because the Emperor of Heaven kills the black dragon in the north, your skin is so black that it is ominous for you to go northwards.”

墨子根本不听，继续朝北走去。但过了不久，他又返了回来。因为北边的淄水泛滥，没办法渡过河去。

Mo Zi didn’t listen to him at all and continue to go northward, but after a while he returned, because he couldn’t cross the Zi River due to floods.

这时，墨子又见到了那个算命先生，他得意地对墨子说：“怎么样，我说你不能往北走，遇到麻烦了吧？”

At this moment, Mo Zi met that fortune-teller again, who said to him complacently, “Look! I said you shouldn’t go northward, now you have met troubles!”

墨子微微一笑，说：“淄水泛滥，南北两个方向的行人全都受到阻隔。行人中有皮肤黑的，也有皮肤白的，怎么都过不去呢?”

Mo Zi smiled and said, “Due to floods of the Zi River, people from the north and south are all blocked, and among those people, some have black skin and some have white skin, why all of them are blocked?”

算命先生支吾着说不出话来。墨子又说：“假如

The fortune-teller stammered with nothing to say. Mo Zi said again, “If the Emperor

天帝在东方杀了青龙，在南方杀了赤龙，在西方杀了白龙，再在中央杀了黄龙，岂不是让天下的人都动弹不得了吗？所以，你的谎言是敌不过真理的，就像拿鸡蛋去碰石头，把全天下的鸡蛋全碰完了，石头还是毁坏不了。”

of Heaven kills cyan dragon in the east, red dragon in the south, white dragon in the west and yellow dragon in the center, then all people can't go anywhere? So your lie can not surpass the truth, just like you strike an egg against a rock, even if all the eggs are destroyed, the stone will still keep undamaged.”

算命先生听完以后，羞愧地走了。

The fortune-teller felt ashamed and went away.

067

以貌取人

Judge people by outward appearance

出自 《史记·仲尼弟子列传》。

释义 根据外貌来判断一个人的优劣。

春秋时期的大儒学家孔子，门下有弟子三千，其中杰出的有七十二人，被称为

Confucius was a great Confucian in the Spring and Autumn Period, and had 3000 disciples, and among which 72 disciples were

"七十二贤人"。

在这些弟子中，有一个叫宰予的，能说会道，是孔子学生中"言语"方面的高才生。他开始给孔子的印象不错，但后来渐渐地露出真相——他既没有仁德又十分懒惰。曾经有一次，他大白天不读书听讲，却躺在床上睡大觉，为此被孔子骂作"朽木不可雕"。最后，宰予因为参与田常作乱的事，被砍了头，灭了族。

孔子的另外一个弟子，叫澹台灭明，字子羽，他最早是经子游的推荐来到孔子门下。孔子见他相貌丑陋，认为他资质低下，不会成才，所以并不看重他。澹台灭明却毫不气馁，更加勤奋学习。他学成以后，南游到吴楚讲学，跟从他学习的有三百多人，为当地培养了一大批人才。他也成为第一个

excellent and honored as the 72 Learned Persons.

Among these disciples, there was a person called Zai Yu, who was an eloquent talker as a gifted disciple in the area of language. At the very beginning, he gave Confucius a good impression, but gradually his true personality was exposed, and Confucius found that this disciple was lack of kindheartedness and diligence. Once, Zai Yu was scolded by Confucius as "a rotten wood unworthy to be sculptured", because he slept in daytime without reading or learning. Finally, because Zai Yu participated in the revolt by Tian Chang, he was beheaded and his family was exterminated.

Another disciple of Confucius called Tantai Mieming with alternate name as Zi Yu, he was formerly recommended by Zi You. Confucius considered Tantai Mieming as untalented due to his ugly appearance, so Confucius didn't care about him at all. But Tantai Mieming was not downhearted and studied even harder. After he finished study, he went southward and gave lectures in Wu and Chu with over 300 students, which was a great contribution for local talents cultivation. Tantai Mieming also became the

到南方讲学的儒学大师，其才干和品德传遍了各诸侯国。

为此，孔子感慨说："我只凭言辞判断人的好坏，结果错识了宰予；我只凭相貌判断人的优劣，结果又看错了子羽。"

first Confucian giving lectures in the south, and his talents and virtues spread around the vassal states.

Thus Confucius said, "I once judged a person by his words, then I mistakenly judged Zai Yu; I once judged a person by his appearance, then I mistakenly judged Zi Yu."

068

出尔反尔

To go back on one's word

出自 《孟子·梁惠王下》。

释义 指人的言行前后不一，反复无常。

战国时期，邹国和鲁国发生战争。邹穆公率领邹国的军民去抵抗，最终吃

In the Warring States Period, Zou and Lu were at war. The Duke Mu of Zou led troops to resist, but was defeated finally. In

了败仗。他手下的官吏死了三十三个人，而百姓却一个也没有死，而且在战斗的时候，他们像在旁边看热闹一样，压根没人去冲锋杀敌。

邹穆公很不开心，于是问孟子："在这次战争中，官吏被杀死这么多，可是百姓却没有一个为他们去拼命的。他们眼看着长官被杀而不去营救，我想杀了这些人，可是数量太多；如果不杀的话，又让人难消愤恨，该怎么办才好呢？"

孟子说："这不怪百姓，要怪就得怪您自己。记得有一年闹灾荒，百姓们有的饿死，有的外出逃荒。大王的粮仓满满的，钱库也很充足，而管钱粮的官员却不把灾情报告给您，他们高高在上，根本不关心百姓的疾苦。曾子说过，'要警惕呀！你怎样对待别人，别人也怎样对待你。'现在百姓

the battle, 33 officials died, but not a single civilian died. Moreover, those civilians were just like watching the scene of bustle instead of charging forward to kill the enemies.

The Duke Mu of Zou was very upset and asked Mencius, "So many officials were killed in this battle, but not a single civilian was willing to put up a desperate fight to save them, I really want to kill these civilians, but the quantity is too big; but if I don't kill them, it is really difficult to eliminate my resentments, so what should I do?"

Mencius said, "It is not the fault of civilians, it is your fault. I remember one year when famine broke out, some civilians were starved to death and some fled for a living. Both your granary and coffer were full enough, but the responsible officials conceal the situation of famine from you. They kept aloof from the masses without any concern about the suffering of the civilians. Zeng Zi once said, 'Be cautious! The way you treat others will be the same as others treat

有了这个报复的机会，当然会用同样的手段来对待那些长官。”

邹穆公问道：“那要怎么办呢？”

孟子说：“您可以实行仁政，这样老百姓都感激您，也会敬爱他们的长官，就都愿意为国冲锋杀敌了。”

邹穆公听了孟子的话，面带愧色，默然不语。

you'. Now those civilians have the chance to revenge, they certainly will treat those officials with the same means."

The Duke Mu of Zou asked, "Then what should I do?"

Mencius said, "You can implement benevolent government, then the civilians will be grateful to you, and they will respect their officials, so they will be willing to charge forward to kill the enemies for the country."

The Duke Mu of Zou kept silent with an ashamed look.

069

叶公好龙

Professed love of what one really fears

出自 汉·刘向《新序·杂事》。

释义 比喻表里不一。

春秋时期，孔子有个弟子叫子张，他听说鲁哀公很喜欢招纳贤才，便从很远的地方

In the Spring and Autumn Period, one of Confucius disciples called Zi Zhang, he heard the Duke Ai of Lu liked to recruit

赶到鲁国，请求拜见鲁哀公。可是他在鲁国一直待了七天，也没见到鲁哀公的影子。子张大失所望，便给鲁哀公的车夫讲了一个故事，让他把这个故事转述给鲁哀公。然后，子张就悄然离去了。

talents, so he went from far away to Lu and requested to visit the Duke Ai of Lu. But he didn't see the Duke Ai of Lu at all for seven days, he was very disappointed and told a story to the cart driver and asked him to forward to the Duke Ai of Lu. Then Zi Zhang left Lu in private.

后来有一天，鲁哀公记起子张求见的事情，准备让自己的车夫去把子张请来。车夫告诉他子张早走了。鲁哀公很纳闷，问车夫说："他不是投奔我来的吗，为什么又走掉了？"于是，车夫向鲁哀公转述了子张留下的这个故事。

Afterwards one day, the Duke Ai of Lu remembered the visit of Zi Zhang and asked his cart driver to receive him, but was told that Zi Zhang had already gone. The Duke Ai of Lu was very curious and asked, "He came to visit me, why did he leave?" Then the cart driver forwarded the story which Zi Zhang told him as following.

楚国叶县有个叫叶子高的人，大家都叫他叶公。叶公平日总向人吹嘘自己如何如何喜欢龙，他在衣带钩上画着龙，在酒具上刻着龙，房屋卧室的墙上也全都雕刻着各式各样龙的图案。

In the Ye County of Chu, there was a person called Ye Zigao, people all called him as Lord Ye. Lord Ye always boasted to others how he loved dragon. The patterns of dragon were painted on his clothes hook and engraved on his wince set, and even the walls of his house were painted with various patterns of dragon.

天上的真龙听说叶公这么喜欢龙，很是感动，想去

The real dragon in the heaven was very moved when it knew Lord Ye loved dragon so

拜访一下。一天，真龙降落到了叶公的家里，它刚把头伸进窗户里，就被叶公看见了，他立刻吓得浑身发抖，脸都变了颜色，惊恐万状，回头就跑。

其实叶公并非真的喜欢龙，只不过是表现在口头上，徒有形式而已。

much, so it decided to visit Lord Ye. One day, the real dragon descended in the home of Lord Ye. Lord Ye saw the dragon when its head went through the window. He was scared to tremble all over the body and even lose the normal color of his face, then he went away in consternation.

Actually Lord Ye didn't really love dragon, his love on dragon was only expressed in his words, which was a kind of pretense.

070

司空见惯

A common occurrence

出自 唐·孟棨《本事诗》。

释义 经常见到，不足为奇。

刘禹锡是唐朝中期一位杰出的诗人，出身于书香门第，才学过人。他

Liu Yuxi was an excellent poet in the middle of Tang Dynasty, who was born in a family of scholars and brilliant than ordinary people. He

十九岁的时候到京城长安游学，二十一岁考中进士。在朝廷任职期间，他曾参与政治改革，改革失败后，被贬到江南一带做官。

一直到了晚年，刘禹锡才回到长安。当时，长安城中还有一个诗人，名叫李绅。李绅做过司空，家里很富有，喜欢讲排场。李绅对刘禹锡的诗名仰慕已久，于是就请刘禹锡来到家里，摆了丰盛的酒席招待他。酒过三巡，李绅叫来歌女唱歌陪酒，两人一边饮酒，一边畅谈。几杯酒下肚，刘禹锡有些微醉，他面对如此奢华的场面，想起自己坎坷的命运，不禁诗兴大发，他举着酒杯站起来，高声吟出了一首七绝：

高髻云鬟宫样妆，
春风一曲杜韦娘。
司空见惯浑闲事，

studied abroad in the capital Chang'an at his nineteen years old, and he passed the exam and became the imperial scholar at his twenty-one years old. During his term of office, he once joined in the political reform, but failed and was demoted to the office in Jiangnan area.

Liu Yuxi came back to Chang'an in his old age. At that time, there was a poet called Li Shen, who was the former minister and indulged in ostentation and extravagance due to his richness. Li Shen had admired Liu Yuxi's poetic talents for a long time, so he invited Liu Yuxi to home for a splendid banquet. After a few drinks, Li Shen asked hostess to accompany, and they chatted freely and glowingly during drinking. Liu Yuxi was a little drunk, in face of such a luxurious scene and in consideration of his bumpy fate, with the wine cup in his hand he couldn't help to speak out a poem of seven-character quatrains, "The hostess has the imperial makeup with high and pretty hair bun, and she plays the song of Lady Du Wei in the spring breeze. All the splendid scene seems so common to the former minister Li Shen, but I fell in love with the hostess so

断尽江南刺史肠。

诗的意思是说，这样美丽的女子，司空大人见得多了，早已习以为常，我却为她想断肝肠。李绅一听，就把这个歌女送给了刘禹锡。这段佳话也成为“司空见惯”成语的来历。

deeply.”

This poem means that beautiful hostess was so common in the eyes of the former minister Li Shen, but Liu Yuxi fell in love with hostess deeply. By hearing this poem, Li Shen gave this hostess to Liu Yuxi. The idiom of “a common occurrence” derives from this story.

071

叹为观止

Acclaim something as the acme of perfection

出自 《左传·襄公二十九年》。

释义 所见事物非常完美，令人赞叹。

季札是春秋时期吴国人，曾经被孔子赞美为具有最高品德的人。季札的父

In the Spring and Autumn Period, there was a person of Wu called Ji Zha, who was reputed as the most virtuous person by

亲是吴国国王，非常看重季札，一直有意要传位给他。他的三位哥哥也都特别疼爱他，认为季札的德行才干最适合继承王位，所以在父亲去世后，哥哥们都争相拥护他即位。但是季札不肯接受，坚持把王位让给了哥哥。

有一次，吴国派遣季札访问鲁国。到了鲁国以后，季札请求欣赏聆听周朝的音乐和舞蹈，鲁国国君就让人为他一个个地进行表演。季札一面欣赏各种音乐和歌舞，一面指出它们的优缺点。当看完表演赞颂虞舜的《韶箾》歌舞后，他大声称赞道："虞舜的功德无人能比啊！就像无垠的上天，没有什么不被它覆盖；又像广阔的大地，没有什么不被它承载。再没有什么能超过这部歌舞所表现出来的虞舜的功德了，如果还有其他

Confucius. The father of Ji Zha was the king of Wu, who regarded him highly and intended to enthrone him. The other three elder brothers of Ji Zha also particularly loved him and regarded him as the suitable person to ascend the throne due to his virtue and capability, so after their father passed away, his brothers all supported him to enthrone, but Ji Zha refused and insisted on giving up throne to his brothers.

One time, the emperor of Wu dispatched Ji Zha to visit Lu. After he arrived, he requested to enjoy Zhou's music and dance, so the emperor of Lu arranged people to show one by one, and Ji Zha pointed out the merits and demerits of the music and dance when enjoying. After the show of *Shao Xiao* which praised Yu Shun, Ji Zha acclaimed "The virtue of Yu Shun is so unparalleled that it is just like the infinite sky covering all and the immense earth bearing all. There's no more music and dance can express more than *Shao Xiao* in Yu Shun's virtue, so I dare not request to enjoy any other more!"

乐舞，我也不敢再请求欣赏了！”

后来，人们便从季札的话里引申出了“叹为观止”这个成语。

Afterwards, the idiom of “acclaim something as the acme of perfection” derives from this story.

072

外强中干

Outwardly strong and inwardly weak

出自 《左传·僖公十五年》。

释义 外表强大，内里空虚。

春秋时期，晋献公死后，公子夷吾继承王位当上了国君，称为晋惠公。夷

In the Spring and Autumn Period, after the Duke Xian of Jin passed away, the prince Yi Wu ascended the throne as the Duke

吾当初因为内乱一度逃亡国外，在秦国的帮助下才得以回国。他曾经答应过秦穆公，如果有一天能够有机会当上国君，就把晋国的五座城池割让给秦国，来报答救命之恩。可是，当上国君的晋惠公并没有实现诺言。后来秦国发生饥荒，向晋国求助，晋惠公也没有帮助秦国，反而趁机发兵去攻打秦国。

Hui of Jin. At first Yi Wu fled due to civil disorders and then came back by the help of Qin. Yi Wu once promised to the Duke Mu of Qin that he would cede five cities to Qin when he became the emperor as a reward, but the Duke Hui of Jin neither fulfilled his promise nor helped Qin when Qin turned to Jin due to famine, nevertheless the Duke Hui of Jin took advantage of this chance and launched attacks on Qin.

秦穆公大怒，亲自率军攻打晋国，一连三仗获胜，晋国形势危急。晋惠公决心亲自出征，于是叫人给他的战车套上郑国出产的名马。在一旁的庆郑劝阻他说："古代有祭祀活动或打大仗的时候，一定要用本国产的马，因为本国的马在本国的国土长大，熟悉本国的水土，听从本国人的使唤，而且熟悉道路，使用起来随人心意。郑国的马虽然身形高大，但它一遇到意外情况，

The Duke Mu of Qin was furious, he led troops in person to attack Jin and won three battles in succession, thus Jin was in a critical situation. The Duke Hui of Jin decided to go for a battle, so he asked people to harness Zheng's famous horse to his chariot, but Qing Zheng who stood beside persuaded him, "In the ancient time, upon occasions of sacrificial activity or big war, people must use native horses, because native horses are familiar with the local environment and routes and obedient to the orders of native soldiers, so people can drive the horses freely. Nevertheless, although Zheng's horses are tall and big, upon any accidental occasion, they will

就会血管膨胀，血液循环加快，呼吸急促，狂躁不安。它的外表看似强壮，而内部已经气虚力竭，到那时，进退两难，后悔就晚了。”

become manic with blood vessels expanded, blood circulation accelerated and breaths shortened. They seem to be strong in outward appearances but internally exhausted already, at that time, it will be difficult for you to charge forward or withdraw.”

可是晋惠公一意孤行，没有接受庆郑的劝告，还是套上郑国的马出征了。不久，秦晋两国的军队交战，战斗十分激烈。正在这时，晋惠公乘坐的战车陷入了泥泞之中，战马受惊，狂嘶乱叫，拼命挣扎，反而越陷越深，进退不得。晋军因此大败，晋惠公也成了秦国的俘虏。

But the Duke Hui of Jin neglected his advice and insisted on his own way to go for the battle, with Zheng’s horse harnessed to his chariot. After a while, troops of Qin and Jin were in fierce battle, at this critical moment, the chariot of the Duke Hui of Jin trapped in mud, and the horse was frightened and neighed crazily, but the more it struggled desperately, the deeper it was trapped, finally it couldn’t move at all. Thus Jin’s troops were defeated utterly and the Duke Hui of Jin became the captive of Qin.

073

宁为玉碎，不为瓦全

Better a glorious death than a shameful life

出自 《北齐书·元景安传》。

释义 宁愿保持高尚的气节死去，而不愿屈辱地活着。

南北朝时期，东魏的丞相高洋逼迫孝静帝退位，自己当上了皇帝，建

In the Southern and Northern Dynasty, the Prime Minister Gao Yang of the Eastern Wei compelled the Emperor Xiao Jing to abdicate

立北齐。高洋为了不留后患，又毒死了孝静帝和他的三个儿子。

the throne and became the emperor of the newly-established Northern Qi. In order to avoid future troubles, he poisoned the Emperor Xiao Jing and his three sons to death.

在高洋当皇帝的第十个年头，有一天发生了日食，他担心这是个不祥的兆头，于是就问自己的亲信：“西汉末年王莽篡夺了刘家的天下，为什么后来光武帝刘秀又能夺回天下呢？”这名亲信说不清楚，就随意应付说是因为王莽没有斩草除根，把刘氏宗室的人杀干净。高洋信以为真，于是把东魏的宗室近亲44家共七百多人全部杀掉，连婴儿也不放过。

In the 10th year of the Northern Qi, one day Gao Yang saw solar eclipse, since he believed it was an ominous sign, he asked his trusted follower, “By the end of the Western Han Dynasty, Wang Mang usurped the throne of Liu Xiu, but why the Emperor Guang Wu Liu Xiu regained his throne afterwards?” This trusted follower had no idea and randomly explained that it because Wang Mang didn’t exterminate the clan of Liu Xiu. But Gao Yang took it as truth, so he killed over seven hundred people of forty-four close clan relatives of the Eastern Wei’s emperor, and even the babies were not spared.

消息传开后，东魏宗室的远房宗族感到很害怕，担心他们自己什么时候也会被杀掉，于是聚在一起商量对策。有个叫元景安的人说，眼下要保命的唯一办法，就是请求高洋准许他们脱离原

When this news spread out, the distant clan relatives were very scared and afraid of being killed in the future, so they gathered together for discussion. A person called Yuan Jingan said that the only life-saving method was to ask for Gao Yang’s permit to break away from the original surname Yuan of the

来东魏宗室的元姓，改姓高。元景安的堂兄元景皓坚决反对这种做法，他气愤地说："怎么能用抛弃本宗，改为他姓的办法来保命呢？大丈夫宁做玉器被打碎，也不愿做瓦器得到保全！"

clan family of the Eastern Wei and follow the surname of Gao. But Yuan Jinghao, the cousin of Yuan Jingan firmly disagreed and angrily said, "How could you discard the clan and follow other surname for life-saving? A great man should rather be a jade ware to be broken than an earthen ware to be preserved!"

元景安偷偷地把元景皓的话报告给高洋，高洋立即逮捕了元景皓，并将他处死，元景安因告密有功，被赐姓高，并且升了官。不过，仅仅过了三个月，高洋就因病死去，年仅三十一岁。

Yuan Jingan forwarded Yuan Jinghao's words to Gao Yang in private, and Yuan Jinghao was immediately arrested and condemned to death. Then as reward, Yuan Jingan was granted the surname of Gao and promoted in office. Nevertheless only three months later, Gao Yang died due to illness at his merely thirty-one years old.

074

对牛弹琴

Cast pearls before swine

出自 汉·牟融《理惑论》。

释义 说话时不看对象，白费口舌。

东汉时，有个对佛教教义很有研究的学者，叫牟融。他引用儒家的诗书向人

In the Eastern Han Dynasty, there was a scholar called Mou Rong who was deeply-knowledgeable in Buddhist doctrines. He quoted

们宣讲佛经，受到了一些儒者的责难，指斥他为什么不直接依据佛经来回答问题。牟融讲了一个故事作为回答。

Confucian poems to preach Buddhist scriptures, but was blamed by certain Confucians for not referring to Buddhist scriptures, but Mou Rong answered via the following story.

春秋时期，鲁国有个著名的音乐家，叫公明仪。他对音乐有着极深的造诣，善于弹琴。琴声优美动听，往往让人如醉如痴。有一年的春天，公明仪带着琴来到城郊的田野散步，青草的芳香，伴随着和煦的春风阵阵吹来，让他的心情非常舒畅。他环顾四周，发现不远处有一头大黄牛正在悠闲地吃草，于是兴致勃发，拨动琴弦，对着这头牛弹奏了一首高雅的《清角之操曲》。

In the Spring and Autumn Period, there was a famous musician of Lu called Gong Mingyi, who was well versed in music and good at playing Chinese zither, and the sound was so pleasant and make people fascinated. One year in spring, he went to suburb with his Chinese zither, he felt so relaxed when the scent of grass flew with warm spring breeze constantly. He looked around and found a big yellow cattle eating grass leisurely nearby, so he was excited and began to play a piece of the elegant music to that cattle.

虽然公明仪弹奏的曲子非常悦耳动听，但是那头大黄牛却根本不理会，仍然低着头一门心思地继续吃草。

Although the music was very pleasant and melodious, that yellow cattle didn’t care at all and continued to eat grass.

公明仪见美妙的琴声并不能打动这头不懂音乐的牛，非常无奈。过了一会

Gong Mingyi felt helpless when he realized the pleasant music couldn’t influence the cattle at all, because it knew nothing about

儿，他又想出了一个办法，抚动琴弦，弹出一段段奇怪杂乱的声音，有的像嗡嗡的蚊蝇声，有的像迷路的小牛犊发出的叫声。这时候，大黄牛才像突然明白了什么似的，摇摇尾巴，竖起耳朵，听了起来。

music. Shortly after, he had a good idea and moved the strings to make strange and noisy sounds just like the flies and mosquitoes flying or a lost little calf mooing, and that big yellow cattle seemed to understand suddenly and began to wave its tail and pricked up its ears to listen.

所以，对那些没有读过佛经的人直接讲佛经中的道理，就像对牛弹奏美妙的乐曲一样，不也是等于白讲吗？

Therefore, if you directly preached Buddhist scriptures to those people who never read Buddhist scriptures, it was just like playing pleasant music to cattle, wasn't it useless at all?

075

对症下药

Apply medicine according to indications

出自 《三国志 · 魏志 · 华佗传》。

释义 针对事物的问题所在，采取有效措施。

华佗是东汉末年著名的医学家，他救死扶伤，医术高明，深受人们的

Hua Tuo was the famous Medical scientist by the end of the Eastern Han Dynasty, who healed the wounded and rescued the dying with

敬仰。

his excellent medical skills, and was deeply respected by people.

有一次，地方上的小官吏倪寻和李延二人一同到华佗那里看病。两人诉说的病症相同，都是头痛发热。华佗分别给两人诊了脉，然后说："倪寻应该用泻药，而李延要吃发汗的药。"

Once, two local petty officials Ni Xun and Li Yan went to visit Hua Tuo. The symptoms they described were the same as headache and fever, Hua Tuo took their pulse individually and said "Ni Xun should take laxative medicine, and Li Yan should take sweating medicine."

两人看了药方，感到非常奇怪，问："我们两人的症状相同，病情一样，为什么吃的药却不一样呢？"

They looked at the prescription and asked curiously, "We have the same symptoms, why should we take different medicine?"

华佗解释说："倪寻的身体外部并没有什么问题，病是由于身体内部食物消化不良引起的；李延的身体内部很健康，病是由于外感风寒，受了凉而引起的。所以虽然你们两位的病情表现是一样的，但是病因不同，我当然得对症下药，给你们用不同的药治疗了。"

Hua Tuo explained, "Ni Xun's illness is due to dyspepsia instead of any problems in bodily exterior; Li Yan's illness is due to exogenous cold instead of any problems in bodily interior. So although your symptoms are the same, the causes of illness are different, and you should take different medicine accordingly."

华佗随即给他们分别开了药方，没过多久，两人的

Then Hua Tuo prescribed for them individually, and shortly afterwards they

病就全好了。

recovered completely.

后来，人们就把“对症下药”作为成语，来比喻针对不同的客观实际情况，采取不同的方法加以应对，从而妥善地处理问题。

Afterwards, people use the idiom of "apply medicine according to indications" to describe to take different methods according to different situations, thus all the problems will be solved properly.

076

尔虞我诈

Each trying to cheat or outwit the other

出自 《左传·宣公十五年》。

释义 互相猜疑，互相欺骗。

春秋时期，楚庄王派大夫申舟出使齐国，他自恃国力强大，所以指示申舟经

In the Spring and Autumn Period, the Emperor Zhuang of Chu dispatched the official Shen Zhou to visit Qi, and he

过宋国的时候，不必向它借路。申舟估计这样一来势必会惹怒宋国，说不定因此而被杀死。但楚庄王坚持要他这样做，并向他保证，如果他被宋国杀死，自己一定出兵讨伐宋国，为他报仇。申舟没有办法，只好把儿子托付给楚庄王，然后出发。

果然不出申舟所料，他经过宋国时，由于没有借路而被宋国人抓住杀害。消息传到楚国，楚庄王气得鞋子来不及穿，宝剑也没时间佩戴，就下令讨伐宋国。然而围了宋国都城很长时间，还是没有把它打下来。

一天深夜，宋国大夫华元悄悄潜入楚军主帅子反的营里，对他说："我们的粮草早已吃光，柴草也已经烧光。但即使如此，如果你们想迫使我们订立丧权辱国的和约，那我们宁肯灭亡也

indicated Shen Zhou not to ask for a permit from Song. Shen Zhou estimated that it would provoke Song and he was probable to be killed, but the Emperor Zhuang of Chu insisted and promised to attack Song if Shen Zhou was killed by Song. Shen Zhou had no choice and entrusted his son to the Emperor Zhuang of Chu, and then left.

As expected by Shen Zhou, when he passed through Song, because he didn't ask for a permit from Song, he was seized and killed. When the news spread to Chu, the Emperor Zhuang of Chu was too furious to wear shoes and sword and immediately ordered to launch attacks on Song. However, despite besieging the captial of Song for a long time, it was still not defeated.

Late one night, Song's official Hua Yuan slipped into the campsite of Zi Fan, who was the commander in chief of Chu, and Hua Yuan said, "We have already run out of our provisions and firewood, but even so, if you force us to sign any agreement to humiliating our country and forfeit our sovereignty, we

不会接受。现在你们如果能退兵三十里，那么您怎么吩咐，我就怎么办！”

would rather choose death than obedience. If you could withdraw for thirty miles, then we will obey any orders of you!”

子反当即和华元私下约定，然后再禀告楚庄王。楚庄王本来就想撤军，听了自然同意，第二天，下令退兵三十里。华元到楚营中去订立盟约，盟约上写着：“我无尔诈，尔无我虞。”意思是说：我不欺骗你，你也不必防备我!

Zi Fan agreed and sign agreement in private and then reported to the Emperor Zhuang of Chu, and the emperor readily agreed because he intended to withdraw before. The next day, Chu's troops withdrew for thirty miles. Hua Yuan went to Chu's campsite for signing the treaty of alliance which said, “we don't cheat you and you don't cheat us”, which means that I don't cheat you, so you don't have to take precautions against me!

后人由这个故事引申出了成语“尔虞我诈”。

Afterwards, the idiom of “Each trying to cheat or outwit the other” derives from this story.

077

巧夺天工

Art beats nature

出自 宋·无名氏《采兰杂志》。

释义 人工的技艺十分精巧，胜过天然。

魏文帝曹丕的皇后甄氏，最初是袁绍二儿子袁熙的夫人。袁绍在官渡之战

The Empress Zhen of the Emperor Wen Cao Pi was the ex-wife of Yuan Xi who was the second son of Yuan Shao. In the Battle

中被曹操打败，不久吐血而亡，袁熙后来也被杀死。曹丕进入袁府，见到甄氏，被她的美貌所惊呆，看到甄氏脸上有泪痕，还递过去手帕让她擦脸。不久，曹丕派人把甄氏接到自己府里，与她喜结良缘。

曹丕建立魏国称帝后，甄氏被立为皇后。当时甄氏已年过四十，为了能得到曹丕的长久宠幸，她每天早晨都要花很长的时间梳洗打扮。据说在她宫室前的庭院中，有一条长得非常漂亮的绿色的蛇，每当甄皇后梳妆打扮的时候，它就在她面前摆出奇巧的形状，从来不重复。于是，甄皇后就模仿它的形状梳理发型，她的头发虽然是人工梳成的，但精致巧妙，曹丕非常喜欢，称赞她的发型是“巧夺天工”。后宫的人都称之为“灵蛇髻”。

of Guandu, Yuan Shao was defeated by Cao Cao and died after vomiting blood, and Yuan Xi was also killed afterwards. After Cao Pi entered Yuan's mansion, he was amazed by the good looks of Ms. Zhen, and handed over a handkerchief to her for wiping tears. Shortly afterwards, Cao Pi dispatched to pick her up and married her.

After Cao Pi became the emperor of Wei, Ms. Zhen was established as the empress. In order to keep attracting Cao Pi, the Empress Zhen spent a lot of time to dress up every morning, and at this moment, a pretty green snake would always make artful and distinct poses in her yard, so the Empress Zhen imitated its shapes for hairdressing. Although her hair was dressed by people, it was always fine and ingenious, and Cao Pi liked it very much and praised her hair style as “art beats nature”, and the people of imperial harem all described it as “fairy snake bun”.

不过，随着时间的消逝，甄皇后的容貌日渐衰退，年轻貌美的郭皇后终于取代了她的地位。而她由于失宠，心生不满，惹怒了曹丕，最后被下诏赐死。

But as time went, the good looks of the Empress Zhen decayed and was replaced by the young and pretty Empress Guo. Thus the Empress Zhen became resentful after falling into disgrace, which irritated Cao Pi and was finally condemned to death.

078

打草惊蛇

Beat the grass and frighten away the snake

出自 明·郎瑛《七修类稿》。

释义 做事不谨慎，反而使对方有所戒备。

五代十国时期，有个叫王鲁的人，是南唐的当涂县令，他利用手中的权

In the period of Five Dynasties and Ten Kingdoms, there was a person called Wang Lu, who was the county magistrate of Dangtu in

势，贪赃枉法，假公济私，搜刮了不少钱财。而衙门中大大小小的官吏，见到县令如此，也都照猫画虎，收受贿赂，敲诈勒索，无恶不作，百姓苦不堪言。

the Southern Tang Dynasty. By the advantage of his power, he took bribes and violate the law, sought private profit in public affairs and extorted money from the civilians. Thus both high and petty officials in the government office imitated his doings to take bribes, extort money and commit all manners of crimes, and the civilians suffered a lot unspeakably.

有一次，朝廷派人下来巡察地方官员的治理情况，当涂县的老百姓一看机会来了，于是大家联名写了状子，控告县衙里的主簿等人营私舞弊、贪污受贿的种种不法行为。状子到了王鲁手中，他打开一看，不免在心中打起了寒战。因为状子上写的那些罪行，都是证据确凿的事实，而且很多就是在他的包庇纵容下做出来的。于是，他在案卷上批了八个字：“汝虽打草，吾已惊蛇。”意思是说，你们这样做，虽然目的是打地上的草，可是我就像藏在草中的

Once the imperial court dispatched officials for inspection on the local governance, the civilians of Dangtu thought it a good chance and they jointly wrote complaint against the local officials for corruption and bribery. When Wang Lu received this complaint, he couldn’t help to shiver because all the crimes written on the complaint were all absolute facts, and many crimes were committed under his harbor and connivance, so he made a note of eight words on this complaint “Beat the grass and frighten away the snake”, which means, although you intend to disclose the crimes of the local officials like beating trass, I am shocked and frightened indeed as a hiding snake.”

蛇一样，可是被大大地吓了一跳！

后来，人们就根据王鲁所写的这八个字引申出了“打草惊蛇”这一成语。

Afterwards, the idiom of “beat the grass and frighten away the snake” derives from the eight-word note of Wang Lu.

079

瓜田李下

In a melon patch or under a plum tree

出自 《北史·袁翻传》。

释义 比喻容易引起嫌疑的场合。

袁聿修是北齐时期的人，少年老成，很有见识。他年龄不大就出来做官，因

In the period of Northern Qi, there was a person called Yuan Sunxiu, who was young but prudent and capable, he became an official at

为政绩突出，又很有声望，一直官至尚书。

在担任尚书的十多年里，袁聿修最为人们称颂的是他为官清白，从不收受任何贿赂，哪怕是别人的一滴酒他也不会喝。因此，当时有不少文人联名为他立碑表彰，并且送给他一个“清郎”的雅号。

有一次，朝廷派袁聿修到各地考察地方官吏，途经兖州。兖州刺史正是他的老朋友邢邵，二人见面叙旧。袁聿修将要动身离开的时候，邢邵派人送了一匹白绸给袁聿修，作为留念。袁聿修很为难，不收的话，怕得罪老朋友；收下来，又怕招来什么不必要的嫌疑。反复思索之后，袁聿修还是谢绝了，并给邢邵留了一封信，说：“我这次路过这里，与平日出行不同。古人说过，走在瓜田里不要弯腰提鞋子，走在李树下不要伸手整

young ages and was promoted to minister due to his prestige.

In over ten years of his office, he was praised highly for his clean hands because he neither took any bribes nor a drop of wine, thus many scholars jointly made a tablet inscription for his good reputation, and addressed him a gracious name “the upright official”.

Once, the imperial court dispatched Yuan Sunxiu to inspect the local officials. When he passed through Yanzhou, he met and chatted with his old friend Xing Shao, who was the local governor. When Yuan Sunxiu prepared to leave, Xing Shao asked people to send him a bolt of white silk cloth as a memento. Yuan Sunxiu felt awkward beacuse it would offend his old friend if he refused and would incur unnecessary suspicion if he accepted. After thought it over, Yuan Sunxiu refused the gift and left Xing Shao a letter “It is different for me to pass over here this time. The ancient people once said that you should neither bend to make shoes in a melon patch nor stretched out your hand to adjust your hat under a plum

帽子，只有这样，才能躲避嫌疑。你的心意我领了，但白绸不能收，希望你能体谅。”

tree, only in this way, you can avoid suspicions. I appreciate your kindness, but I really can't accept your gift, I hope you could understand me."

邢邵明白袁聿修的心思，回信说：“先前赠送白绸的事，是我过于草率，匆忙之间没有想到这个问题。看到你的来信，我完全明白你的意思，不会怪你的。”

Xing Shao understood the scruple of Yuan Sunxiu and wrote back, "Due to lack of consideration, it is rash for me to give you the white silk cloth. Now I completely understand your scruple after read your letter and will not blame you."

080

妙笔生花

Write like a fairy

出自 五代·王仁裕《开元天宝遗事》。

释义 比喻写作技巧高超。

李白是唐朝的著名诗人，据说他从小就开始读书作诗，非常聪明。七岁的时

Li Bai was a famous poet of Tang Dynasty, and it was said that he was very clever and capable to read and compose poems as a child.

候，父亲想给他起个正式的名字，可是又不知道什么名字合适。一天，他看着院落中的葱翠树木，繁花似锦，来了诗兴，开口念道："春国送暖百花开，迎春绽金它先来。"李白的母亲在一旁接了一句："火烧叶林红霞落"，然后停下来思索下一句该怎么说。这时，李白走到盛开的李树花前，顺口说道："李花怒放一树白"。父母一听，非常高兴，决定把这句的头尾"李"和"白"两个字作为孩子的名字，取名为"李白"。

When Li Bai was seven years old, his father wanted to give him a formal name but had no good idea. One day, upon seeing the lush trees and blooming flowers in the yard, his father was in a poetic mood and spoke out "The Spring is warm and hundreds of flowers are blooming in profusion, and the golden winter jasmines bloom attractively", Li Bai's mother continued beside "The red fallen sun-glow fully cover the trees" and stopped to consider the next sentence. At this moment, Li Bai walked to the blooming plum tree and said offhandedly "The flowers of plum trees are in full bloom and the whole trees are in white". His father and mother were very glad to hear this and decided give him the name of "Li Bai" by taking the first word "Li" and the last word "Bai" in Chinese.

李白的诗之所以写得好，还有一个传说。他少年时代，曾经做过一个奇特的梦。他梦到自己随风飘到了海上的一座仙山上，只见一支巨大的毛笔高耸在云海之间，足有十多丈高。不一会儿，忽然有五颜六色的光芒

There was a legendary about Li Bai's capability of composing poems. When Li Bai was a child, he once had a strange dream that he flew with wind to a fairy mountain on the sea, and he saw a huge writing brush standing between the clouds and sea, which was about over three meters high, and after a while, varicolored lights came out from the

从笔端射出，接着，竟然在笔尖开放出一朵鲜艳的红花。那支生花之笔渐渐朝着他飘然而来。李白眼看着笔越来越近，便想伸手去取，当快要摸到笔杆的时候，突然惊醒，原来刚才只是做了一个梦。

end of the writing brush, and then a bright-colored flower bloomed at its tip, and that writing brush flew towards him closer and closer, when he stretched out his hand and nearly touched the writing brush, he was suddenly awake and found it was only a dream.

自从李白梦中见到笔头生花以后，名诗佳句便源源而出，一发不可收，以“诗仙”之名被天下人所知。

After Li Bai dreamed a flower blooming at the tip of the writing brush, he was capable to compose endless famous poems and well-turned phrases, and then he was well known as “Fairy Poet”.

081

目无全牛

A master butcher sees through parts and joints of a cow without cutting

出自 《庄子·养生主》。

释义 比喻技术熟练，得心应手。

战国早期，有一个赫赫有名的魏惠王，因为魏国都城为大梁，魏国又被称为梁

In the early period of the Warring States, there was an illustrious Emperor Hui in Wei, because the capital of Wei was called Daliang,

国，所以魏惠王也被称为梁惠王。

so Wei was also called Liang, and the Emperor Hui of Wei was also addressed as the Emperor Hui of Liang.

有一次，梁惠王观看厨师宰牛，只见他举手投足之间，牛的骨肉噼噼啪啪地应声分离，牛的分裂声和刀的切割声，都与音乐节拍十分协调。

Once, the Emperor Hui of Liang was watching the butcher slaughtered cattle, upon every move the butcher made, the flesh and bones of the cattle crackled and separated, and the crackling sound and cutting noise were perfectly coordinated with the music beat.

梁惠王看了，不禁赞叹说："好极了！你的技术怎么能精巧到这样的地步？"

The Emperor Hui of Liang sighed with praises "Marvelous! How can your skills be so subtle and ingenious?"

厨师放下刀回答说："我追求的是自然规律，已经超过一般的技术了。我开始宰牛的时候，眼里看到的只有牛；三年以后，眼里就见不到整头的牛了。现在，我是凭精神和牛接触，而不用眼睛去看，即使感官停止了，而精神仍然在活动。依照牛的生理上的天然结构，砍入筋骨相接的缝隙，顺着骨节间的空处进刀，这样的话，筋脉经络相连的地方和

The butcher put aside the knife and said "What I pursue is the natural law instead of the ordinary skills. At the beginning when I slaughter the cattle, I can only see the cattle; after three years, I can't see the whole cattle. And now, I touch the cattle by my spirits instead of my eyes, so even if the senses stop, the spirits will go on. According to physical natural structure of the cattle, I gash the gaps between the bones and muscles and cut the empty space between the joints, in this way, the knife can't touch the connected arteries and veins at all, letting alone the big bone! Until

筋骨结合的地方，尚且不曾拿刀碰到过，更何况大骨呢！如今，我的刀用了十九年，所宰的牛有几千头了，但刀刃锋利得就像刚在磨刀石上磨好的一样。虽然是这样，每当碰到筋骨交错聚结，很难下刀的地方，我就要提高警惕，视力集中到一点，动作缓慢下来，动起刀来非常轻，哗啦一声，牛的骨和肉一下子就解开了，就像泥土散落在地上一样。这时候，我提着刀站起来，举目四望，就会感觉志得意满，浑身畅快。”

now, I have used this knife for nineteen years and slaughtered several thousands of cattle, but the knife is so sharp that it seems to be sharpened on the knife grinder just a moment ago. Nevertheless, for the point that bones and muscles are interlaced and very difficult to gash, I will raise my vigilance, focus my eyes on one point, slow my movements and gently cut the cattle, and by a crash, the bones and flesh immediately split just as soil scattering to the ground. At this moment, I stand up with knife and look around, feeling complacent and refreshed.”

梁惠王说：“好啊！听了你的这番话，我懂得养生的道理了。”

The Emperor Hui of Liang said “Good! I finally understand the principle of health preservation!”

082

鸟尽弓藏

Cast aside the bow once the birds are gone

出自 《史记·越世家》。

释义 事情成功后，就把为其出过力的人抛弃或杀死。

春秋末期，吴国和越国争夺霸主地位，越国被吴国打败，屈服求和。从

By the end of the Spring and Autumn Period, Wu and Yue were in battle for supremacy, and Yue was defeated and surrendered for peace. From

此以后，越王勾践卧薪尝胆，任用大夫文种、范蠡，整顿国政，使国家由弱转强，最终打败吴国。吴王夫差兵败出逃，连续七次向越国求和，都被拒绝，夫差无奈只好拔剑自刎。

then on, the Yue's emperor Gou Jian slept on the brushwood and tasted the gall, and appointed the officials Wen Zhong and Fan Li to rectify the national affairs and strengthened Yue and finally defeated Wu. The Duke, Fu Chai, of Wu fled and sued for peace from Yue for seven times in succession, but finally was refused, so he drew the sword to suicide.

越国灭掉吴国以后，越王宴请群臣时，却发现范蠡已经不知去向，第二天在太湖边上找到范蠡的外衣，大家都以为范蠡投湖自杀了。过了不久，范蠡托人给文种送来一封信，上面写着：飞鸟打尽了，弹弓就被收起来；野兔捉光了，猎狗就被杀掉煮了吃；敌国灭掉了，谋臣就被废弃。越王这个人只可和他共患难，不宜与他同享乐。你如今不离他而去，不久难免有杀身之祸。

After Yue eliminated Wu the emperor of Yue held a banquet for ministers, but Fan Li disappeared without a trace, and later they found Fan Li's coat besides the Tai Lake and believed that Fan Li committed suicide. Shortly afterwards, Fan Li send Wen Zhong a letter which said, "When all birds are shot, the bow will be set aside; when all hares are killed, the hounds will be stewed and eaten; when the hostile countries are eliminated, the ministers will be discarded. The emperor of Yue is an ungrateful person, who will not share prosperity with you, you'd better leave in order to avoid fatal disaster".

文种不听范蠡的劝告。结果，没过多长时间，越王勾践就送给他一把剑，对他

Wen Zhong didn't followed Fan Li's advice, and shortly afterwards, the Yue's emperor Gou Jian gave him a sword and

说："先生教给寡人七种杀人的办法，寡人只用了三种办法就把吴国给灭了，还剩下四种没有地方用，你是不是去先王那里试一试呢？"文种明白勾践的用意，后悔不该不听范蠡的劝告，只得引剑自尽。

这就是"鸟尽弓藏，兔死狗烹"的来历。

said, "You must remember the seven killing means you taught me, I only use three of them to eliminate Wu, would you please try the other four means in front of the late emperor? " Wen Zhong understood what Gou Jian meant and was regretful for not taking Fan Li's advice, and finally he had to kill himself.

This is the origin of "when all birds are shot, the bow will be set aside; when all hares are killed, the hounds will be stewed and eaten".

083

买椟还珠

Get the casket and return the pearl

出自 《韩非子·外储说左上》。

释义 只重视外表，而不顾实质，舍本求末。

春秋时期，楚国有一个商人，专卖珠宝。有一次他

In the Spring and Autumn Period, there was a merchant selling jewelry exclusively.

得到一颗漂亮的珍珠，打算把它卖出去。为了卖个好价钱，他便想着要把珍珠好好包装一下。

Once he got a beautiful pearl and intended to sell it at a good price, so he decided to make a nicely package of it.

这个楚国商人找来名贵的木材，又请来手艺高超的匠人，为珍珠做了一个盒子，用香料把盒子熏得香气扑鼻。然后，在盒子的外面精雕细刻了许多好看的花纹，还镶上漂亮的金属花边，看上去闪闪发亮，就像一件精致美观的工艺品。随后，商人把珍珠小心翼翼地放进盒子里，拿到市场上去卖。

This merchant bought rare wood and hired a highly-skilled craftsman to make a box, which he fumigated with spices and sculptured with many beautiful decorative patterns, as well as inlaid with metal laces. The box looked glittery just like an exquisite and beautiful handicraft, then the merchant cautiously put the pearl into the box and went to the market.

到了市场后，很多人都围上来欣赏。有个郑国人把盒子拿在手里看了半天，爱不释手，最后出高价把楚人的盒子买了下来。郑国人交过钱后，便拿着盒子往回走。可是没走几步又返了回来。他走到楚国商人跟前，把盒子里的珍珠取出来交给

After the merchant arrived in the market, many people surrounded for appreciation. A person of Zheng took the box to look for a good while and reluctant to put it down, and finally bought it at a high price. After this person of Zheng paid, he took the box and went away, but after a few steps he returned and took the pearl out of the box, “You must forget a pearl in the box, and I’m back to return.” Then he gave the

他，说："先生，你把一颗珍珠忘放在盒子里了，我特意回来还珠子的。"然后把珍珠交给了楚国商人，一边低头欣赏着手中的盒子，一边慢慢地回家去了。

pearl to the merchant of Chu. He gazed at the box in his hand and admired it while heading home slowly.

084

名落孙山

Fall behind Sun Shan

出自 宋·范公偁《过庭录》。

释义 考试没被录取。

在宋朝的时候，有一个名叫孙山的秀才，为人幽默，很擅长说笑话，所以人

In the Song Dynasty, there was a scholar called Sun Shan, who was humorous and good at joking, and was nicknamed as "Funny wit"

们就给他取了一个“滑稽才子”的绰号。

by people.

有一次，孙山去京城参加考试，有位邻居的儿子也跟他一起去，邻居一直拜托孙山要多多照顾他的儿子。到了京城以后，两人住在一起，也一同进入考场。放榜的时候，孙山得了最后一名，而邻居的儿子却没考上。邻居的儿子心里很难过，于是决定留下来准备参加下一次的考试。

One time, he went to the capital for exam, and the neighbor's son went with him, and his neighbor asked Sun Shan to take care of his son. When they arrived in the capital, they lived together and entered the examination hall together. When the examination results were released, Sun Shan came in the bottom of the list. The neighbor's son was upset because he failed the exam, and he decided to stay for the next exam.

孙山一回到家里，乡亲们都跑来探望他，关心地问他考得如何。邻居也跑来问他儿子的考试情况。

When Sun Shan arrived home, the fellow villagers all came out to welcome him and asked about the exam, and the neighbor also came over to ask about the exam result of his son.

孙山笑了笑，回答他说：“你的儿子还在京城呢！”

Sun Shan smiled and said, “Your son is still in the capital!”

邻居着急地问：“怎么回事？我儿子到底有没有考中？”

The neighbor asked anxiously, “What's the matter? Did my son pass the exam or not?”

孙山看了看他，并没有直接回答，而是说了一句

Sun Shan answered him by a poem, “Sun Shan is the last one on the list of exam result,

诗："解名尽处是孙山，贤郎更在孙山外。"解名又叫解额，也就是考中举人的名额。这句话的意思是：在中举的榜单上，最后一名是我，你的儿子还在我的后面，那么当然就是没有考中了。

but your son falls behind Sun Shan". The list of exam results shows the scholars who pass the exam, and this poem means that in the list of exam result, I'm the last one, your son is after me, then your son certainly fails the exam.

从此，人们便根据这个故事，把参加考试没有被录取，称作"名落孙山"。

Afterwards, according to this story, people use the idiom of "fall behind Sun Shan" to describe people who fail exam.

085

后生可畏

The younger generation will surpass the older

出自 《论语·子罕》。

释义 常用来称赞有志气有作为的年轻人。

项橐是春秋时期的一位神童，聪明伶俐。

In the spring and Autumn Period, there was a child prodigy called Xiang Tuo, who was clever and quick-witted.

一天午饭后，项橐在路上玩耍。他找来一些小石头，想要垒成一个城堡。他正玩得高兴，忽然从西南驿道上来了辆马车，上面坐着位长者，后面跟着一些弟子。原来是孔子东游来到这里，驾车的是孔子的得意弟子子路。子路正驱车前行，猛然看见一个小孩蹲在路中间，就大声吆喝道："闪开！闪开！"项橐却像没听到一样，照样玩他的。子路停下车来，伸手要揍项橐，被孔子禁止了。

One day after lunch, Xiang Tuo was playing on the path. He found some little stones and intended to establish a castle, as he was enjoying the game, a carriage came from the southwest path, with an elder and some disciples sitting on it. It was Confucius who traveled eastwards and the driver was his favorable disciple Zi Lu. Zi Lu was driving the carriage forward and suddenly saw a child playing in the middle of the path, so he yelled "Stand aside! Stand aside!" Xiang Tuo continued to play as if he didn't hear it at all. Then Zi Lu stopped the carriage and intended to beat Xiang Tuo, but was prevented by Confucius.

孔子从车上下来，问："你这小孩子怎么不让路？"项橐说："是城躲马，还是马躲城呢？"孔子不知该怎么回答，只好绕"城"而过。

Confucius came down from the carriage and asked, "Why you child didn't make way for us?" Xiang Tuo answered, "Should the castle avoid the horse, or should the horse avoid the castle?" Confucius didn't know how to response and had to bypass the so-called castle.

第二天一早，孔子便派弟子去找项橐来交谈。这时，有一群鹅在池塘里戏水。项橐就问孔子："鹅

The next morning, by the invitation of Confucius, Xiang Tuo came to talk with Confucius. At this moment, a flock of geese were paddling in the pond, and Xiang Tuo

的叫声为什么这么大？”孔子说：“因为它的脖子长。”项橐说：“蛤蟆和青蛙的脖子很短，叫声也不小。”孔子无言以对。项橐诚恳地说：“人们都说你上知天文，下知地理，是无所不知的圣人，怎么这些事都给我讲不清楚呢？”孔子长叹一声，俯下身子对项橐说：“后生可畏，我当拜你为师。”

asked, “Why are those geese gaggling so loudly?” Confucius answered, “Because they have long necks.” Xiang Tuo said, “The toads and frogs have short necks, but they also cry loudly.” Confucius didn’t know how to response. Xiang Tuo said sincerely, “People always address you as an omniscient saint knowing astronomy and geography, but why you can’t explain these problems for me?” Confucius heaved a long sigh and bent over to Xiang Tuo and said, “The younger generation will surpass the older, I will take you as my teacher.”

086

多多益善

The more, the better

出自 《史记·淮阴侯列传》。

释义 越多越好。

秦朝末年，各地起义风起云涌。有一个军事才能出众的人，名叫韩信，他先是

By the end of Qin Dynasty, the uprisings burst vigorously. There was an person called Han Xin, who had outstanding military

参加了项羽领导的起义军，但项羽并不重用他，于是他又投靠了另一支起义军的领袖刘邦，被任命为大将军，经过数年征战，帮助刘邦建立了汉朝。

capability. Firstly, he joined in the insurrection army of Xiang Yu, but was not taken seriously, so he turned to another insurrection army of Liu Bang and was appointed as the senior general. He supported Liu Bang to establish Han Dynasty after many years of battles.

刘邦当了皇帝后，对大功臣韩信逐渐失去了信任，于是就用计把他抓了起来，但并没有治罪，只是降了他的官职，把他从楚王贬为淮阴侯，然后又放了他。韩信知道刘邦这样做是因为畏惧他的才能，担心他谋权夺位，因此经常装病不参加朝会。

After Liu Bang became the emperor, he began to lose trust on the major contributor Han Xin. So he seized Han Xin by tricks and downgraded him from the King of Chu to the Duke Huaiyin instead of punishment, and then let him go. Han Xin understood that Liu Bang feared his capability and afraid of being usurped, so Han Xin was always absent from the morning court meeting by the excuse of illness.

刘邦明白韩信的心思，于是就常常找韩信来聊天，讨论国事。有一次，刘邦问韩信：“你觉得我能统率多少军队呢？”韩信回答说：“陛下最多能统帅十万人的军队。”刘邦接着问道：“那你呢？”韩信从容地回答说：“我带兵越多越好

Liu Bang understood the consideration of Han Xin, so he always invite Han Xin for talking about the state affairs. One time, Liu Bang asked Han Xin, “How many troops do you think I can lead?” Han Xin answered, “Your Majesty can lead 100 000 troops at most.” Liu Bang went on, “How about you?” Han Xin answered leisurely, “The more, the better!” Liu Bang smiled and said, “If the

啊！”刘邦笑道：“既然你带兵打仗越多越好，为什么以前还是被我抓住了呢？”韩信说：“陛下虽然不善于带领士兵打仗，但是您很善于指挥将领，所以我就被您抓住了。”刘邦听了，不由得哈哈大笑起来。

more the better, why were you seized by me before?” Han Xin said, “Although Your Majesty is not good at leading troops, you’re excellent at commanding, so I was seized by you.” Then Liu Bang couldn’t help to laugh out.

087

如坐针毡

Sit on pins and needles

出自 《晋书·杜预传》。

释义 心神不定，坐立不安。

晋惠帝昏庸无能，皇后贾南风趁机干预朝政。由于太子司马遹不是贾南

Since the Emperor Hui of Jin was stupid and incompetent, the Empress Jia Nanfeng took this advantage to interfere state affairs. Because

风亲生的儿子，所以贾南风视司马遹为眼中钉、肉中刺。她不仅把太子跟他的生母分开，而且还暗中指使太子身边的人放松管教，司马遹当时只有13岁，一旦失去大人的约束和管教，自然像脱了缰的野马，肆意妄为。

the prince Si-ma Yu was not her biological son, so she regarded Si-ma Yu as a thorn in her flesh. She not only seperated the prince from his biological mother, but also instigated the people around the prince to loosen disciplines. As a child of thirteen years old, once he was free from the constraint and discipline by adults, Si-ma Yu was just like a runaway wild horse and always acted recklessly.

晋朝名将杜预的儿子杜锡，性格非常耿直，他做了太子中舍人以后，多次规劝司马遹远离小人，修养德行，但司马遹不但不听劝告，反而对杜锡心怀怨恨。

The famous general of Jin, Du Yu, had a son called Du Xi, who was very upright. When he assumed the imperial assistant to prince, he always persuaded Si-ma Yu to keep away from the villain and cultivate his virtues, but Si-ma Yu didn't take his advice, nevertheless he was resentful against Du Xi.

有一次，司马遹故意在杜锡坐的毡垫内放了一些针。杜锡没有发觉，结果屁股被扎得鲜血直流，疼痛不堪。第二天，司马遹故意问杜锡说：“你昨天出了什么事？”杜锡难以开口，只好说：“昨天喝醉了，不知道干了些什么。”司马遹说：

One time, Si-ma Yu intentionally hid some pins in Du Xi's mattress, but Du Xi didn't discover and was pricked to blood with great pains. The next day, Si-ma Yu intentionally asked Du Xi, “What was the matter of you yesterday?” Du Xi felt awkward and said, “I was drunk yesterday and had no idea of what I did.” Si-ma Yu said, “You like to blame others, but why

“你喜欢责备别人，为什么自己也做错了事呢？”

did you do the wrong thing?”

后来，贾南风设计陷害司马遹，废除了司马遹的太子之位，发配到许昌。不久，贾南风又派宦官携带毒药到许昌，逼迫司马遹服用。司马遹坚决不从，宦官就趁着司马遹上厕所的时候，把他杀害，当时司马遹年仅23岁。

Afterwards, Jia Nanfeng set up Si-ma Yu and abolished his position of prince, and then Si-ma Yu was banished to Xuchang. Soon after, Jia Nanfeng dispatched the eunuch to Xuchang with poison and forced Si-ma Yu to drink. But Si-ma Yu firmly refused, so the eunuch killed him by the chance when he went to toilet. At that time, Si-ma Yu was only twenty-three years old.

088

妄自尊大

Have too high an opinion of oneself

出自 《后汉书·马援传》。

释义 狂妄自大，轻视别人。

马援是中国古代著名的军事家，东汉开国功臣之一。

Ma Yuan was a famous militarist in Chinese ancient times, who was one of the great contributors during the founding of the Eastern Han Dynasty.

东汉初年，刘秀称帝，也就是光武帝。但是当时天下还没有统一，各路豪强都拥有自己的军队，霸占一方，各自为政。在这些豪强中，在成都称帝的公孙述最为强大。

At the beginning of the Eastern Han Dynasty, Liu Xiu became the Emperor Guang Wu. Due to the disunity at that time, the powerful lords held their own lands and troops, they were independent politically. And therein, Gong-sun Shu in Chengdu was the most powerful one.

马援当时还在陇西的隗嚣手下，很受器重。有一次，隗嚣派马援去公孙述那里去商讨事务。马援接受命令以后，满怀信心地出发了。因为公孙述是他的同乡，两人早年又彼此很熟悉，所以他想着一定能受到热情的欢迎和款待。

At that time, Ma Yuan was the subordinate of Wei Xiao in Longxi, and was regarded highly. One time, Wei Xiao dispatched Ma Yuan to discuss state affairs with Gong-sun Shu, Ma Yuan accepted the order and wen confidently. Because Gong-sun Shu was his fellow villager and they were familiar with each other in early years, so Ma Yuan expected for warm welcome and gracious hospitality.

马援到了以后，公孙述一听说马援要见他，竟然摆出了皇帝的架势，自己高高地端坐在大殿上，许多侍卫站在台阶前面。公孙述让马援用参见帝王的礼节来见他，而且没说几句话就退朝回宫，派人把马援送回宾馆去了。

When Ma Gong arrived, Gong-sun Shu unexpectedly assumed the posture of a king in the imperial hall with many imperial bodyguards before the steps. Gong-sun Shu required Ma Yuan to greet him with the etiquette of visiting the emperor, and withdrew to the palace after few words, and Ma Yuan was sent back to the inn.

接下来，公孙述又以皇帝的名义，给马援封官，赐马援官服。对此，马援心里很不痛快，他对手下的人说：“现在各路豪强争夺天下，还不知道谁胜谁败。公孙述这样大摆排场，自以为强大，有才能的人能留在这里跟他一起建功立业吗?”

马援于是告辞回去，对隗嚣说；“公孙述就好比井底的青蛙，看不到外面的广阔天地，妄自尊大，我们不如到东边的光武帝那里去寻找出路。”

后来，马援投靠了光武帝刘秀，成为光武帝手下的大将，他竭尽全力，打败公孙述等豪强，帮助光武帝统一了天下。

Then Gong-sun Shu intended to appoint Ma Yuan as the official and grant him official costume. Ma Yuan was very upset and said to his followers, “Nowadays many powerful lords are struggling for unification, it is still unknown that who will win. But Gong-sun Shu showed so much extravagance, will any competent people stay here and support him for the establishment of dynasty?”

So Ma Yuan left and said to Wei Xiao, “Gong-sun Shu is just like a frog at the bottom of the well, which can’t see the vast external world and thinks too highly of himself, we’d better turn to the Emperor Guang Wu in the east for development.”

Afterwards, Ma Yuan followed the Emperor Liu Xiu and became the senior general. He tried his utmost to defeat Gong-sun Shu and other lords, and help Liu Bang to accomplish unity.

089

守株待兔

Wait by the stump for a hare to dash itself against it

出自 《韩非子·五蠹》。

释义 不经过努力而希望得到成功。

春秋战国时期，宋国有个农夫，种了几亩地。每天早上天一亮，他就起床扛着

During the Spring and Autumn Period and the Warring States Period, there was a farmer in Song, who tilled a few acres of land. He carried

锄头去田里，傍晚太阳快落山了，又扛着锄头回家，非常辛苦。

hoe to the land when the sun was rising and carried hoe back home when the sun nearly set, it was tough work every day.

有一天，农夫正在地里干活，忽然看见一只兔子箭一般地飞奔过来，猛地撞在田地旁边的一截树桩上，一下子把脖子折断了，很快就咽气了。农夫放下手中的农活儿，走过去捡起兔子，高兴地说："一点劲儿没费，白捡了个大便宜，回家可以美美地吃上一顿了。"

One day, he was tilling the land, and suddenly a hare came running like an arrow and dashed against a stump besides the land, and its neck was broken and died immediately. The farmer put aside the hoe and went to pick up the hare and happily said, "I'm so lucky to get this hare without any efforts, and my wife and I can have a wonderful meal."

晚上回到家，农夫的妻子做了香喷喷的兔肉，两个人美美地吃了一顿。

After he came back home at night, his wife cooked a nice meal of hare meat and they had a wonderful dinner.

第二天，农夫照旧到地里干活儿，可是他老是想着还能遇到昨天的美事，干一会儿活儿就朝草丛里瞅一瞅，希望再有一只兔子窜出来撞在树桩上。可是直到天黑，也没见到有兔子出来，他很不甘心地回家了。

On the second day, the farmer went to the land as usually, and he always thought of the lucky thing yesterday, so he looked over the grass after tilling from time to time. But he didn't see any hare until night and went home reluctantly.

第三天，农夫来到地

On the third day, when the farmer went

里，把农具放在一边，自己就坐在树桩不远处，专门等着兔子窜出来。可是又白白地等了一天。

to the land, he put aside his farm tools and sat not far away from the stump, specially waiting for a hare dashing out, but nothing to gain.

后来，农夫天天什么活儿都不干，就守在树桩边，希望再捡到兔子，可是始终没有再得到。而地里的野草却越长越高，好端端的庄稼都被淹没了。

Afterwards, the farmer began to give up tilling and specially wait for a hare dashing against the stump, but still nothing to gain. Nevertheless, the weeds grew higher and higher, and finally the crops were destroyed.

090

安步当车

Go leisurely on foot is as good as riding in a chariot

出自 《战国策·齐策四》。

释义 以从容的步行代替乘车。比喻安于现状，不求显贵。

战国时期，齐国有一位隐士，名叫颜斶。齐宣王因为仰慕他的名声，就召见

In the Warring States Period, there was a recluse called Yan Chu, and the Emperor Xuan of Qi called him in due to his good

了他。

颜斶进宫后，齐宣王傲慢地对他说："颜斶，你过来！"

颜斶不卑不亢地对齐宣王说："大王，你过来！"

齐宣王很不高兴，旁边的大臣也都责怪颜斶。于是颜斶说："我走到大王面前去，说明是我羡慕他的权势；如果大王走过来，说明他礼贤下士。与其让我羡慕大王的权势，还不如让大王礼贤下士的好。"

齐宣王恼怒地问他："那到底是大王尊贵，还是士人尊贵？"

颜斶说："当然是士人尊贵了。从前秦国进攻齐国的时候，秦王下令说：谁敢在距离高士柳下惠坟墓五十步以内的地方砍柴，格杀勿论；另外还悬赏，谁能砍下齐王的脑袋，就封他为万户侯，赏金两万两。由此可

reputation.

When Yan Chu entered the imperial palace, the Emperor Xuan of Qi said to him arrogantly, "Yan Chu, come here!"

Yan Chu answered in a neither haughty nor humble way, "Your Majesty, come here!"

The Emperor Xuan of Qi was unhappy and the ministers besides all blamed Yan Chu, and Yan Chu said, "If I walk to the emperor, it shows that I admire his power; if the emperor walk to me, it shows that he treats worthy scholar with courtesy. Rather than that I admire the emperor's power, it would be better that the emperor shows his courtesy to the worthy scholar."

The Emperor Xuan of Qi asked angrily, "The emperor or the scholar, who is honorable after all?"

Yan Chu said, "Certainly the scholar! When Qin attacked Qi, the emperor of Qin once ordered that anyone who dared to cut firewood within fifty steps from the tomb of the famous scholar Liuxia Hui would be killed; and anyone who cut the head of Qi's emperor would be conferred as duke with reward of twenty-two thousand gold. Thus it shows that the head of

见，一个活着的大王的头，还抵不上一个死去的士人坟墓呢。”

an alive emperor is much unworthy than the tomb of a dead scholar.”

齐宣王觉得自己理亏，就请求做颜斶的学生，并且说：“你和我在一起，吃饭有美味，出行有车坐，妻子儿女也可以穿上华美的服装。”

The Emperor Xuan of Qi felt indefensible and asked to be Yan Chu’s student, “If you follow me, you will have delicious meals, luxurious chariot and delicate clothes for your wife and children.”

颜斶毫不动心，坚决辞谢说：“我还是希望回去，每天晚点儿吃饭，也像吃肉那样香；慢慢地走路，就当是坐车一样。清静无为，自足自得，多么开心啊！”

Yan Chu was not tempted and declined, “I still wish to go home, when I have late meals, I will take it as delicious meat, and when I walk slowly, i will take it as riding in a chariot. It would be very happy to have a peaceful and complacent life!”

说完，颜斶便告辞而去。

Then Yan Chu bid farewell and left.

091

曲高和寡

Highbrow songs find few singers

出自 战国·宋玉《对楚王问》。

释义 言论或作品不够通俗，能理解的人很少。

宋玉是战国后期的楚国辞赋作家，相传是屈原

Song Yu was a famous composer of Chu poems and odes in the late Warring States

的学生。据说他不但文章写得出色，人也长得十分俊美。

Period, who was legendarily regarded as the student of Qu Yuan, and it is said that he not only had an outstanding literary talent, but also eminently good looks.

宋玉在楚襄王的时候做过“文学侍从”一类的官。楚襄王也一直对宋玉很赏识，但是总有人在他面前说宋玉的坏话。有一天，他问宋玉说：“现在不少人对你有意见，你是不是有什么做得不对的地方？”

In the reign of the Emperor Xiang of Chu, Song Yu once assumed the position of literary assistant, although the Emperor Xiang of Chu regarded him highly, a few people always spoke evil of him. One day, the emperor asked Song Yu, “Now a few people criticize you, do you have any wrong doings?”

宋玉回答说：“确实有这种情况，请允许我为您解释一下。有位歌者在都城的广场上演唱，开始唱《下里》《巴人》这些通俗歌曲时，有几千名听众跟着唱起来；当他唱到《阳春》《白雪》这类高雅的歌曲时，能跟着唱的只有几十人；而唱到更高深的歌曲时，跟着和唱的就只有几个人了。这样看来，歌曲越是高雅，和唱的人就越少。所以杰出人才的美好操行，往往会超出

Song Yu answered, “This situation indeed exists, let me explain for you. There was a performance in the square of the capital, when he sang popular songs such as *Village and People of Shu*, thousands of audience followed him; when he sang elegant songs such as *Spring and White Snow*, only dozens of people followed him; when he sang more profound songs, only several people followed. So in this way, the more elegant the songs are, the less people follow. The good virtues of excellent people always greatly exceed the ordinary

普通人很多，一般的人又怎能了解我的所作所为呢？因此有人说三道四也就难免了。”

people, so how could the ordinary people understand my doings? So it is common that some people make carping comments on me.”

092

有恃无恐

Be emboldened by the support

出自 《左传·僖公二十六年》。

释义 有所倚仗，毫无顾忌。

春秋时期，称霸中原的齐桓公死后，他的儿子齐孝公继承了王位。

In the Spring and Autumn Period, after the death of the Duke Huan of Qi, who once dominated the Central Plains, his son, the Duke

Xiao of Qi ascended the throne.

有一年，鲁国遭到了严重的灾荒，齐孝公乘机亲自率领大军，去讨伐鲁国。鲁僖公得知消息，知道自己无法和齐军对抗，便派大夫展喜带着牛羊、酒食去犒劳齐军。

One year, Lu suffered serious calamities, and the Duke Xiao of Qi led troops to attack Lu. Upon this news, the Duke Xi of Lu was fully aware that he was powerless to resist, so he dispatched officials to treat Qi's troops with cattle, sheep, wine and food.

展喜日夜兼程，在齐鲁边界上与齐军相遇，他前去拜见齐孝公，说：“我们的君王听说大王亲自来到我国，特地派我前来慰劳。”

Zhan Xi pressed forward day and night without rest and met Qi's troops at the boundary between Qi and Lu, so he went to visit the Duke Xiao of Qi and said, “It is heard that Your Majesty come to our country, so he specially dispatched me to send you the rewards.”

齐孝公傲慢地说：“你们鲁国人感到害怕了吗?”

The Duke Xiao of Qi said arrogantly, “Are the people of Lu afraid?”

展喜语气平静地回答说:“那些没有见识的人可能有些害怕，但我们的国君和大臣们却一点也不害怕。”

Zhan Xi answered calmly, “Those ordinary people maybe afraid, but our king and ministers are not afraid at all.”

齐孝公轻蔑地说：“你们国家国库空虚，百姓家中缺粮，地里没有庄稼，连青草也看不到，你们凭什么不害怕呢？”

The Duke Xiao of Qi said contemptuously, “For your empty coffers, lack of rice, no corps and even no grass, how can't you fear?”

展喜不慌不忙地说："当初，鲁国的祖先周公和齐国的祖先姜太公，忠心耿耿，齐心协力辅助成王，使天下大治。成王对他俩十分感激，让他俩立下盟誓，告诫后代的子子孙孙，要世代友好，不互相侵害。我们的祖先这样友好，大王您又怎么会贸然废弃祖先盟约，进攻我国呢？我们正是倚仗着这一点，才不害怕。"

Zhan Xi answered unhurriedly, "At the very beginning, the Duke Zhou and Master Jiang respectively as the ancestors of Lu and Qi were all loyal and devoted to support the King Cheng to accomplish unification. The King Cheng was so grateful to make an oath of alliance that all the descendants should be friendly without infringement on each other. Our ancestors were so friendly, how can Your Majesty abandon the oath and attack us? We are not afraid just because we secure this in knowledge."

齐孝公觉得展喜的话很有道理，就打消了讨伐鲁国的念头，班师回国了。

The Duke Xiao of Qi thought it was very reasonable and gave up the idea to attack Lu and went back.

093

江郎才尽

At one's wits' end

出自 南北朝·钟嵘《诗品》。

释义 人的才思减退或是本领用尽。

南北朝时期，有个著名的才子叫江淹，从小与母亲相依为命，尽管家境贫寒，

In the Southern and Northern Period, there was a famous gifted scholar called Jiang Yan, who mutually depending on each other

但凭着自身的努力，青年时代的江淹就已写得一手好文章。后来，江淹的才名传到了南朝宋建平王刘景素那里。刘景素很欣赏江淹的才华，于是便给江淹写信邀请他。随后，江淹去拜访刘景素，二人谈得十分投机。不久，刘景素就提拔江淹做了南兖州的官吏。

for living with his mother. In spite of his poor family, Jiang Yan could write excellent articles in his youth, then his good reputation spread to Liu Jingsu as the Duke Ping of the Southern Song, who regarded Jiang Yan highly and wrote to invite him. Then Jiang Yan went to visit Liu Jingsu and they had a nice talk. Shortly after, Liu Jingsu promoted Jiang Yan to be the official of the southern Yanzhou.

后来萧道成灭宋立齐，请江淹做了史官。有一次，襄阳发掘出一座古墓，出土了一面玉镜和一些竹简。竹简上刻着的古体字谁也看不懂，人们于是便把竹简拿给江淹看，江淹一眼就认出上面写的是周宣王时候的事情。从此，江淹的名气更大了。

Afterwards, Xiao Daocheng eliminated Song and established Qi, so he invited Jiang Yan to assume office. One time, an ancient tomb was excavated in Xiangyang, and a jade mirror and some bamboo slips were unearthed. No one could recognize the ancient characters on the bamboo slips, so people took them to Jiang Yan, who immediately understood that it was about the history of the Emperor Xuan of Zhou, thus Jiang Yan became much more famous.

随着官越做越大，江淹过惯了养尊处优的生活，再也不愿意动笔写文章了。时间一长，才思减退，有时勉强写出一点东西，但人们读

As his official position became higher and higher, Jiang Yan was used to a comfortable life, and was not willing to write any articles. After a long time, his wits began to decrease and could barely write something, but people

了以后感到十分乏味。当时的人传说：有一天，江淹在凉亭里睡觉，做了一个梦。梦中有一个叫郭璞的人对他说："我有一支笔放在你那里已经很多年了，现在应该是还给我的时候了。"江淹摸了摸怀里，果然掏出一支五色笔来，于是他就把笔还给郭璞。从此以后，江淹就再也写不出美妙的文章了。因此，人们都说江郎的才华已经用尽了。

thought it as boring. There was a legendary story about Jiang Yan which said: One day, Jiang Yan was sleeping in the pavilion and had a dream. In the dream, a person called Guo Pu said to him, "I have a writing brush in your hold for many years, now it is time to give it back to me." Jiang Yan touched a five-colored writing brush as expected and gave it to Guo Pu. Afterward, Jiang Yan could not write any excellent articles, so people all said that Jiang Yan's wits had exhausted.

094

百发百中

One hundred shots, one hundred hits

出自 《战国策·西周策》。

释义 箭术高明，每次都能命中目标。

战国时期，秦国大将白起将要带兵攻打魏国都城大梁。谋士苏厉对周王说：

In the Warring States Period, the great general Bai Qi of Qin was preparing to attack the capital Daliang of Wei, and the adviser Su Li said

“白起这几年打败韩、赵等国，夺取了许多土地。现在他将要带兵攻打大梁，大梁一旦被攻下，周王室就危险了，您应当想办法阻止白起出兵。”于是，周王就派苏厉去到了秦国。

to the Emperor of Zhou, “Bai Qi has defeated Han, Zhao and other several countries and seized many lands during these years, now he prepares to attack Daliang, as long as Daliang is captured, Zhou’s imperial family will be very dangerous, so you should figure it out to stop him.” Thus the Emperor of Zhou dispatched Su Li to Qin.

苏厉见到白起，给他讲了下面这个故事。

Su Li saw Bai Qi and told him a story as follows.

“从前，楚国有一个名叫养由基的人，箭术高明。他距离柳树一百步外，每箭都能射中柳叶的中心，百发百中。旁边看的人都夸射得好，可是一个过路的人却说，这个人，可以教他该怎样射箭了。

Once upon a time, there was a person called Yang Youji, who was excellent in archery. He could shoot at the center of a leaf with a distance of one hundred steps from the willow with great accuracy. All the onlookers praised him, but only one passer said, “This person should be taught how to shoot.”

养由基心里很不舒服，就说，那让我们也开开眼界，看看你是怎么射的吧！

Yang Youji felt upset and said, “Now let us broaden our eyesight and have a look at how you shoot!”

那个人说，我不能教你射箭的本领。不过你有没有想过，你射柳叶百发百中，却不善于休息，等一会疲倦了，有一箭射不中，就会前

That passer said, “I can’t teach you how to shoot, but have you ever thought that you are good at shooting with great accuracy instead of shooting with reasonable rest. After a while, when you’re tired and missed one shot, you will

功尽弃。”

讲完这段故事，苏厉话锋一转，说：“您已经打败韩、赵等国，取得许多土地，功劳很大。现在听说又要派您带兵去进攻大梁，如果这一仗不能取胜，就会前功尽弃。您不如假称自己生病，不要出兵为好。”

白起笑着说：“我所向披靡，百战百胜，怎么会不能取胜呢？”结果，他并没有被苏厉说动，率兵攻打魏国，大获全胜，夺取了魏国的几十座城池。

waste all your previous efforts.”

When Su Li finished the story, he switched the conversation to other subject and said, “You have defeated Han, Zhao and other several countries and seized many lands, as well as made great contributions. Now it is heard that you will be dispatched to attack Daliang, and if you failed this time, you will waste all your previous efforts. It would be better if you pretend to be ill and decline to attack.”

Bai Qi smiled and said, “I’m invincible and ever-victorious, how can’t I gain a victory?” Finally, he was not persuaded by Su Li and led troops to attack Wei. He gained a complete victory and seized dozens of cities.

095

约法三章

Agree on a three-point rule

出自 《史记·高祖本纪》。

释义 订立简单的共同遵守的条款。

秦朝末年，刘邦和项羽一同起义反秦。后来，刘邦的人马首先攻入秦国都城咸

By the end of Qin Dynasty, Liu Bang and Xiang Yu joined together to attack Qin. Afterwards, the troops of Liu Bang firstly

阳。咸阳宫里富丽豪华，美女如云，让小吏出身的刘邦大开眼界，待在宫中饮酒作乐，不愿意离开。

charged into the capital Xianyang. The magnificent luxury of the imperial palace and numerous beauties broadened the eyesight of Liu Bang, who was once only a petty official, so he stayed for drinking and pleasure in the imperial palace and reluctant to leave.

后来，在樊哙和张良的再三劝说下，刘邦才醒悟过来，派人封了贮藏金银财宝的库房，带兵回到灞上。

Afterwards, thanks to the repeated persuasion by Fan Kuai and Zhang Liang, Liu Bang awakened to the truth and asked people to seal up the treasure coffers, and then brought troops back to Bashang.

为了收买人心，几天以后，刘邦又把各县有威望的父老豪杰召集到灞上，告诉大家说："你们已经吃尽了秦朝的苦头，今天，我跟诸位父老约定三条法令。第一，杀人的偿命；第二，打伤人的治罪；第三，偷盗的治罪。除了这三条，其余秦朝的法律一概废除。"

Several days later, in order to buy popularity, Liu Bang called in the prestigious fellow countrymen to Bashang from all the counties and said, "You have suffered a lot in Qin Dynasty, so today I'd like to make a three-point rule with you as follows. Firstly, life for a life; secondly, punishment for injury; thirdly, punishment for theft. And additionally, all the Qin's laws will be abandoned."

父老们听了刘邦的约法三章，高兴极了，赶快回去向老百姓宣传。老百姓听说刘邦如此宽大仁慈，也都很高兴。他们争先恐后地拿着

The fellow countrymen were very happy to hear this three-point rule and hurried to propagate to other civilians. And the civilians were also very happy for Liu Bang's leniency, so they competed to contribute wine and meat

酒肉和粮食来慰劳士兵。刘邦再三辞谢说："军中有的是粮食，不可接受你们的礼物，如果任意收礼，就违背了我进关的初衷了。"

由此，刘邦得到了百姓的拥护和支持，最后取得天下，做了皇帝。

to reward the soldiers. Liu Bang declined over and over again and said, "There are plenty of food in our campsite, we can't accept your gifts, otherwise, my preliminary intention will be violated."

Thus, Liu Bang gained support from civilians and finally accomplished the unification as the emperor.

096

老马识途

An old horse knows the way

出自 《韩非子·说林上》。

释义 有经验的人熟悉情况，能在某个方面起到指引作用。

齐桓公成为中原各国的盟主以后，有一次，北方一个叫作山戎的少数民族侵

After the Duke Huan of Qi dominated the Central Plain, one time a minority called Shanrong attacked Yan by robbing rice,

犯燕国，抢夺粮食、牲畜和财物，燕国派人来向齐桓公求救。齐桓公征求管仲的意见，管仲说："山戎经常骚扰中原，使中原不得安宁，一定要征服它。"齐桓公听了管仲的话，亲自率领大军去援救燕国。

livestock and treasure, and the emperor of Yan dispatched people to seek help from the Duke Huan of Qi. The Duke Huan of Qi asked for Guanzhong's advice, and Guanzhong said, "Shanrong always harass the Central Plain, so it should be conquered." Then the Duke Huan of Qi personally led the troops to rescue Yan.

齐国军队在春天的时候出征，到打败山戎凯旋时已是冬天，周围的自然环境已经大变了样。大军在崇山峻岭里穿行，来到一个山谷里，转来转去，最后迷了路，怎么也找不到出去的道路。齐桓公派出多批探子去探路，但仍然弄不清楚该从哪里走出山谷。时间一长，军队的粮食都快没了，情况非常危急。

It was spring when Qi's troops went out to battle, and turned winter when they defeated Shanrong and went back triumphantly, so there were great changes for the natural surroundings. The troops went through the high mountains and lofty hills, and when they went into a valley, they moved back and forth, but finally got lost and couldn't find the way out. The Duke Huan of Qi dispatched several scouts to explore but still unable to find the way out. Being trapped here, the troops was going to run out of their food and was in critical condition.

后来，管仲思索了好久，有了一个主意，于是他对齐桓公说："大王，我认为老马走过的路多，一定有认路的本领，可以利用它们在前面领

Afterwards, Guanzhong considered for a long time and came up with an idea, he said to the Duke Huan of Qi, "Your Majesty, I think the old horses will probably know the way, we can let them guide us out of the

路，带着大军走出山谷。”

valley.”

齐桓公同意了。管仲立即挑出几匹老马，解开缰绳，让它们在军队的最前面自由行走。也真是奇怪，这些老马都毫不犹豫地朝着一个方向行进，身后的军队于是紧跟着它们，东走西走，最后终于走出山谷，找到了回国的大路。

The Duke Huan of Qi agreed. Guanzhong selected several old horses, he released their reins and let them walk freely at the very head of the troops. It was strange that all the old horses walked towards a same direction without any hesitance, so the troops followed them closely. Finally, they walked out of the valley and found the way back to their country.

大家死里逃生，都很佩服管仲的足智多谋。从此，“老马识途”也成为一个广为流传的成语。

All the people barely escaped with their lives and highly admired Guanzhong's resourcefulness. From then on, the saying of “An old horse knows the way” becomes a popular idiom.

097

老牛舐犊

An old cow licks the calf

出自 《后汉书·杨彪传》。

释义 比喻父母疼爱子女的深挚感情。

三国时期，曹操手下有一个掌管文书的官吏，名叫杨修，博学多才，聪明过

In the period of the Three Kingdoms, Cao Cao had a subordinate in charge of documents called Yang Xiu, who was knowledgeable and

人。一次，有人给曹操送来了一盒他很喜欢吃的酥点，盒子上面写着“一合酥”三个字。曹操因为有事顾不上吃就出去了。杨修马上打开盒子，招呼众人把酥点分着吃完了。曹操查问此事，杨修说：“盒子上写着‘一合酥’，不就是一人一口酥吗？我们怎敢违背您的命令，就把它吃了！”曹操虽然很不高兴，但也无话可说。

clever than the ordinary. One time, someone had brought Cao Cao a box of his favorite crisp pastries, with three chinese characters of “a box of crisp pastries” on the package. Cao Cao left the pastries and hurried out. Yang Xiu immediately opened the box and distribute the pastries to people on site. Later when Cao Cao queried, Yang Xiu answered, “There are characters of ‘a box of crisp pasties’ on the package, isn’t it mean that each person takes a bite of the crisp pastries? We ate it because we dare not violate your order.” Cao Cao was not glad to hear that, but had noting to say.

又有一次，曹操领兵攻打蜀国汉中，正处于进退两难的境地，进攻并不有利，撤退又怕丢面子。这时，厨师送来鸡汤，曹操正准备吃，夏侯惇来请示行军口令，曹操随口说道：“鸡肋！鸡肋！”杨修听到口令之后，马上收拾行装。夏侯惇见了，问他为什么，杨修说："鸡肋食之无味，弃之可惜。宰相把汉中当作鸡

Another time, Cao Cao led troops to attack Hanzhong of Shu, and when he was in a dilemma that it would be disadvantageous to attack and shameful to withdraw. At this moment, the cook send him a bowl of chicken soup. When Cao Cao prepared to eat, Xia-hou Dun went in for the orders, and Cao Cao said randomly “Chicken ribs! Chicken ribs!” Yang Xiu heard it and immediately packed up, and Xia-hou Dun asked the reason, Yang Xiu said “The chicken ribs are tasteless but regrettable to throw away. Our minister takes Hanzhong

肋，意思就是没有必要留在这里，要准备回去了。所以我先收拾好行李。"后来，曹操果然下令回师。

杨修多次猜中曹操的心思，曹操对他很是嫉恨，后来就借口杨修扰乱军心，把他杀了。杨修死后，他的父亲杨彪非常悲痛。一次，曹操问杨彪说："你为什么瘦得这么厉害？"杨彪悲伤地说："人都怀着老牛舔小牛一样的爱子之心，现在小牛死了。我这老牛怎么能不瘦呢？"曹操听了，默默无语。

as the chicken ribs, which means there's no necessity to stay here and prepared to go back, so I pack up firstly." Afterward, as expected, Cao Cao ordered to go back.

Since Yang Xiu had figured out Cao Cao's meanings for several times, Cao Cao was jealous and resented towards him , and by the excuse of undermining the morale, he killed Yang Xiu. After Yang Xiu's death, his father Yang Biao was deeply grieved. One time, Cao Cao asked Yang Biao, "Why are you thin so badly?" Yang Biao said sadly, "Everyone has a heart of parental love just like the old cow licks the calf, now the calf is dead, how can't I become thin so badly?" Cao Cao heard and sank into silence.

098

老骥伏枥

An old steed in the stable still aspiring to gallop

出自 三国·魏·曹操《步出夏门行》诗。

释义 虽然年老，仍怀有雄心壮志。

东汉末年，曹操在官渡之战中以少胜多，大败袁绍，军威大振。不久以

By the end of the Eastern Han Dynasty, Cao Cao defeated Yuan Shao with a force inferior in number in the battle of Guandu. Shortly

后，曹操又统领大军远征乌桓。大军一到柳城，就大败乌桓骑兵，杀死了单于蹋顿。这样曹操北征乌桓、统一北方的大业算是完成了。

after, Cao Cao led troops to conquer Wuhuan, as soon as his troops arrived in the city of Liu, the Wuhuan cavalrymen were seriously defeated and the chief Ta Dun was killed. Thus Cao Cao had completed the north expedition to Wuhuan and unification of the north.

回到军营，曹操仍心潮起伏，久久不能平静。他想到北方的袁绍、蹋顿虽然已讨伐平定，而南方的孙权、刘备却仍然雄踞一方。自己虽然是五十三岁的人了，但历史的重任肩负在身，统一国家的使命仍在召唤着他。想着想着，他激情难耐，豪情又起，大踏步走到案前，挥笔写下：

After Cao Cao came back to the campsite, he still felt an upsurge of ups and downs for a long time. He thought that although Yuan Shao and Ta Dun in the north were already suppressed, Sun Quan and Liu Bei still prominently dominated in the south. And he had to undertake momentous historical task of unification at his fifty-three years old. He thought it over with great passion and aspiration, and he stepped to the desk in big strides and wrote the following poem:

神龟虽寿，
犹有竟时；
螣蛇乘雾，
终为土灰。
老骥伏枥，
志在千里；
烈士暮年，
壮心不已。

Though Long May Live the Sacred Turtle,
There is time it has to die;
The Flying Snake on mist arises,
At last to dust it has to turn.
The aged steed that lies in the stable,
Aspires to race a thousand miles;
The hero in his evening years,
Never lets droop his noble ideal.

盈缩之期，
不但在天；
养怡之福，
可得永年。

It is not with Heaven along that rests,
The fullness or abridgment of life;
By keeping peace of mind and body,
One will secure longevity.

从这首诗可以看出，曹操认识到了人的生老病死，却并不消极懈怠，他要用建功立业来弥补人生这一憾事，表现了曹操老当益壮、志在千里的积极进取精神。

From this poem, although Cao Cao realized the truth of life and death, he was ambitious to accomplish the career of unification in order to make up the regret of life, which reflects Cao Cao's positive enterprising spirit at his old but vigorous age.

099

自相矛盾

To contradict oneself

出自 《韩非子·难一》。

释义 说话做事前后抵触。

楚国有一个卖兵器的人，到市场上去卖矛和盾。一到市场，就有好多人围过来看，这个人便举起他的盾，向大家夸口说："我的

A man of the state of Chu had a spear and a shield for sale. When he arrived in the market, many people gathered around to have a look, so he was loud in praises of his shield, "My shield is so strong that nothing can pierce it through."

盾是世界上最坚固的，无论什么样的锋利尖锐的武器也不能刺穿它！”

夸完他的盾之后，接下来，这个卖兵器的人又拿起一支矛，大言不惭地夸了起来：“我的矛是世界上最尖利的，无论怎样牢固结实的东西也挡不住它，只要一碰上，马上就会被它刺穿!”

Then he also sang praises of his spear, “My spear is so sharp that it can pierce through anything.”

说完，他十分得意，又大声吆喝起来：“快来看呀，快来买呀，这里有世界上最坚固的盾和最锋利的矛!”

Finally, he praised loudly, “Come and look! Come and buy! Here are the strongest shield and sharpest spear!”

这时，一个看客上前拿起一支矛，又拿起一面盾，问他说：“如果用这支矛去刺这面盾，会怎样呢?”

At this moment, a passer took up a spear and lift a shield, and asked, “What would happen if your spear is used to pierce your shield?”

“这——”卖兵器的人支支吾吾，说不出话来。围观的人群爆发出一阵大笑，便都散去了。

“Ah...” This man made an ambiguous statement with nothing to say, and the surrounding people had a burst of laughter and dispersed.

那个卖兵器的人也灰溜溜地扛着矛和盾走了。

And the man also walked away despondently with his spear and shield.

100

讳疾忌医

Conceal one's ailment and refuse medical treatment

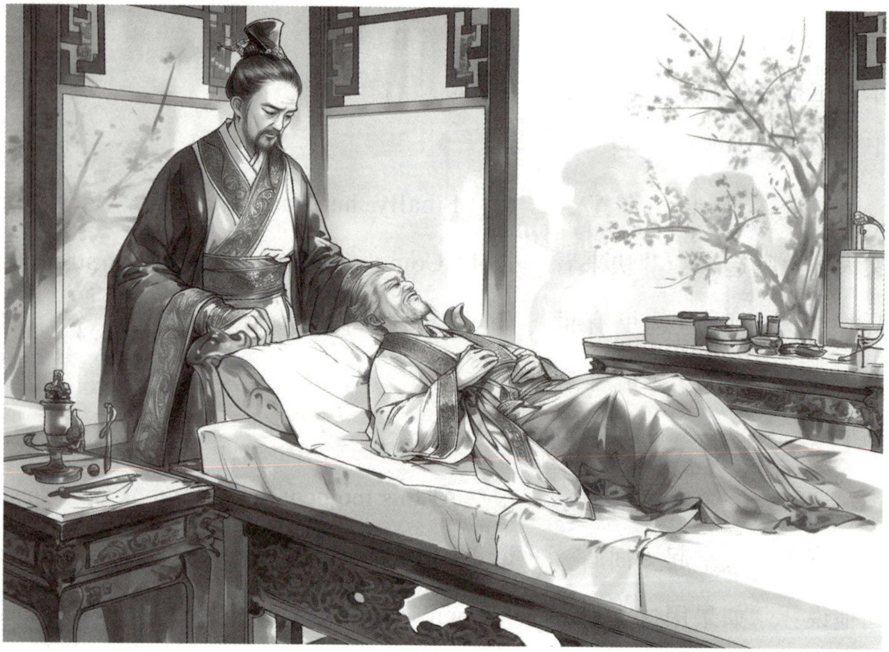

出自 《韩非子·喻老》。

释义 怕人批评而掩饰自己的缺点。

扁鹊是战国时的一位名医，本名秦越人，因为他医术高超，所以当时的人们

In the Warring States Period, there was a famous doctor called Bian Que, his autonym name was Qinyue Ren, because of his superb

借用了上古时期的神医“扁鹊”的名号来称呼他。

medical skills, people addressed him as Bian Que, which was the name of a miracle doctor in the ancient times.

有一天，扁鹊去见蔡桓公。这个蔡桓公，也就是齐桓公田午。扁鹊端详了一番蔡桓公的气色，对他说：“大王，您得病了。现在病只在皮肤表层，赶快治，很容易就会治好。”蔡桓公不以为意地说：“我没有病，用不着你来治。”扁鹊走后，蔡桓公对身边的人说：“这些医生成天想给没病的人治病，好用这种办法来证明自己医术高明。”

One day, Bian Que went to visit the Duke Caihuan, who was also called Tian Wu as the Duke Huan of Qi. Bian Que carefully observed the complexion of the Duke Caihuan and said, “Your Majesty, you’re ill. Now the illness only lies on the skin surface, it will be easily cured with immediate treatment.” But the Duke Caihuan took it carelessly and said, “I’m not ill and don’t need your treatment.” After Bian Que left, the Duke Caihuan said to his followers, “Those doctors always want to cure the healthy people in order to prove their superb medical skills.”

过了十天，扁鹊又去见蔡桓公，他着急地说：“您的病已经发展到肌肉里去了，要抓紧治疗啊!”蔡桓公把头一歪，说：“我根本就没有病，你走吧!”扁鹊走后，蔡桓公很不高兴。

Ten days later, Bian Que visited the Duke Caihuan again and said anxiously, “Now your illness has developed into the muscle, please hurry up to cure!” The Duke Caihuan slanted his head and said, “I’m not ill at all, you can go now!” After Bian Que left, the Duke Caihuan was very upset.

又过了十天，扁鹊又去见蔡桓公。他看了看蔡桓

Another ten days later, Bian Que visited the Duke Caihuan again and said anxiously after

公的气色，焦急地说：“大王，您的病已经进入了肠胃，不能再耽误了!”蔡桓公连连摇头说：“我哪来的什么病！”扁鹊走后，蔡桓公更不高兴了。

又过了十天，扁鹊再一次去见蔡桓公。这次，他只是远远地望了一眼，掉头就走了。蔡桓公心里很纳闷，就派人去问扁鹊：“您去见大王，为什么掉头就走呢?”扁鹊说：“有病不怕，只要治疗及时，一般的病都会慢慢好起来的。怕的是有病说没病，不肯接受治疗。病在皮肤里，可以用热敷；病在肌肉里，可以用针灸；病到肠胃里，可以吃汤药。但是现在大王的病已经深入骨髓，只能听天由命了，所以，我也不敢再请求为大王治病了。”

observing his complexion, “Your Majesty, now your illness has developed into gastrointestinal organs, please don’t delay any more!” The Duke Caihuan kept shaking his head and said, “How can I become ill!” After Bian Que left, the Duke Caihuan was even more upset.

Then another tens days later, Bian Que visited the Duke Caihuan again. This time, he only looked at him from a distance, and then turned his head and walked away. The Duke Caihuan was curious and dispatched people to ask for the reason, “You came to visit our majesty, why did you turn your head and leave?” Bian Que said, “Illness is not terrible, because it can be gradually cured with timely treatment. It is terrible to pretend to be not ill and refuse treatment. When illness lies on skin surface, it can be cured by hot compress; when illness lies in muscle, it can be cured by acupuncture; when illness lies in gastrointestinal organs, it can be cured by medical soup. But now the illness has developed into bone marrow, the fate of our majesty can only be submitted to the will of Heaven, so I dare not request to cure his illness.”

五天以后，蔡桓公的病果然发作了，他急忙让人去请扁鹊，但是扁鹊已经到别的国家去了。没过几天，蔡桓公就病死了。

Five days later, as expected, the illness of the Duke Caihuan began to show, so he hurried to invite Bian Que, who had already went to other countries. Several days later, the Duke Caihuan died due to illness.

弘扬华夏经典历史文化精髓

中国成语故事

Chinese Idiom Stories

汉英对照 ②

张　羿◎编著

雅　雅◎译

天津出版传媒集团

天津科技翻译出版有限公司

图书在版编目（CIP）数据

中国成语故事.2：汉英对照 / 张羿编著；雅雅译.
天津：天津科技翻译出版有限公司，2025.5 - - ISBN
978-7-5433-4658-1

Ⅰ.H319.4

中国国家版本馆CIP数据核字第2025VS4967号

出　　版：天津科技翻译出版有限公司
出 版 人：方　艳
地　　址：天津市和平区西康路35号
邮政编码：300051
电　　话：022-87894896
传　　真：022-87893237
网　　址：www.tsttpc.com
印　　刷：运河（唐山）印务有限公司
发　　行：全国新华书店
版本记录：710mm×1000mm　16开本　38印张　500千字
2025年5月第1版　2025年5月第1次印刷
定价：136.00元（全2册）

目录

CONTENTS

目录

CONTENTS

101

过河拆桥

Kick the bridge after crossing the river

出自 《元史·彻里帖木儿传》。

释义 目的达到后，将帮助自己的人一脚踢开。

元朝有个大臣叫彻里帖木儿，有一年在浙江任职，正好赶上科举考试，从

In Yuan Dynasty, there was a minister called Cheli Tiemuer, one year during taking office in Zhejiang, he happened to witness the

官府到考生都花费了许多钱财，而且还有营私舞弊的情况。彻里帖木儿便暗暗下决心，等到自己掌握大权，一定要促使朝廷废除这种制度。

imperial examination, and he found that both government and the candidates spend lots of money in malpractice and corruption. Thus he was inwardly determined to push the imperial court to eliminate this corrupt system as soon as he took hold of power in the future.

后来，彻里帖木儿当了副宰相，便奏告元顺帝，请求废除科举制度。元顺帝虽然昏庸，但对于废除科举制度这一建议倒是赞成的。不久，他就命人起草了废除科举制度的诏书，准备颁发下去。当时，有一个地位略低于副宰相的参政官许有壬，他最早就是通过科举考试进入官场，逐渐被提升起来的。所以当朝廷准备废除科举制度时，许有壬坚决表示反对。

Afterwards, when Cheli Tiemuer became the vice minister, he submitted memorials to the Emperor Shun of Yuan for eliminating the imperial examination system. Although the Emperor Shun of Yuan was muddle-headed, he approved of this suggestion. So shortly after, he ordered to draft an imperial edict to for eliminating the imperial examination system and prepared to announce. At that time, there was a person called Xu Youren, whose position was relatively lower than the vice minister, and he was firstly selected into the imperial court through the imperial examination and then promoted gradually, so he firmly objected this imperial edict.

第二天，满朝文武被召到崇天门，皇帝特地下令让许有壬排在官员的首位，听读皇帝下达的废除科举制度的诏书。许有壬虽然心里非

The next day, all the officials were called up to gather at Chongtian Gate, and the emperor specially arranged Xu Youren to stand before all the officials to hear the announcement of the imperial edict. Xu Youren was very upset,

常不愿意，但又害怕得罪皇帝，只好勉强跪在百官前列听读诏书。

听完诏书后，百官纷纷回府，许有壬满脸不高兴地低头走着，有个名叫普化的御史特地走到他旁边，凑着他的耳朵，冷嘲热讽道："参政，你这下可成为过河拆桥的人了。"他的意思是，许有壬是靠科举当官的，现在却带头听读废除科举制度的诏书，就好像一个人过了桥以后就把桥拆掉一样。

许有壬听了，又羞又恨，加快脚步离开。此后他便借口有病，再也不上朝了。

but also afraid of offending the emperor, so he reluctantly knelt before all the officials to hear the announcement.

After the announcement, all the officials went back, only Xu Youren bowed his head and walked, totally miserable. A censor called Pu Hua specially walked to him and whispered with cynicism, "Now you become the person who kicks the bridge after crossing the river." He meant that Xu Youren was selected to the imperial court through the imperial examination, now he took lead to hear the announcement for eliminating the imperial examination, it is just like a person kicks the bridge after crossing the river.

Xu Youren heard and felt shameful and hateful, and he hurried to walk away. Afterwards, he didn't go to the imperial court any more by the excuse of illness.

102

闭门思过

Shut onself up amd ponder over one′s mistakes

出自 《汉书·韩延寿传》。

释义 犯了错误之后进行自我反省。

西汉时期有一个非常贤明的官吏，叫韩延寿。因为他在担任淮阳太守

In the Western Han Dynasty, there was a wise official called Han Yanshou. Due to his prominent performance as the prefecture chief

时政绩显著，朝廷又派他到更难治理的颍川任太守。

有一次，韩延寿出去巡视各地情况，经过高陵县的时候，看到有兄弟二人为了争夺田产而大打出手。韩延寿见此情景十分沮丧，觉得这违背了他一贯推行的礼义教化。于是自责说："我有幸成为这个地方的长官，却没有给老百姓做出表率，百姓没有接受教化的熏陶，以致兄弟失去和气，闹到衙门来打官司。这全都是因为我无德无能造成的，我必须引咎辞职，关起门好好反省自己的过失，听候朝廷处分。"说完之后，他就回到住处，整日不出门，反省自己的不足。

其他的官员都不知所措，最后只好也一个个把自己捆起来，进入监狱，表示请罪。这下为争夺田产打

in Huaiyang, the imperial court dispatched him to assume the prefecture chief in Yingchuan, which was harder for governance.

One time, Han Yanshou went out for inspection, when he passed by the county of Gaoling, he saw two brothers were fighting for farm lands, and he was upset and thought that it violated the etiquette education which he kept carrying forward. So he blamed himself, "I was lucky to become the local prefecture chief, but I didn't give civilians a good example, so civilians were not influenced by the etiquette education, thus those two brothers fought against each other and went to the local government for a lawsuit. All of this was caused by my incompetence, so I have to resign, shut up the door, and ponder over my own faults, waiting for the punishment by the imperial court." Then he stayed at home for pondering his faults, and didn't come out all day long.

Other officials had no idea and finally they all tied themselves up to the prison, waiting for the punishment. In this way, those two brothers were dumbfounded and their family people

官司的兄弟俩全傻了，他们的家里人也都惶恐不安，指责他俩犯了大罪。兄弟俩痛悔自己的错误，于是剃光了头，裸着上身来到县衙请罪。两人都表示愿意把田产让给对方，希望韩太守能原谅他们。韩延寿这才出门，和县里官员及兄弟俩见面，并且摆设酒宴与他们一起庆贺。

also felt insecure and blamed them for their wrong doings. Those two brothers seriously regretted and shaved their head clearly, and went to the local government for pardon, naked to the waist. They said they were willing to give the farm lands to the other and hope the local prefecture chief could forgive them. Then Han Yanshou went out and met the officials and those two brothers, and celebrated with them in a banquet.

103

两袖清风

Be clean-handed

出自 明·都穆《都公谭纂》。

释义 为官清廉，手头没有一点积蓄。

于谦是明朝著名的民族英雄和诗人，他在十二岁的时候就写下《石灰吟》一诗，来

Yu Qian was the famous national hero and poet in Ming Dynasty, and he wrote a poem called *The Recitation of Lime* to express

抒发他的志向。于谦性格耿直，为官廉洁，虽然他生活的那个年代朝政腐败，贪污成风，但他却一直秉持自己高洁的品性，不同流合污。

his ambition. Yu Qian was upright and incorruptible, although he lived in a dynasty full of corruption and embezzlement, he still kept his upright character and refused corruption.

明朝正统年间，宦官王振掌握大权，干涉朝政。每到朝会的时候，各地官吏为了讨好王振，都要献给他许多珠宝白银。当时于谦在外地做官，每次进京奏事，总是不带任何礼品。他的同僚劝他说："你虽然不献金银财宝，攀附权贵，也应该带一些著名的土特产，像线香、蘑菇、手帕等物，送点人情呀！"于谦举起双手，笑着说："我带有两袖清风啊！"为此，他还曾写了一首《入京诗》：

During Ming Dynasty Zhengtong, the eunuch Wang Zheng took hold the imperial power, and he always interfered in the state affairs. Upon each morning court, officials from all over the country would contribute lots of treasure and money to him. Each time Yu Qian went to join in the morning court, he never brought any gifts, and many fellow officials persuaded him, "Even if you don't bring any treasure and money pleasing the superiors, you should bring some local products such as the joss-stick, mushroom and handkerchief as gifts!" Yu Qian lifted his hands and said, "I bring two sleeves of breeze!" He also wrote a poem called *the Poem of Entering the Capital* as follows:

绢帕蘑菇与线香，
本资民用反为殃；
清风两袖朝天去，
免得闾阎话短长。

The handkerchief, mushroom and joss-stick are originally used for civilians, but now they become scourge; now I bring two sleeves of breeze to join the morning court, to avoid gossips by civilians.

诗的意思是说，绢帕、蘑菇、线香这些东西本来是供百姓享用的，可是因为贪官污吏的搜刮，它们反而给百姓带来了灾难。所以我什么也不带，只带两袖清风去朝见天子，免得人说长道短。

后来，于谦被奸臣捏造罪名，判处死刑。在查抄他的住宅时，家徒四壁，除了书籍以外，没有一点值钱的东西。连抄家的士兵看到这种情形，都不禁潸然泪下。

This poem means that handkerchief, mushrooms and joss-stick are used for the civilians, but due to the embezzlement of corrupt officials, these things bring disasters to civilians, so I bring nothing but two sleeves of breeze to visit the emperor to avoid any gossips.

Afterwards, Yu Qian was condemned to death due to fabricated charges by some treacherous officials. When soldiers searched his house, nothing valuable was found except for books, which made the soldiers shed tears.

104

余音绕梁

The tune lingers in the house

出自 《列子·汤问》。

释义 歌声高亢悦耳，使人经久不忘。

春秋战国时期，韩国有一位擅长歌唱的女子，名叫韩娥。有一次，她经过齐

In Han during the Spring and Autumn Period, there was a lady called Han E, who was good at singing. One time she passed by Qi,

国，因为盘缠用尽，便在齐国都城的雍门卖唱来换取钱物。韩娥的声音清脆嘹亮，婉转悠扬，十分动听。一直到她演唱完了，大批的齐国听众还聚在雍门，徘徊留恋，不愿意散去。

due to run-out of money, she sang for exchange of money at the Yong Gate of capital. Her voice was so melodious and pleasant that many people were reluctant to leave even if her song had finished, still lingering at Yong Gate instead of dispersing.

后来，韩娥来到一家旅店投宿时，旅店老板见她穷困潦倒，便当众羞辱她。韩娥忍不住拖着长音放声大哭，哭声悲伤凄楚，附近居民都被感动得流下泪来。

Afterwards, Han E wanted to put up for night at an inn, but she was penniless and frustrated, so the boss scolded her in public. And Han E couldn't help to cry loudly, and her cry was full of sorrow and misery, even the nearby residents were moved to tears.

韩娥在旅店里难以安身，被迫离开了。人们听说后，急忙分头去追赶她，苦苦挽留。韩娥经不住人们的请求，就返回来，为大家又演唱了一次。人们把她围得水泄不通，听得非常出神，干活的停了手，行路的歇了脚，吵架的住了嘴，开店的关了门。韩娥唱完以后，人们纷纷解囊资助她。

Since it was impossible to stay at the inn, Han E had to leave, and people hurried to find her and persuaded her to stay, finally she couldn't refuse anymore and came back for singing. People surrounded her tightly and listened to her song so infatuatedly that people even stopped working, walking, quarreling and doing business. When Han E finished singing , all the people offered her money and food.

韩娥离开三天之后，人

Three days after Han E left, people felt

们都还觉得她那优美的歌声仍然在梁间萦绕不断，就好像她没有离去一样。后人称其为“余音绕梁”，并作为成语世代流传了下来。

her melodious song still lingered in the house just like she never left. Afterwards, the idiom of “the tune lingers in the house” spread for generations.

105

初出茅庐

Just come out of thatched cottage

出自 罗贯中《三国演义》。

释义 崭露头角。

东汉末年，诸葛亮隐居在南阳隆中，号称“卧龙”。刘备曾三次去拜访

By the end the Eastern Han Dynasty, Zhuge Liang stayed in recluse in Longzhong of Nanyang, known as “crouching dragon”. Liu

他，请求他出山辅佐自己打天下。诸葛亮被刘备的诚意打动，终于出来做了他的军师，并得到了他的高度信任。但是刚开始的时候，关羽、张飞等将领对诸葛亮的才能并不认可。

没过多久，曹操派大将夏侯惇率领十万大军攻打新野，刘备找诸葛亮前来商议。诸葛亮说："我担心众将不听我的命令，希望借主公的印剑一用。"刘备立即将印剑交给诸葛亮。诸葛亮开始给各将领分派任务，命关羽带着一千人马埋伏在豫山，放过敌军的先头部队，看到起火，迅速出击；张飞带着一千人马埋伏在山谷里，等起火后，杀向博望城；关平、刘封带着五百人马，在博望坡后面分两路等候，敌军一到，立刻放火。接下来又把赵云从樊城调来当先锋，只许败

Bei had visited him thrice for requesting him to support the career of unification. Zhu-ge Liang was moved by Liu Bei's sincerity, so he agreed to be his military adviser and won great trust. But at the beginning, Guan Yu, Zhang Fei and other generals didn't recognize the capability of Zhu-ge Liang.

Shortly afterwards, Cao Cao dispatched the great general Xia-hou Dun to lead one hundred thousand of troops for conquering Xinye, so Liu Bei asked Zhu-ge Liang to have a discussion. Zhu-ge Liang said, "I'm afraid that the generals will not follow my orders, so I'd like to borrow your seal and sword." Liu Bei immediately handed them over to Zhu-ge Liang. Then Zhu-ge Liang began to assign tasks. Zhu-ge Liang assigned Guan Yu with one thousand of troops for ambush in Yu Mount, and ordered him to let off the leading troops of the enemy and quickly launch attacks upon the signal of fire; Zhu-ge Liang assigned Zhang Fei with one thousand of troops for ambush in valley, and ordered him to launch attacks on Bowang City upon the signal of fire; Zhu-ge Liang assigned Guan Ping and Liu Feng with five hundreds of troops for

不许胜；刘备带着一千人马作为后援。

waiting at the slopes of Bowang in two teams, and ordered them to set fire as soon as the enemies arrived; Zhu-ge Liang transferred Zhao Yun from Fan City to play a vanguard role, solely aiming at failure instead of victory; Zhu-ge Liang assigned Liu Bei with one thousand of troops as reinforcements.

分派完毕，关羽忍不住问："我们都去打仗，先生干什么？"诸葛亮说："我在城中坐等。"张飞大笑道："我们都去拼命，先生你却这般逍遥！"诸葛亮脸一沉，说道："印剑在此，违令者斩！"关羽、张飞不敢再吭声，冷笑着走了。

When the assignment finished, Guan Yu couldn't help to ask, "All of us will go for battle, but what are you doing?" Zhu-ge Liang answered, "I will wait inside the city." Zhang Fei laughed and said, "All of us will risk our lives, but you will just wander in leisure!" Zhu-ge Liang turned sour on his face and said, "Here are the seal and sword, whoever violates my orders will be killed!" Guan Yu and Zhang Fei dared not say anything and went away with a sneer.

战斗开始以后，各将领按照诸葛亮的吩咐行事，直杀得曹兵丢盔弃甲。诸葛亮神机妙算，初次用兵就大获全胜，使关羽、张飞等将领都佩服得五体投地。

As the battle began, all the generals strictly followed Zhu-ge Liang's orders, Cao Cao's troops were defeated so seriously that all the soldiers cast their amours. Thanks to the divine strategy and shrewd tactics of Zhu-ge Liang, they won a complete victory for the first battle, and Guan Yu, Zhang Fei and other general extremely admired Zhu-ge Liang.

因此，后来有人作诗称赞诸葛亮说："直须惊破曹公胆，初出茅庐第一功。""初出茅庐"的成语由此而来。

Afterwards, someone wrote a poem to praise Zhu-ge Liang, "the courage of Cao Cao's troops are heavily broken up, this is the first great contribution after Zhu-ge Liang comes out of his thatched cottage." Thus the idiom of "just come out of thatched cottage" drives from this story.

106

别开生面

Break fresh ground

出自 唐·杜甫《丹青引》。

释义 另创一种新的形式或局面。

曹霸是唐代的一位著名画家，擅长画人物和马。由于画术高超，他的名声传到

Cao Ba was a famous painter in Tang Dynasty, who was good at painting human portraits and horses. Due to his superb art of painting, his good

了京城长安，唐玄宗于是召他进宫，命他当场作画，并给予丰厚的赏赐。由于曹霸受到皇帝的宠幸，长安城里的王公贵族和官宦人家，都以收藏他的画为荣，大家不惜花费很高的价钱来收购他的墨迹。

reputation had spread to the capital Chang'an, so the Emperor Xuanzong of Tang Dynasty called in him to the imperial palace and ordered him to paint on the spot, and rewarded him generously. Since Cao Ba was greatly favored by the emperor, the princes, aristocrats and officials were all proud of collecting his paintings, and they spared no costs to buy his paintings.

长安的宫殿中，有一座著名的凌烟阁。阁内的四壁上绘有唐朝二十四位开国功臣的肖像。这些肖像是七十多年前著名画家阎立本画的，由于年代已久，现在大部分已经剥落，难以辨认。因此玄宗把曹霸召来，让他重新描画。

In the palace of Chang'an, there was a famous Lingyan Pavilion. There were twenty-four portraits of meritorious generals as the founding fathers on the inner walls, which were painted by the famous painter Yan Liben over seventy years ago, and most of the desolated paintings had peeled off and became indecipherable. So the Emperor Xuanzong called in Cao Ba to repaint.

曹霸接到任务后，为了更好地还原这些功臣的英姿，他阅读了大量史料，对照墙壁上已经暗淡模糊的肖像，仔细琢磨，然后开始精心绘制。四十九天后，二十四位功臣的肖像重新描绘完成，以崭新的面貌，栩

After Cao Ba received this assignment, in order to restore the valiant looks of these meritorious generals, he read lots of historical materials and considered carefully, then he began to paint meticulously according to the obscure and ambiguous portraits on the walls. Forty-nine days later, he accomplished repainting and twenty-four portraits showed

栩如生地展现在人们面前。

后来，安禄山、史思明叛乱，曹霸因为一幅作品有影射朝廷之嫌，被免去左武卫将军的官职，离开长安，流落到成都，靠在街头替人画像维持生计。

一次，著名诗人杜甫在朋友家里看到曹霸画的《九马图》，得知这位名噪一时的画家也在成都，便马上去寻访，几经打听，终于在街头找到了曹霸。杜甫对曹霸的遭遇非常同情，写了一首诗赠给他。诗中有两句这样写道：凌烟功臣少颜色，将军下笔开生面。意思是，凌烟阁中的功臣肖像已失去往日鲜艳夺目的色泽，幸亏在将军的笔下才使它们重放光彩。后人从这两句诗中提炼出了“别开生面”这一成语，沿用至今。

vividly.

Afterwards, due to rebellion of An Lushan and Shi Siming, one of Cao Ba's painting was believed to hint obliquely at the imperial court, so he was removed from the post of Left Guard General, and then he was stranded to Chengdu and made a living by painting at the street.

One time, the famous poet Du Fu saw *the Painting of Nine Horses* at his friend's home, and got to know the once-famous painter was also in Chengdu, so he decided to pay a visit. After several times of inquiring, he finally found Cao Ba at the street. Du Fu was very sympathetic towards Cao Ba's misfortune and wrote him a poem as a gift. Two sentences of this poem were "the portraits of meritorious generals faded their colors in Lingyan Pavilion, it is Cao Ba who makes it show a fresh look." It means that those portraits of meritorious generals have lost their brilliant colors, but thanks to Cao Ba, they renew their brilliance again. Afterwards, people derived the idiom of "break fresh ground" from these two sentences and popularly used until today.

107

励精图治

Make vigorous efforts

出自 《汉书·魏相传》。

释义 振奋精神，力求治理好国家。

西汉时期，汉宣帝刘询即位后，由于年龄幼小，朝政大权都由大将军霍光

In the Eastern Han Dynasty, after Liu Xun ascended the throne as the Emperor Xuan of Han, due to his young age, the imperial power

掌握。霍光辅佐汉朝几代皇帝，从政将近四十年，是当时无可取代的权臣，连皇帝都要忌惮他几分。

was totally held by the great general Huo Guang, who had assisted several generations of emperors for nearly forty years. Huo Guang was so irreplaceable that even the emperor was afraid of him.

虽然霍家显贵至极，但霍光的妻子霍显仍然不满足，她为了让小女儿成为皇后，巩固霍家地位，居然勾结御医毒死了许皇后。霍光知道以后，不但没有揭发，反而利用权势袒护了御医。

Although Huo Guang's family was in extreme dignity, Huo Guang's wife Huo Xian still felt unsatisfied, in order to make her youngest daughter the Empress and consolidate the position of Huo's family, she even bribed the imperial doctor to poison the Empress Xu to death. But when Huo Guang knew, instead of exposing, he took advantage of his power to shield the imperial doctor from punishment.

后来霍光病死，不久，霍显毒害许皇后的事情败露，汉宣帝听取魏相的意见，免去了霍氏的爵位，并任命魏相为丞相。霍氏一家对魏相恨之入骨，他们开始谋划造反，想先除掉魏相，再废掉汉宣帝，拥立霍光的儿子霍禹为帝。结果这件事被人揭发，霍家被满门抄斩。

Afterwards, Huo Guang died due to illness, and Huo Xian's evil deeds were exposed, then the Emperor Xuan of Han took the advice of Wei Xiang to remove Huo's family from the rank of nobility and appointed Wei Xiang as the Prime Minister. Huo's family hated Wei Xiang to the marrow of bones and began to plot rebellion, in order to enthrone Huo Guang's son Huo Yu as the emperor by eliminating Wei Xiang and deposing the Emperor Xuan of Han. But finally this plot was exposed and the entire Huo's family was exterminated.

从此以后，汉宣帝开始振奋精神，亲自处理国家政事，力图把国家治理得繁荣富强。在君臣的共同努力下，当时已经日渐衰败的西汉王朝又开始强盛起来。

From then on, the Emperor Xuan of Han began to arouse all his efforts to handle the state affairs in person and strive to make the country prosperous and strong. Upon the common efforts by the emperor and ministers, the decaying Western Han Dynasty became strong again.

108

呆若木鸡

Motionless like a wooden cock

出自 《庄子·达生》。

释义 愣着不动，像只木鸡。

战国时期，斗鸡游戏风行一时，是一种非常受大众欢迎的娱乐活动。

In the Warring Sates Period, the game of cock fighting became popular as a greatly favorable entertainment activity.

齐国的君主齐宣王，就十分热衷于这一游戏。他为了能够在斗鸡场上获胜，特地邀请了一个叫纪渻子的驯鸡高手，专门来为他训练斗鸡。

The Emperor Xuan of Qi was extremely keen on this game, and in order to win the game, he even specially invited a training master called Ji Shengzi to train the fighting cocks.

齐宣王求胜心切，没过几天，就派人来催问纪渻子："鸡已经训练好了吗？"纪渻子回答说："还没有，这只鸡一见对手就气势汹汹，跃跃欲试，沉不住气。"

Since the Emperor Xuan of Qi was eager to win, he dispatched people to hasten Ji Shengzi only after few days, "Have you trained the fighting cock well?" Ji Shengzi answered, "Not yet, this fighting cock can't retain its composure and itches to fight with overweening arrogance as soon as the opponent appears."

过了几天，齐宣王再次派人询问，纪渻子说："还不行，它一看到其他鸡的身影，马上就紧张起来，说明还有好斗的心理，不够沉稳。"

Several days later, the Emperor Xuan of Qi dispatched people to hasten again, and Ji Shengzi said, "Still not yet, this fighting cock immediately becomes nervous as soon as the opponent appears, this shows that it is still aggressive and not sufficiently calm."

又过了几天，纪渻子终于对齐宣王派来的人说："请你告诉齐王，我把鸡训练好了。它虽然偶尔还会叫几声，但已经有些呆头呆脑，看上去就像木鸡一样，

Another several days later, Ji Shengzi told the person dispatched by the Emperor Xuan of Qi, "Please inform the emperor, the fighting cock is trained well. Although it will occasionally crows, it seems to be jolter-head just like a wooden cock, this

说明它已经进入完美的精神境界了。”

早已等得不耐烦的齐宣王，一听说鸡训好了，就迫不及待地下令召开斗鸡大会。他把纪渻子训练好的鸡放入斗鸡场，无论对手的鸡如何又叫又跳，如何示威，这只鸡都不动声色，没一点反应。结果，别的鸡竟都被它吓跑了。齐宣王于是靠着这只“木鸡”，在斗鸡场上所向披靡，无往不胜。

shows that it has entered a perfect spiritual state.”

The Emperor Xuan of Qi was already impatient and urgently convened cockfighting game upon this news, he put the trained cock into cockfighting ring, and no matter how the opponent cock crowed, jumped or provoked, this fighting cock retained its composure without any reaction. Finally, the other cocks were scared away by it. So from then on, the Emperor Xuan of Qi kept invincible in cockfighting games with this “wooden cock”.

109

呕心沥血

Make painstaking efforts

出自 唐·韩愈《归彭城》诗。

释义 极度劳心苦思。

李贺是唐朝中期的一位著名诗人，他的诗写得非常好，作品风格与李白十

Li He was a famous poet in the middle period of Tang Dynasty, since he wrote very good poems with similar styles as Li

分相像，当时的人都称李白为“仙才”，而把李贺称为“鬼才”。

Bai’s poems, people at that time addressed Li Bai as “fairy talent” and Li He as “wizard talent”.

李贺写诗非常勤奋。十四五岁的时候，他每次外出游玩，总是骑着一头瘦弱的小毛驴，背一个书袋，里面装着纸和笔。每当遇到好的题材，口中吟得佳句，李贺就赶紧记下来放到书袋里。等晚上回到家里，他就迫不及待地从书袋里把诗稿取出来，继续在灯下整理加工，常常一直忙到天明。他的母亲每次看到这种情形，总是心疼地说：“我儿把全部的精力和心血都放在了写诗上，真是要把心呕出来才罢休啊！”

Li He was very industrious in writing poems. At the age of fourteen or fifteen, each time he traveled outside, he always rode on a skinny donkey and carried a book pocket filled with paper and writing brushes. As soon as he came out good subjects and well-turned sentences, Li He hurried to write it down and put it into book pocket. When he came back home at night, he eagerly took them out and continued to reorganize and polish until the next morning. Each time his mother saw he was making such painstaking efforts, she always said lovingly, “My son put all of energy and heart into writing poems, he wouldn’t stop until he throws up his heart!”

李贺到十八岁左右，就已经诗名远播，当时的名人韩愈、皇甫湜等都对他十分器重。不过，由于他把自己的全部心力都倾注在诗歌创作中，加上得不到朝廷的重

At the age of eighteen, Li He’s good reputation on poems had already spread extensively, and he was highly regarded by the celebrities of that time such as Han Yu and Huang-Fu Shi. Nevertheless, due to his wholehearted devotion on poems and ignorance

用，精神抑郁苦闷，严重地损害了健康，二十七岁便离开了人世。

by the imperial court, he suffered from anxiety and depression, which seriously damaged his health, and finally he died at his twenty-seven years old merely.

110

囫囵吞枣

Gulping down a whole date

出自 元·白珽《湛渊静语》。

释义 对事物不加分析思考。

从前有个读书人，看书的时候常常会大声地念出来，可是却从来不动脑筋想一

Once upon a time, there was a scholar, who always read loudly during reading, but he never thought about the essence of the articles,

想文章的道理，还自以为看了很多书，懂得很多道理。

有一天，这个人去参加朋友的聚会，大家边吃边聊，其中有一位客人感慨说：“这世上很少有两全其美的事，就拿吃水果来说，梨对牙齿很好，但是吃多了伤胃；枣能健胃，可惜吃多了会伤牙齿。”大家都觉得很有道理。

那位读书人为了表现自己懂得多，知识渊博，就抢过话头说：“这很简单嘛！吃梨子的时候不要吃进果肉，就不会伤胃；吃枣的时候整个吞下去，就不会伤到牙齿了！”

当时桌子上正好有一盘枣，他刚说完，就拿起一个大枣放在嘴里，整个吞了下去。大家怕他噎到，连忙劝他说：“千万别吞，卡在喉咙里多危险啊！”有个喜欢开玩笑的人说：“你这真是囫囵吞枣呀！”

and he always presumingly thought he had read lots of books and knew lots of knowledge.

One day, this person went to join in his friends' party, all the people were eating and talking happily, one of the guests sighed, "There are seldom things which can satisfy both sides. Let's take eating fruit for example, pears are good for teeth, but will harm stomach if too much; dates are good for stomach, but will harm teeth if too much." All the people thought it make sense.

In order to show off his wide range of knowledge, that scholar eagerly followed up, "It is easy! It will not harm stomach if you don't eat the flesh of pears; it will not harm teeth if you gulp the whole date!"

There was just a plate of dates, so he immediately took a big date into his mouth and gulped down. For worrying that he would be choked, all the people hurried to persuade him "Don't gulp, it will be dangerous if the date choked at your throat!" One person said jokingly, "You are really gulping down the whole date!"

大家听了，都笑得前仰后合。这个读书人自作聪明，如果照他说的方法把枣整个连核吞下去，连消化都困难，又哪里谈得上什么健胃呢?

Then people all laughed into convulsions, this scholar thought him clever, but if gulping down the whole date according to his method, it would be difficult to digest, not to speak of benefiting stomach.

111

围魏救赵

Besiege Wei to rescue Zhao

出自 《史记·孙子吴起列传》。

释义 袭击敌人后方以迫使其放弃进攻。

战国时期，魏惠王派大将庞涓带兵去攻打赵国，团团围住了赵国都城邯郸。赵

In the Warring States Period, the Emperor Hui of Wei dispatched the great general Pang Juan to attack Zhao, and the capital Handan of

国国君派人到齐国去请求援助，齐国立刻任命田忌为大将，孙膑为军师，带兵去救赵国。

Zhao was surrounded tightly. The emperor of Zhao turned to Qi for help, and the emperor of Qi immediately appointed Tian Ji as the great general and Sun Bin as military adviser to lead troops for relieving besiegement.

田忌打仗非常勇敢，但智谋不足，接到命令后，便想立刻赶到邯郸去解围。孙膑劝阻他说："要解开纷乱的丝线，不能强拉硬扯；要给别人劝架，不能直接加入进去厮打。解人之围，要避实就虚，击中要害。现在魏国和赵国打了一年的仗，双方都疲惫不堪。魏国的精兵都集中到了邯郸，国内只剩下老弱病残，兵力空虚。咱们不如直奔魏国都城大梁，占据它的交通要道，袭击它空虚的地方。魏军一定会放弃邯郸，回来援救。我们可以在半道设下伏兵拦截，这样不但解了赵国之围，还可一举打败魏军。"

Tian Ji was very brave in battle, but lacking of resourcefulness, as he received the orders, he immediately intended to relieve besiegement of Handan. But Sun Bin stopped him and said, "To untie messy threads, it's not a good idea to pull hard; to stop people from fighting, it's not a good idea to join in fighting. To relieve besiegement, we should avoid strongholds and strike weak parts, and then hit the vital point. Now Wei and Zhao were in battle for one year, both of them were terribly fatigued. Wei's picked troops centralized in Handan, only elderly and sick troops stayed in Wei. We had better charge into the capital Daliang of Wei, conquer its vital traffic thoroughfares and strike their weakest points, then Wei's troops will certainly give up Handan and go back to rescue. We can arrange troops in ambush at the halfway, in this way, we can relieve besiegement of Zhao and defeat Wei's troops at one stroke."

田忌采纳了孙膑的计划，于是带兵直奔大梁，并且在中途设下埋伏。庞涓得知齐兵要攻打大梁的消息，立刻下令从赵国退兵去援救大梁，半路上受到埋伏的齐军袭击，死伤两万多人，狼狈逃去。这样，齐军既解了赵国之围，又打败魏军，一举两得。

Tian Ji followed Sun Bin's plan and led troops directly to Daliang, and set ambush at halfway. As soon as Pang Juan got the news that Qi's troops planned to attack Daliang, he immediately ordered to withdraw from Zhao to rescue Daliang, and Wei's troops were attacked by Qi's ambush at halfway and fled destructively, with over twenty thousand of soldiers killed and wounded. Thus, Qi relieved besiegement of Zhao and defeated Wei, just like killing two birds with one stone.

112

完璧归赵

Return the jade intact to Zhao

出自 《史记·廉颇蔺相如列传》。

释义 把原物完好地归还本人。

战国时期，赵王得到了一块美玉，名为和氏璧。秦王听说后，想把和氏璧占为

In the Warring States Period, the emperor of Zhao got a fine jade called the jade of He, when the emperor of Qin got the news, he intended

己有，就派人送信给赵王，说秦国愿用十五座城池换取这块宝玉。赵王于是派蔺相如带着和氏璧去出使秦国。

蔺相如来到秦国，拜见秦王，献上和氏璧。秦王满心欢喜，把玉璧传给大臣和妃嫔们观看，却压根儿不提划给赵国十五座城池的事。

蔺相如看秦王没有诚意，便上前说道："这块美玉有点小毛病，让我指给您看。"秦王信以为真，就把玉璧还给蔺相如。蔺相如拿到和氏璧，后退几步，背靠着柱子，说："大王只顾观赏宝玉，根本不提交城的事，所以我将璧收回。大王要是逼迫我，我就撞死在这根柱子上，这块宝玉也一块儿撞碎。"秦王赶紧道歉，并派人拿来地图，把准备给赵国的十五座城池的位置指给蔺相如看，还答应过几

to have it for his own and send letters to the emperor of Zhao that Qin was willing to exchange this jade with fifteen cities. So the emperor of Zhao dispatched Lin Xiangru to Qin with the jade of He.

When Lin Xiangru arrived in Qin, he visited the emperor of Qin and presented the jade of He. The emperor of Qin was very glad and passed it on ministers and concubines for appreciation, without mentionning the fifteen cities for Zhao.

Lin Xiangru perceived the emperor of Qin was not sincere and went up and said, "There is a minor flaw in this jade, let me show you." The emperor of Qin believed and returned the jade to Lin Xiangru, but when Lin Xiangru got the jade, he withdrew for several steps against the pillar and said, "Your Majesty was only apreciating this jade instead of mentioning handing over the fifteen cities, so I have to take it back. If Your Majesty intends to force me, I will strike myself on this pillar to death and also crash this jade." The emperor of Qin hurried to apologize, he dispatched people to bring the map and indicated the locations of the fifteen cities, and also promised that

日举行盛典，正式接见蔺相如。

蔺相如知道秦王言而无信，当天夜里就让手下人偷偷地把和氏璧送回了赵国。

秦王斋戒五天后，在正殿里隆重地接待了蔺相如。蔺相如对秦王说：“我看大王并无诚意，因此早将和氏璧送回赵国了。如果大王先交出十五座城池，赵国一定不敢不把宝玉拱手相送。请您好好考虑一下。”

秦王很生气，但又无可奈何，只得放他回去了。

he would hold ceremony to welcome Lin Xiangru formally.

Lin Xiangru believed the emperor of Qin would eat his words, so he dispatched people to send the jade back to Zhao at the very night.

Five days after fasting, the emperor of Qin formally welcomed Lin Xiangru, but Lin Xiangru said, “I know Your Majesty has no sincerity, so I have already sent the jade back to Zhao. If Your Majesty hand over the fifteen cities first, Zhao will certainly dare not to keep the jade back. Please think it through.”

The emperor of Qin was very angry and had no alternative but to let Lin Xiangru go back.

113

弄巧成拙

To overreach oneself

出自 宋·黄庭坚《拙轩颂》。

释义 本想要弄聪明，结果做了蠢事。

北宋时期有位画家叫孙知微，擅长人物画。一次，他受寺庙委托画一幅《九曜

In the Northern Song Dynasty, there was a painter named Sun Zhiwei who was good at figure painting. Once, he was

星君图》。他已经把图画的线条用笔勾好，只剩下着色最后一道工序。恰好这时有朋友请他去饮酒，他放下笔，把画仔细看了一会儿，觉得还算满意，便对弟子们说："这幅画的线条我已全部画好，只剩下着色，你们小心些，不要着错了颜色。等我回来时，希望你们已经画好了。"

commissioned by a temple to paint *Nine-star God portrait*, he had already drawn its outline, only the last step of coloring left. Coincidentally, one of his friends inviteed him for drinking, he put down the painting brush and looked over the painting carefully, he felt fairly satisfied and said to his disciples, "I've already finished the outline, you should be careful enough not to mistake coloring, and I wish it would be completed when I come back."

孙知微走后，弟子们都过来围着画，七嘴八舌，纷纷议论哪些地方应该用什么颜色。其中有个叫童仁益的弟子，平时喜欢卖弄小聪明，哗众取宠，这会儿却装模作样地一言不发。

After Sun Zhiwei left, the disciples came around the picture and lively discussed which colors should be used in different places. There was a disciple named Tong Renyi, who ordinarily liked to show off smart and act ostentatiously to impress others, but at this moment he kept silence in a pompous manner.

有人问他："你怎么不说话了，莫非这幅画有什么欠缺？"童仁益故作高深地说："水曜星君身边的童子神态传神，只是他手中的水晶瓶好像少了点东西。"众弟子说："没发现少什么

Someone asked him, "Why you keep silence this time? Could it be something defective?" Tong Renyi pretended to be profound and said, " Look at the boy besides the Water-star God, his expression is vivid, but it seems something missing in his hand-held crystal bottle." The other disciples said,

啊。”童仁益说：“老师每次画瓶子，总要在瓶中画一枝鲜花，可这次却没有。也许是急于出门来不及画，我们还是画好了再着色吧。”他一边说着，一边在瓶口处画上了一枝莲花。

“We don’t see anything missing.” Tong Renyi said, “Our master always drew a flower in the bottle, but this time he didn’t. Maybe our master was too hurry to forget, let’s finish drawing a flower and then coloring.” As he said, he finished drawing a lotus flower at the bottle neck.

孙知微回来后，发现童子手中的瓶子生出一朵莲花，生气地说：“这是谁干的蠢事，简直是弄巧成拙！童子手中的瓶子，是水曜星君用来降服水怪的镇妖瓶，你们给添上莲花，把宝瓶变成了普通的花瓶，岂不成了天大的笑话。”说着，把画撕了个粉碎。

When Sun Zhiwei came back and saw the lotus flower at the bottleneck in the boy’s hand, he angrily said, “Who is so stupid and overreach himself? The bottle in the boy’s hand is used to surrender the sea monster, but now it turned to be a plain vase by adding a lotus flower. It is really a big joke!” Then he tore up the picture.

众弟子看着童仁益，都不知道该说什么是好。

The other disciples stared at Tong Renyi and felt nothing to say.

114

投笔从戎

To renounce the pen for the sword

出自 《后汉书·班超传》。

释义 指文人从军。

班超是东汉时期著名的军事家和外交家，他的父亲班彪、哥哥班固都是非常有

Ban Chao was a famous militarist and diplomatist in the Eastern Han Dynasty, whose father Ban Biao and brother Ban Gu were all

名的历史学家，《汉书》这部巨著就是班固所编撰的。

very famous historians, and *the History of Han Dynasty* was written by Ban Gu.

班超年轻的时候就很有抱负，肯动脑筋，能言善辩，读了不少书。公元62年，班固被汉明帝召到洛阳，做了一名校书郎，班超和他的母亲也跟着到了京城。当时，他们的家境并不富裕，班超便找了个替官府抄书的差事挣钱养家。

When Ban Chao was young, he was very ambitious, intelligent, eloquent and well-read. In AD 62, Ban Gu was commissioned to be the Official Collator in Luoyang by the Ming Emperor of Han Dynasty, with his mother accompanied to the capital. As they were not rich, so Ban Chao choose to copy books for local government for make a living.

班超一直怀有远大志向，日子久了，他就不太甘心做这种乏味的抄写工作了。一天，他正在抄书，突然感到一阵莫名的厌烦，于是停下来，把笔扔在地上，感叹说："身为男子汉大丈夫，应当学学当年的傅介子和张骞，在外建立功勋，获得封侯，怎么能够把时间都花在替人抄书上面呢！"

Because Ban Chao always had great ambitions, so he felt reluctant to do the boring job. One day, when he was copying books, he suddenly felt inexplicable boredom and threw down the writing brush, he sighed, "As a man, I should take Fu Jiezi and Zhang Qian of the year as examples to perform exploits and be ennobled, how can I waste time on copying books?"

公元73年，班超随军出击匈奴，立下战功，被派去出使西域。他凭借着自

In AD 73, Ban Chao joined in army to attack Xiongnu and established feats, and he was sent on a diplomatic mission to the western

己的机智和勇敢，克服重重困难，经过数年，使西域的五十多个国家归附汉朝。班超也因此被封为定远侯。他一直在西域待了三十一年，为保护边境安全，促进人民的友好往来作出了卓越的贡献。

territories. With his witness and braveness, he overcame many difficulties and made over fifty countries submit to Han Dynasty after years, thus he was ennobled as Ding Yuan vassal. He had been staying in the western territories for thirty-one years, and made great contributions for border security and friendly exchanges of peoples.

115

投鞭断流

Throw whips into the stream to stop its flowing

出自 《晋书·苻坚载记》。

释义 比喻人马众多，兵力强大。

东晋时期，前秦王苻坚统一北方后，决心率领百万大军，乘势一举消灭东晋，

In the Eastern Jin Period, when the former Qin emperor Fu Jian unified the North, he decided to lead millions of armies to wipe out the Eastern

统一中国。为此，他召集群臣商议，说：“自我称王二十多年来，国富民安，可是只有南方的东晋还没有被征服，每每想到这件事，我连饭都吃不下。我打算亲自率军去攻打晋国，大家意见如何？”

Jin at one stroke for the final unification of Central Plains. Therefore, he called up ministers and said, “Since I have been the emperor for over twenty years, the country flourishes and people live a peaceful life, but only the Eastern Jin of the South is not surrendered, which makes me feel the food tasteless.So I decide to lead the army to attack Jin, what’s your opinions?”

话音刚落，一位谋士站起来说：“陛下英明，以我们九十多万的人马，东晋怎能抵挡得了呢？”苻坚听了很高兴。

Hardly had his voice faded away, an adviser stood up and said, “Your Wise Majesty, how can the Eastern Jin withstand our over nine hundred thousand solders?” Fu Jian was very glad to hear that.

这时，有一位名叫石越的下属劝阻说：“从星象来看，今年不适合南进。何况东晋占有长江天险，君臣和睦，上下一心，眼下要灭晋是很困难的。我们不如暂时巩固国力，训练军队，等晋朝内部松动，再找机会攻伐。”

At this time, a subject named Shi Yue persuaded, “From the point of aspect astrology, it’s unfavorable to attack the South this year. Moreover, the Eastern Jin took up the natural barrier of the Changjiang River, its emperor and subjects are united and harmonious, it seems very difficult to wipe out the Jin. We’d better consolidate national strength and train the soldiers, and wait for the chance until some internal fluctuation happens in Jin.”

苻坚不以为然地说：“过去周武王伐纣之前，占卜不吉利，但还是取得

But Fu Jian disapprovingly said, “In the past, when the King Wu of Zhou attacked the Emperor Zhou of Shang, although the divination

了胜利；春秋时的吴王夫差和三国时的吴主孙皓，他们都有长江天险，最后仍不免灭亡。现在凭我这百万大军，只要把每个士兵的马鞭扔到江中，就可以截断长江的流水，还怕什么天险！”

was unlucky, they finally triumphed; the King Fu Chai of Wu in the Spring and Autumn periods and the king Sun Hao of Wu in the Three Kingdom period, although they all took up the natural barrier of the Changjiang River, they were finally wiped out. Now we have millions of soldiers, as long as we threw each one's horsewhips into the Changjiang River, its current would be stemmed, so we don't have to be afraid of the natural barrier!"

苻坚一意孤行，亲自率领八十万大军，前去攻打东晋。东晋派大将谢玄、谢石带领八万精兵抗敌。苻坚由于轻敌，被晋军在淝水一役中大败，他自己也差点做了俘虏。

So Fu Jian persisted in his own course arbitrarily and personally led eight nundred thousand of soldiers to attack the Eastern Jin. The Eastern Jin appointed senior generals Xie Xuan and Xie Shi with eighty thousand of picked troops to completely defeated Fu Jian in the battle of Fei Shui. And Fujian, nearly became a captive due to his underestimation of the enemy.

116

抛砖引玉

To throw out a minnow to catch a whale

出自 宋·释道原《景德传灯录》。

释义 比喻以较差的作品或是较粗浅的意见引出别人的佳作或高见。

唐朝时，有一个叫赵嘏的人，诗写得很好，他曾经写过一句："长笛一声人倚

In the Tang Dynasty, a person named Zhao Gu, who was good at writing poems, as he once written a sentence as "a person

楼”，从而得到了一个“赵倚楼”的称号。当时还有一个叫常建的人，诗写得也不错，但是他总认为自己没有赵嘏写得好。

leaning upon a balustrade in a sound of flute", he was nicknamed as "Mr Zhao leaning upon a balustrade". There was another person named Chang Jian, who was also good at writing poems, but he always thought that Zhao Gu was superior to him in poem writing.

有一次，常建听说赵嘏要到苏州游玩，他十分高兴，心想这是一个向赵嘏学习的好机会，千万不能错过，可用什么办法才能让他留下诗句呢？他想了又想，终于有了一个主意：赵嘏既然到苏州，肯定会去灵岩寺，如果自己先在寺庙里留下半首诗，他看到后肯定会补全的。于是他就提前跑到寺里，在墙上题下了半首诗。

On one occasion, Chang Jian was happy to hear that Zhao Gu planned to travel to Suzhou, so he took it as a good chance to learn from Zhao Gu. But he was wondered how to make Chang Jian write poems. He thought it over and over and came out an idea, as Lingyan Temple was a must scenic spot in Suzhou, if he written an unfinished poem on the wall of Lingyan Temple, Zhao Gu would positively complemented. Thus Chang Jian went to the temple and left an unfinished poem on the wall.

不久，赵嘏果然来到灵岩寺，当他走到一座墙壁时，发现上面题着两句诗，端详片刻，心想，诗写得不错，不过为什么只写了两句呢？于是他提起笔来，在常建的诗后又补了两句，成为

As expected, Zhao Gu travled to Lingyan Temple. When he saw the unfinished poem on a wall, he thought it over for a moment and added two sentences to the poem as a complete seven-character quatrain.

一首完整的七言绝句。

赵嘏走后，常建赶过来观看，觉得补写的这两句确实比自己高明，便抄写了下来。后来人们说，常建的这个办法，真可谓是“抛砖引玉”了。

When Zhao Gu left, Chang Jian hurried to have a look, and he thought the two sentences which Zhao Gu complemented were indeed better than his poem, so he copied them down. Therefore, people always said the method of Chang Jian was really “ throw out a minnow to catch a whale”.

117

杞人忧天

Fear is often greater than the danger

出自 《列子·天瑞》。

释义 比喻不必要的忧虑和担心。

在古时候的杞国，有一个胆子很小的人，他经常会想到一些奇怪的问题，让人

In the Qi State during the ancient periods, there was a very coward person who always thought about weird and inexplicable

觉得莫名其妙。

problems.

一天，他吃过晚饭后，坐在门前乘凉，突然自言自语道：“假如有一天天塌下来，那该怎么办呢，我们岂不是要被活活地压死？”

One day after dinner, he relaxed in a cool place in front of the gate and suddenly said to himself, “If one day the sky falls, all of us would be crushed to death, what should we do?”

从此以后，他整天担心天会塌下来，自己没有地方安身，他越想越觉得可怕，为此愁得睡不着觉，吃不下饭。

From then on, he always worried that the sky would fall and he felt more and more scared, so that he couldn’t sleep and eat.

朋友们看他整日精神不振，很为他担心，就去开导他说：“天不会那么容易塌下来的，即使天真的塌下来了，也不是你一个人担心就能解决的。何况天是由很厚的气体聚积而成的，放心，它不会塌下来的。”

Since he was depressed everyday, his friends began to worry about him and persuaded him, “It is impossible for the sky to fall, even if it really happens, it will not be solved by yourself only. Moreover, the sky is actually accumulated by thick air and will not fall at all.”

杞人听了朋友的话，又担心道：“如果天是由气体组成的，那么太阳、月亮和星星不就掉下来了吗？”

But he was still worried and asked, “If the sky is accumulated by air, wouldn’t the sun, moon and stars fall down?”

朋友说：“太阳、月亮和星星也都是由会发光的气体积聚而成的，即使掉下

His friend said ,“The sun, moon and stars are also accumulated by air, even if they fall, people will not be hurt.”

来，也不可能把人砸伤。”

可是，无论朋友怎么说，杞人就是不相信。一年又一年过去了，天没有塌下来，日月星辰也好好地挂在天上，但他仍然在为此担忧。后来人们就根据上面这个故事，引申出了“杞人忧天”这一成语。

Nevertheless, no matter what his friends said, he just didn’t believe. Year after year, the sky didn’t fall, and the sun, moon and stars hung up well in the sky, but he had still been worried. Afterwords, an idiom was extended from his story.

118

束之高阁

Put on the shelf

出自 《晋书·庾翼传》。

释义 扔在一边，不去用它。

庾翼是东晋时期的人，从小就才智过人，怀有远大的志向。他从二十三岁便跟

In the Eastern Jin Period, a person named Yu Yi was excellent and ambitious. For fifteen years in Liangzi Lake, he lived and studied

着兄长庾亮一起居住读书，在梁子湖度过十五年，完成了学业的积累，一举成名。当时，他的书法甚至与“书圣”王羲之齐名。后来，庾翼因为在作战中多次立功，被封为都亭侯，官至征西将军。

with his elder brother Yu Liang since he was 23 years old, and he completed his study and bound to fame. At that time, his calligraphy even enjoyed equal popularity with Wang Xizhi as “the saint of calligraphy”. Afterwards, he made many contributions in battles and was ennobled as Duting Vassal and appointed as the Big General Conquering the West.

与庾翼同时代的殷浩，也很有才能，而且很擅长于高谈阔论，二十岁的时候就出了名。镇西将军谢尚年轻的时候，听说殷浩擅长清谈，特意去拜访他。殷浩并没有发表太多的长篇大论，只是给谢尚提示了一些道理，不但谈吐举止有风度，而且所用的辞藻丰富多彩，动人心弦。谢尚全神贯注地听着，不知不觉间汗流满面。

During the same period, a person named Yin Hao was also very talented and eloquent, and became famous at his twenties. Xie Shang, a young General Conquering the West, heard of Yin Hao and paid a special visit to him. Yin Hao didn’t harangue and only showed him some viewpoints in a refined style of conversation and action, with colorful and touching rhetoric. Xie Shang listened with full concentration and turned to be sweated on his face unconsciously.

殷浩后来做了扬州刺史，不久又调任建武将军，但是在讨伐敌人的战役中却多次失败，被革了职。后来

Afterwards, Yin Hao was appointed as the prefectural governor and soon transferred to be General Jian Wu, but he was finally dismissed due to several failures in battles against

有人向庾翼建议，让殷浩重新出来做官。庾翼一向认为殷浩是一个徒有虚名的清谈家，只会高谈阔论，而没有真才实干，于是带着鄙夷的口吻说："像殷浩这类人，只好把他捆绑起来放到高楼上去，等到天下太平后，再来考虑任用他。"

"束之高阁"这个成语便由此而来。

enemies. Someone suggested Yu Yi to reappoint Yin Hao, but Yu Yi always considered Yin Hao as a nominal talker without any true ability, so he said in a contemptuous tone, "People of the kind like Yin Hao should be tied and trapped on the high shelf until the time of peace."

Thus the idiom of "put on the shelf" was extended from this story.

119

沉鱼落雁

Make the fish sink and wild geese fall

出自 《庄子·齐物论》。

释义 形容女子容貌美丽。

在庄子的《齐物论》里有这么一句话："毛嫱丽姬，人之所美也，鱼见之深

In *On the Equality of Things* by Zhuang Zi, there is a saying " The beautiful appearances of Mao Qiang and Li Ji are popularly appreciated

入，鸟见之高飞，麋鹿见之决骤。”意思是说，毛嫱和丽姬是人人都喜欢的美女，连鱼儿见了她们都深深地潜入水底，鸟儿见了她们都高高地飞向天空，麋鹿见了她们，都撒开四蹄飞快地逃离了。

by people, as long as they appear, the fish sink down, the birds fly away and the elks run away".

这是有关“沉鱼落雁”一词最早的记载，后来的人们慢慢地将它与中国古代的两大美女联系了起来。

This is the earliest record of the idiom "make the fish sink and wild geese fall", and afterwards people gradually made a connection between it and the two famous beauties.

第一个是春秋战国时期的西施。西施是越国人，长得粉面桃花，美丽动人。据说她在河边浣纱时，清澈的河水映照着她俊俏的身影，使她显得更加美丽，这时，鱼儿看见她的倒影，竟然忘记了游水，渐渐地沉到河底。从此，西施这个“沉鱼”的代称，在附近流传开来。

One is the famous beauty Xi Shi in the Warring States Period, who was of Yue State, with a charming appearance. It is said that when she was washing gauze besides the river, the river reflected her pretty figure, which made her more beautiful. When the fish saw her charming reflection, they even forgot to swim and slowly sank down the river. From then on, the nickname of "make the fish sink" became popular.

另一个是汉代的王昭君，同样是个才貌双全的

The other one is Wang Zhaojun in the Han Dynasty, who was also endowed with both

美人。汉元帝为了安抚北匈奴，就选她与单于结为姻缘。在离家的途中，她看到远飞的大雁，不由得触景生情，便弹起了琴，以寄托她那无尽的乡思。一群南飞的大雁听到她悦耳的琴声，凝望着她美丽的容颜，竟忘记了抖动翅膀而跌落在地上。王昭君由此便得了个“落雁”的美称。

beauty and talent. For the purpose of pacifying the North Xiongnu, the Yuan Emperor of Han Dynasty married her to the Chief of Xiongnu. When she saw wild geese flying over on her way to north, she began to play the musical instrument for comforting her endless homesickness. When those wild geese flying southward heard the melodious sound, they even forgot to flap their wings and thus fell down the ground. Therefore, Wang Zhaojun was reputed a nickname as “make wild geese fall”.

120

沧海桑田

Sea change into mulberry fields and mulberry fields into seas

出自 晋·葛洪《神仙传·王远》。

释义 比喻世界上的事物变化极大。

汉朝时期，苏州有一个叫蔡经的平民，被仙人王远点化成仙。十年后蔡经回

In the Han Dynasty, there was a civilian named Cai Jing in Suzhou, who was enlightened and turned to be an immortal by the immortal

家，告诉家人说，七月七日仙人王远和麻姑来家作客，到时候要准备如何如何接待，说完就走了。

Wang Yuan. Ten years later, he came back home and told his family that two immortals Wang Yuan and Ma Gu would pay a visit on July, 7th, and he asked his family to make good reception, then he left again.

到了约定的那天，果然王远在一批侍从的簇拥下，坐在五条龙拉的车上，来到蔡经家门前。车子一降落，簇拥着王远的那些人就全部隐没了。接着，王远和蔡家人打过招呼，就独自坐在那里等候麻姑的到来。

On that appointed day, the immortal Wang Yuan came to visit Cai Jing's family, on a cart pulled by five flying dragons with a cluster of his attendants. When the cart landed up, the cluster of attendants disappeared, Wang Yuan greeted Cai Jing's family and then sit there himself for waiting for Ma Gu.

没过多久，麻姑从空中降落了下来，她的随从人员只有王远的一半。麻姑看上去好像只有十八九岁，一头秀发长及腰间，衣服上面绣着美丽的花纹，光彩耀目。

After a while, Ma Gu landed up from the sky, with only half of the attendants compared with Wang Yuan. Ma Gu looked like eighteen or nineteen years old, with beautiful long hair reaching to her waist and the beautiful embroidered patterns in a dazzling brilliance.

麻姑和王远互相行过礼后，王远就吩咐开宴。宴席上的用具全都是用金和玉制成的，制作精巧；餐皿里面盛放的大多是奇花异果，香气扑鼻。所有这些，都是蔡

After Wang Yuan and Ma Gu greeted each other, Wang Yuan commanded the feast. For the first time in the life of Cai Jing's family, they saw that the tableware were all made of gold and jade exquisitely, with a sharp aroma of rare flowers and

经的家人从来没有见过的。

席间，麻姑对王远说："自从得道接受天命以来，我已经亲眼见到东海三次变成桑田。刚才去到蓬莱岛，又看到东海的海水比前一时期浅了一半，难道它又要变成陆地了吗？"

王远叹息道："是啊，圣人们都说，东海的水在下降，那里不久又将扬起尘土了。"

宴饮完毕，王远和麻姑各自召来车驾，告别蔡家人，升天而去。

上面的故事记载在晋朝人葛洪撰写的《神仙传·王远》里，后人就是据此引申出了"沧海桑田"这一成语。

fruits.

During the feast, Ma Gu said to Wang Yuan, "Since I accepted the heavenly destiny, it is the third time for me to see the East Sea turned to be mulberry fields. Just now when I passed by Penglai island, I saw the sea water of the East Sea is half less than the former period, wouldn't it turned to be land again?"

Wang Yuan sighed, "Probably! Many immortals say the sea water of the East Sea begins to fall, it wouldn't be long for dust raising."

As the feast finished, Wang Yuan and Ma Gu individually called in their carts, and they bid farewell to Cai Jing's family and flew up to the heaven.

The above story is recorded in *the Legend of Immortals on Wang Yuan*, by Ge Hong in the Jin Dynasty, from which extended the idiom "Sea change into mulberry fields and mulberry fields into seas".

121

纵虎归山

Let the tiger return to the mountain

出自 《三国演义》。

释义 把老虎放回山去。

三国时期，曹操亲自率领大军战胜吕布后，刘备跟着曹操到了都城许昌。当

In the period of the Three Kingdoms, after Cao Cao personally led the great army to defeat Lu Bu, Liu Bei followed Cao Cao to the

时，被曹操挟持到许昌的汉献帝，暗地里组织一些汉朝旧臣，准备诛杀曹操。刘备也参与了这一秘密活动。为了避免引起怀疑，他常常关着大门，躲在院子里种菜，装出一副胸无大志的样子。

capital Xu Chang. Since the Emperor Xian of Han was captured to Xu Chang by Cao Cao, he organized some former ministers of Han and prepared to kill Cao Cao. Because Liu Bei was also involved, so he closed his door and cultivated vegetables everyday, and pretended to be a mediocre person without any ambition.

谋士程昱对曹操说："我看刘备志向不小，如果现在不杀他，将来一定会成为祸患。"曹操拿不定主意，征求另一位谋士郭嘉的意见。郭嘉认为现在正是用人之时，刘备是因为失败了才投奔曹操，如果杀了他，会落得个杀害人才的坏名声。曹操认为他说得对。

An adviser named Cheng Yu said to Cao Cao, "I think Liu Bei was an ambitious person, he would probably become a big calamity if you don't kill him now." Cao Cao was indecisive and asked another adviser Guo Jia, Guo Jia said, "Now it is a crucial moment in need of many talents, since Liu Bei failed and submitted to you, if you kill him, you will gain a bad reputation of killing talents", and Cao Cao agreed.

不久，曹操打败袁术，担心他去投奔袁绍，便准备派人去拦截袁术。刘备趁机向曹操请求率兵前往。曹操同意了，让刘备带着五万兵马出发。郭嘉和程昱听说曹操放走了刘备，急忙去见曹操，说："即使丞相不

Before Long, after Cao Cao defeated Yuan Shu, he was worried that Yuan Shu would submit to Yuan Shao, so he prepared to seize Yuan Shu, Liu Bei took the chance to lead the army. Cao Cao agreed and permitted Liu Bei for fifteen thousand solders. When Guo Jia and Cheng Yu heard this news, they hurried to meet Cao Cao and said, "Even your Prime Minister

把他杀掉，也不该轻易放他离去，而且又给了他许多兵马，这等于把蛟龙放回大海，把猛虎放归深山啊。以后再想制服他，能够办得到吗？” 曹操这时也感到非常后悔，可是已经晚了。

don’t kill Liu Bei, you should not let him go with such a big quantity of soldiers, which equally letting dragon back to the sea and the fierce tiger back to the forest. How could you subdue him in the future?” Cao Cao felt regretful, but it was too late.

122

纸上谈兵

Talk about stratagems on paper

出自 《史记·廉颇蔺相如列传》。

释义 比喻不切实际的空谈。

公元前264年，秦国攻打赵国，赵国将领廉颇退到长平关，构筑营垒，坚守不

In BC 264, after Zhao state was defeated by Qin state, Zhao's General Lian Po withdrew to the Chang Ping pass, he built and stick to

出。秦国于是派人在赵国首都邯郸散布流言说：“廉颇太老了，已经丧失了锐气，因此不敢出战。秦国最害怕的是赵括，只要赵括不出来当统帅，秦国一定会赢。”赵王听信流言，把廉颇免职，任命赵括接替。

the barracks without any attack. Thus Qin state sent people to the Zhao’s capital Han Dan for spreading rumors, “Lian Po is an old man without any invincible spirit, so he dares not to attack. Qin state is actually afraid of Zhao Kuo, if Zhao Kuo is appointed as the General, Qin will certainly win the battle.” The king of Zhao listened to the gossip and ordered Zhao Kuo to replace Lian Po.

赵括是赵国名将赵奢的儿子，从小钻研兵法，口才一流，自认为他的军事才能天下无双。赵奢在世的时候，父子谈论起用兵之道，赵奢往往被儿子驳得哑口无言。有人称赞说：“真是将门出虎子啊。”但赵奢却不以为意地说：“战争是关系到生死的大事，他说起来如此轻松，一旦担任大将，必定失败。”

Zhao Kuo was the son of the famous general Zhao She, who was eloquent and kept delving into military strategy since young, and he imposed himself as unparalleled in military talents. When Zhao She was alive, every time he discussed military strategy with his son, he was always retorted and rendered speechless. Someone praised, “Zhao Kuo is really a capable young man from an distinguished family!” But Zhao She disagreed, “Battle is a matter of life and death, how could he think it so simple? He will probably fail if he is appointed as the General.”

赵括就任之后，立刻下令撤除防御工事，亲自率领精锐士兵向秦军营垒发起进攻。秦国将领白起下令后退。赵括一心扩大战果，

As Zhao Kuo assume the General, he immediately ordered to remove the fortifications, and he personally led picked soldiers to attack Qin’s army base. But Bai Qi, the General of Qin, ordered to withdraw. Zhao Kuo blindly

继续进攻秦军。白起一边下令撤退，一边暗中派出部队切断赵括的退路，赵国大军被一分为二。赵括多次发动攻击，想冲出包围圈，但全部失败。赵军勉强支持了四十六天，最终失败，赵括死在乱箭之下，剩下的四十万士兵被迫投降，被秦军全部活埋。

concentrated on expanding his achievements by continuing his attack. Meanwhile, Bai Qi ordered to withdraw on one hand and secretively sent troops to cut off Zhao's route of retreat on the other hand, which split Zhao's troops into two parts. Zhao kuo pursued attacks many times to break out of the enclosure, but all failed. Zhao's army managed to maintain for forty-six days and was finally utterly defeated. Zhao Kuo was shot to death by thousands of arrows, and the remaining four hundred thousand of soldiers were all forced to surrender and buried alive by Qin's army.

123

言过其实

Paint the devil blacker than he is

出自 《三国志·蜀书·马良传》。

释义 言语浮夸，超过实际才能。

马谡是三国时的蜀国将领，他和哥哥马良都在刘备手下做官。马谡喜欢

Ma Su was the General of Shu Kingdom in the period of Three Kingdoms, whose elder brother Ma Liang also served as an official for

谈论军事，丞相诸葛亮很看重他。但是刘备总觉得马谡这人不踏实，在他临死前曾经对诸葛亮说："马谡言语浮夸，超过他的实际能力，不可重用，丞相要多加留意。"

Liu Bei. Ma Su was good at talking about military strategy, which made the Prime Minister Zhu-ge Liang think highly of him. But Liu Bei didn't consider Ma Su as a down-to-earth person and exhorted Zhu-ge Liang before he died, "Ma Su's exaggerated words are far exceed his actual ability, I suggest you to pay more attention not to entrust him with important tasks."

后来，诸葛亮北伐曹魏，任命马谡为前锋，镇守战略要地街亭。临行前，诸葛亮再三嘱咐马谡："街亭虽小，却关系重大。它是通往汉中的咽喉。如果失掉街亭，我军必败。"并让他靠山近水安营扎寨，小心谨慎，不得有误。

Afterwards, when Zhu-ge Liang attacked the Wei State northward, he appointed Ma Su as the vanguard to defend the strategic rear Jieting. Before departure, Zhu-ge Liang repeatedly emphasized to Ma Su, "Although Jieting is a small rear, it matters most! It is the pass to central plain. If we lose Jieting, we will probably fail." Zhu-ge Liang also instructed Ma Su to pitch the camp near the mountain and river, and asked Ma Su to follow his order strictly.

马谡到达街亭后，自作主张，想把大军部署在远离水源的街亭山上。副将王平提出反对意见，认为街亭一无水源，二无粮道，如果魏军围困街亭，切断水源，断绝粮道，蜀军就会不战自

When Ma Su arrived at Jieting., he made his own decision to pitch the camp on the mountain far away from river, but the deputy General Wang Ping raised objections because Jieting. was not connected to any pass of supporting water and foodstuff, if Wei troops besieged Jieting and cut off the water and

溃。马谡坚持己见，将大军布置在山上。

foodstuff pass, the Shu troops would collapse without a battle. However, Ma Su stubbornly adhered to his own ideas and located the troops on the mountain.

魏国将领张郃侦察到这一情况，心中大喜，立即带兵切断水源和粮道，把马谡的军队围困在山上，然后放火烧山。蜀军军心涣散。张郃乘势进攻，大败蜀军。诸葛亮率领的大军也被迫退回汉中。

The layout of Shu troops were reconnoitered by Zhang He, the General of Wei, who was overjoyed and immediately led soldiers to cut off the pass of water and foodstuff, then he besieged Shu troops and set fire on the mountains. When the morale of Shu troops was undermined, Zhang He took the chance to attack and completely defeated Shu troops. Finally, the troops led by Zhu-ge Liang was also compelled to withdraw to central plain.

事后，诸葛亮想起刘备临终时的嘱咐，后悔自己没有听从，结果铸成大错，于是向后主刘禅上表，要求免去自己的丞相职务，降级三等，以处罚自己用人不当，造成败绩的重大过失。

Afterwards, Zhu-ge Liang remembered the warnings of Liu Bei before his death, he was greatly regretted for not to follow Liu Bei's warnings and made a grave mistake. Therefore, Zhu-ge Liang petitioned to Liu Shan for removing himself of the Prime Minister and demote to the third class, for the penalty of appointing the wrong person to fail the battle.

124

走马观花

Give a hurry and cursory glance

出自 唐·孟郊《登科后》诗。

释义 对事物没有深入细致地观察，粗略而过。

孟郊是唐代著名的诗人，他年轻时经常在河南嵩山一带闲游隐居。后来回到

Meng Jiao was a famous poet in the Tang Dynasty, who lived in seclusion around Mount Song in Henan. When he came back to his

家乡湖州，仍然过着清贫的生活，不愿意出去做官。其间写了大量的诗歌作品，并曾参加当时诗僧皎然在湖州组织的诗会。孟郊写的诗中，最为后人所熟知的应该就是《游子吟》，写尽了人世间的母子之爱。

hometown Huzhou, he still lived a poor life and unwillingly assumed any office. During his lifetime in his hometown, he produced lots of poems and once joined in the poem gathering organized by the monk poet Jiao Ran in Huzhou. The most popular poem by Meng Jiao should be *The Song of the Roamer*, which deeply described the great mother love.

到四十一岁那年，孟郊听从母亲的劝说，到京城长安去应考进士，可是两次都没被录取，受尽了冷落和讥讽。后来在他四十六岁的时候，第三次上京应考，才考上了进士。他当即写了一首诗，题为《登科后》。诗里说道：

At his forty years' old, Meng Jiao was persuaded by his mother to join the imperial exam in the capital Chang'an, but he failed twice and suffered great snub and ridicule. Until the third time of exam at his forty-six, he finally succeeded in Jinshi exam as the third degree scholar. He wrote a poem at once with the title as *Succeeded in Imperial Exam*, which says as the following.

昔日龌龊不足夸，今朝放荡思无涯。

春风得意马蹄疾，一日看尽长安花。

The old shabby and awkward life isn't worth mentioning, and I feel extremely happy today without the depression. In the spring wind the proud horse runs rapidly, and I view the beautiful scenery of Chang'an in a day.

这首诗的后两句，把自己得中进士以后，骑着快马，春风得意地来往京城各

The last two sentences vividly describe Meng Jiao happily rode a horse running rapidly around Chang'an, and afterwards two idioms

处、尽情游览的那种兴奋之情，生动地描绘了出来。后来，人们从这两句诗中总结出了两个成语，一个是“春风得意”，另一个就是“走马观花”。

are extended from these two sentences, one is “in one’s palmy days”, and the other is “give a hurry and cursory glance”.

125

运斤成风

Whirl the hatchet with a noise like the wind

出自 《庄子·徐无鬼》。

释义 比喻手法熟练，技艺高超。

惠子是战国时期宋国人，他是庄子的好友，也是哲学上的对手，两个人经常

In Song state during the Warring States Period, there was a person named Hui Zi, who was both the good friend and the philosophical

为了各自的观点相互争论。惠子死后，庄子去送葬，想到自己从此没有可以推心置腹谈论的对象了，十分感慨，于是对他的门徒讲了如下的故事。

在楚国的郢都有一个人，胆量过人，他的朋友石是个技艺高明的匠人。有一次，他俩联手为人们表演了这样一套绝活：郢人在鼻尖涂上像苍蝇翅膀一样薄的白粉，然后让匠人用斧子把这层白粉削去。只见匠人石不慌不忙地挥动斧头，呼的一声，白粉被全部削掉，而郢人的鼻尖却丝毫没有受到损伤。郢人也依旧面不改色，若无其事地站在那里。

这件事传到了国君那里，他非常佩服匠人石的绝技和郢人的胆量，很想亲眼看一看这个表演，于是就恭恭敬敬地把匠人石请来，让他再表演一次。石说：“我

opponent of Zhuang Zi, and they always argued for their own opinions. Afterwards, Hui Zi died, Zhuang Zi went to his funeral, and when he realized there would be no one to talk heart to heart in the future, he felt emotional and told a story to his disciples as the following.

In the capital Ying of Chu state, there was a courageous person, whose friend was a skillful craftsman named Shi. One day, they joined together and demonstrated a unique skill for the audience. The person of Ying coated on his tip of nose some white powder in a layer as thin as the fly wings, and he asked the craftsman to scrape away with his hatchet. The craftsman Shi steadily wielded his hatchet and scraped away the white power in a whoosh, and the nose tip of his friend remained intact. The person of Ying stood there calmly as if nothing happened.

As this story spread to the emperor, who greatly admired the unique skills of the craftsman Shi and the courage of the person of Ying. Since he strongly wished to see their show with his own eyes, he respectfully invited the craftsman Shi to show again. But Shi said,

的好友已经去世，我失去了唯一的搭档，再也没办法表演了。”

“My good friend died, and I lose the only partner, so the unique skill can not be showed again.”

后来，人们根据上面的故事，引申出了“运斤成风”这一成语，其中的“斤”，在古代即指斧头。

Afterwards, an idiom “whirl the hatchet with a noise like the wind” was extended from the above story, therein, the word “Jin” means hatchet in the ancient times.

126

近水楼台

Waterwide pavilions

出自 宋·俞文豹《清夜录》。

释义 处于能够优先得到便利的某种地位。

范仲淹是北宋时期著名的政治家和文学家。他小的时候，家里非常贫穷，但

Fan Zhongyan was a famous politician and litterateur in the Northern Song Dynasty. Although he lived a poor life as a child, he

他学习刻苦，读了很多书。范仲淹后来一直做到参知政事这样的高官，身为朝廷重臣，他的为人极为正直，尤其善于选拔人才。

studied very hard and read lots of books. As he became government official, he was even promoted to the deputy Prime Minister, because he was very upright and good at selecting talents.

范仲淹在杭州做知府的时候，对属下的官员知人善任，使他们能够充分发挥自己的才干，因此这些官员都很感激范仲淹。有一个叫苏麟的人，由于在外县工作，所以未能得到范仲淹的提拔。一次，苏麟因公事见到范仲淹，乘机给范仲淹写了一首诗。诗中有这样两句："近水楼台先得月，向阳花木易逢春。"意思是说，靠近水边的楼台可以最先得到月光，朝着阳光的花草树木容易成长而开花。

When Fan Zhongyan was the prefecture governor in Hangzhou, he knew his subordinates well and assigned them properly, which made them give full play to their talents, thus those officials were all very grateful. A person named Su Lin worked in another county and was never promoted by Fan Zhongyan. Once he met Fan Zhongyan for business reasons, he took the chance to write a poem to Fan Zhongyan, therein two sentences were "those on the waterside pavilions are the first to see the rising moon, and the flowers and trees in the sunlight are easy to spring".

苏麟借用这首诗，巧妙地指出接近范仲淹的人都得到了好处，自己却始终未见提携。范仲淹读后，心领神会，于是，便按照苏麟的意

Su Lin used this poem to subtly pointed out that people around Fan Zhongyan enjoyed the priority, but he was never promoted. Fan Zhongyan understood at once and later arranged a suitable position for him.

愿，为他安排了一个合适的职位。

这两句诗后来就流传开来，并经过缩减形成了“近水楼台”这个成语。

Afterwards, these two sentences were briefly cut into an idiom “waterside pavilions”.

127

邯郸学步

Copying for copying's sake

出自 《庄子·秋水》。

释义 机械地照搬模仿。

战国时期，燕国寿陵有个年轻人，听说赵国都城邯郸的人都特别有风度，他

In the Warring State Period, a young man of Shouling in Yan state heard that the people of Zhao's capital Handan were all very gracious

们走起路来不紧不慢，姿势优雅，特别好看。于是他带上盘缠，不远千里，专程赶到赵国去学习邯郸人走路的姿势。

and elegant, and they all walked elegantly with unhurried steps, so he took enough money and travelled thousands of miles to Zhao state for learning the walking posture of people in Handan.

到了邯郸，年轻人来到大街上，看着来来往往的人群，发现这里的人走路步法确实比寿陵的要好看多了，于是就跟在人家后面模仿。但是，无论怎么模仿，他都觉得自己学得不像。年轻人心想，学不好的原因肯定是自己走惯了老的姿势和步法，于是，他下决心丢掉自己原来的习惯走法，从头开始学习走路。

As he arrived in Handan, he came to the street and began to observe the people coming and going. He thought that the walking posture of Handan was indeed much better than that of Shouling, so he followed the passersby to learn. But no matter how he imitated, he still felt it unlike, so he decided to throw out his original habit of walking and learn how to walk from the beginning.

可是，一连过了好几个月，年轻人却越学越差劲，眼看身上带着的盘缠已经花光，自己一无所获，他十分沮丧，只好回家了。可是他又忘了自己原来是怎样走路的，不知道怎么迈步，无奈，他只好在地上爬着回了

However, after several months, the more he imitated, the worse his walking posture became, he felt very depressed and had to go back home because he had run out of money. Whereas, he even forgot how to walk and how to step forward, so he had to climb back to Shouling.

寿陵。

唐朝大诗人李白根据这个故事，曾写诗说“寿陵失本步，笑杀邯郸人”，嘲讽了那些一味模仿他人，招致可笑结果的人。

Based on this story, the famous poet Li Bai in the Tang Dynasty once wrote a poem “a Shouling person forget how to walk and was laughed at by Handan people”, which made a mockery of people blindly imitating others and incurring ridiculous results.

128

饮鸩止渴

Quenching a thirst with poison

出自 晋·葛洪《抱朴子》。

释义 用错误的办法解决眼前的困难，而不顾严重的后果。

在中国古代的毒药中，最有名的应该就是鸩酒。鸩据说是一种鸟，它的羽毛含

Among the various poisons in Chinese ancient time, the most famous one is the zhen poison. It is said that the zhen bird is a legendary

有剧毒，只要把羽毛泡在酒里，就会制成毒酒，人喝下去马上毙命。

东汉时期，有一个人叫霍谞，从小勤奋好学，读了大量儒家经书，在当地很出名。霍谞有个舅舅叫宋光，在郡里当官，由于他秉公执法，得罪了一些权贵，被他们诬告篡改诏书，从而被押到京都洛阳，关入监狱。

霍谞当时才十五岁，在得知舅舅下狱后，他的心情一直平静不下来。他从小经常和宋光在一起，对舅舅的为人非常清楚，知道舅舅不可能干这种弄虚作假的事。他日思夜想，最后决定给大将军梁商写一封信，为舅舅申诉冤情。信中有这样一段话："宋光作为州郡的长官，一向奉公守法，得到朝

bird with poisonous feathers. When its feathers are put into wine, the wine turns to be poisonous and people will immediately die as they drink.

In the Eastern Han Dynasty, there was a person named Huo Xu, who was diligent and studious since childhood and read lots of Confucian scriptures, and he was well-known in local area. Huo Xu had an uncle named Song Guang, who took office in county. Since he always enforced the law impartially, he offended some bigwigs and was lodged a false accusation of tampering the imperial edict, and finally he was detained in the prison in the capital Luoyang.

At that time Huo Xu was only fifteen years old, knowing the bad news of his uncle, he couldn't calm down, because he always stayed with his uncle and clearly knew his personality, he believed that his uncle would not practise fraud. He thought it over for day and night, and finally decided to send a letter to the General Liang Shang to complain grievances. There was a paragraph in the letter "As an official of county, Song Guang had been enforcing the law impartially in order to obtain employment by

廷的任用，怎么会冒着死罪的风险去篡改诏书呢？这正好比为了充饥而去吃生附子（生附子为毒品），为了解渴而去喝鸩酒。他怎么可能这样做呢？”

the imperial government, how could he risk his life to tamper the edict? Just like a person eats monkshood to appease his hunger and drinks zhen wine to appease thirst. How could he be so stupid to do this?”

梁商读了这封信，觉得很有道理，对霍谞的才学和胆识也很赏识，便请求皇帝，把宋光免罪释放。

Liang Shang felt reasonable after he read this letter, and he also appreciated Huo Xu’s talents and courage, so he turned to the emperor and asked for pardon for Huo Xu’s uncle, and finally Song Guang was acquitted.

129

鸡犬升天

Fowls and dogs turn immortals

出自 晋·葛洪《神仙卷·刘安》。

释义 一个人得势,与他有关的人也跟着沾光。

西汉时期,有位著名的思想家、文学家,名叫刘安。在十六岁的时候,他

In the Western Han Dynasty, there was a person named Liu An, who was a famous ideologist and litterateur. He inherited his

就继承父亲爵位，被封为淮南王。刘安虽然贵为诸侯王，却偏偏对道教的书籍入了迷，产生了炼丹成仙的念头，四处去寻访有仙方神术的道人。

father's tile of nobility and was ennobled as the king of Huainan, but he was addicted to Taoist books and alchemy to be an immortal, looking for Taoist priests with magic and divine prescription.

有一天，他听说有位名叫八公的仙翁，有炼制仙丹的秘方，但是从不传给别人，于是就去寻访八公。可是八公大部分时间都在四处云游，刘安吃尽了苦头，也没能找到八公。不过刘安仍然一心一意地寻访，最终，他的诚心感动了八公。一天，八公来到刘安家里，把炼制仙丹的方法传授给了他，并且告诉他，仙丹炼成，吃下以后就可以升天成仙。

One day, he heard that an immortal man named Ba Gong had private prescription for producing elixir, but he never taught others, therefore Liu An went to visit Ba Gong. He suffered lots of difficulties because Ba Gong was wandering around for the most of time. Whereas Liu An kept on finding Ba Gong devotedly and finally moved Ba Gong. One day, Ba Gong came to visit Liu An and taught him the method of producing magic and divine prescription, and told him that he would turn to be immortal by eating the elixir.

此后，刘安每天都虔诚地静心修炼，结果真的炼出了仙丹。他知道升天成仙的时刻到了，便沐浴更衣，焚香祷告。他把仙丹吃了下

From then on, Liu An kept on practising reverently and finally made out the elixir. He knew it was time for him to be immortal, so he bathed and dressed himself, and burned incense and prayed to God. Finally, as he ate the elixir,

去，顿时觉得身体轻飘飘的，低头一看，原来自己早已站在了云端之上。

he immediately felt weightless and found him already stand on the cloud.

刘安成仙后，散落在院子里的仙丹，被家里的鸡和狗吃了，它们竟然也都飘然升空，成了神仙。

After Liu An became an immortal, some elixir was scattered in the yard, when the fowls and dogs ate the elixir, they also became weightless and flew to the sky as immortals.

130

鸡鸣狗盗

Crow like a cock and snatch like a dog

出自 《史记·孟尝君列传》。

释义 指微不足道的技能。

战国时期，齐国的孟尝君带着宾客出使秦国，谁知秦昭王却把孟尝君和他的手

In the Warring States Period, the Lord Meng Chang of Qi state led his followers to Qin state as envoy, but the King Zhao of Qin

下人软禁起来，只等找个借口杀掉。

put them under house arrest and planned to kill them by certain excuse.

孟尝君听说秦昭王有个最宠爱的妃子，只要妃子说一，昭王绝不说二，于是派人去求她救助。妃子答应了，但提出要拿齐国那件天下无双的狐裘作为报酬。孟尝君为难了：刚到秦国，他就把这件狐裘献给了秦昭王。就在这时候，有一个门客说："我能把狐裘找来！"说完就走了。

The Lord Meng Chang heard that the King of Qin had a beloved concubine and the king usually fully agreed with what she said, so he sent out to ask for her help. The concubine agreed but asked for the unique fox fur coat of Qi as reward. The Lord Meng Chang felt embarrassed because he gave it as gift to the King Zhao of Qin when he arrived. At this time, one guest said "I can get the fur coat", and then left.

原来这个门客最善于钻狗洞偷东西。晚上，他借着月光，逃过巡逻人的眼睛，轻松地钻进贮藏室把狐裘偷了出来。妃子拿到狐裘，也说话算数，说服秦昭王放弃了杀孟尝君的念头，并准备过两天为他饯行，送他回齐国。

It turned out that this man was very good at going through dog hole for stealing. At night, by eluding the patrol, he easily went through the storage room and stole the fox fur coat out. The concubine got the fox fur coat and kept her promise. She finally persuaded the king of Qin to give up the idea of killing the lord Meng Chang, moreover, she also suggested to prepare a farewell dinner and send the lord Meng Chang back to Qi state.

孟尝君不敢再等，立刻偷偷地率领门客连夜骑马向

The lord Meng Chang dared not to wait anymore and immediately rode eastward

东快奔。到了函谷关时正是半夜，按秦国规定，函谷关每天鸡叫才开门。大家正在发愁时，有一个门客突然学起了鸡叫，声音惟妙惟肖，接着城关外的公鸡都跟着打鸣了。守关的士兵虽然觉得奇怪，但也只得起来打开关门，放他们出去。就这样，孟尝君靠着这些鸡鸣狗盗之士逃回了齐国。

with his followers that very night. It was just midnight when they arrived at Hangu Pass, according to Qin's regulations, the gate would only be opened until the cock crowed. When they were worried, one of the followers suddenly imitated cock crow, which was so vivid that those cocks outside the Pass also followed to crow. Although the guard felt strange, he had to open the gate and let them out. Therefore, the lord Meng Chang escaped back to Qi by the support of those followers with pretty tricks.

131

丧心病狂

As mad as a march hare

出自 《宋史·范如圭传》。

释义 丧失理智，像发了疯一样。

岳飞是南宋时期著名的抗金英雄，他奋勇杀敌，历经数次战斗，收复

Yue Fei was a famous hero conquering the Jin state in the Southern Song Dynasty, who advanced courageously in many battles and

了大片失地，金人都因此悲叹道：“撼山易，撼岳家军难！”

recovered many lost territories. The people of Jin state mournfully sighed, “It is easy to shake the mountains, but it is very difficult to shake the troops of Yue Fei!”

金军将领兀术害怕岳飞，就写信给当时的宋朝宰相秦桧，要他设法杀掉岳飞。秦桧便让皇上连下十二道金牌，命令岳飞班师回朝。等岳飞回朝后，秦桧就找了几个与岳飞有矛盾的人，编造谎言，罗列罪状，上朝弹劾岳飞。皇帝很快罢免了岳飞的官职，解除了他的兵权。

The Jin General Wu Zhu was very afraid of Yue Fei, so he wrote to the current Prime Minister Qin Hui of Song and asked him to kill Yue Fei. Qin Hui persuaded the emperor to continuously send out twelve gold medals to call Yue Fei back. Then Qin Hui asked several Yue Fei's foes to make up crimes to impeach Yue Fei. The emperor soon dismissed Yue Fei from his official position and military leadership.

为杀掉岳飞，秦桧想尽了办法，先是收买岳飞的部下王俊，让他诬告岳飞与部下张宪、岳云谋反，但都找不到证据。接着秦桧又诬陷岳飞曾给张宪写信，让张宪谎报军情，借此引起朝廷的恐惧。但是由于没有信件作为证据，岳飞的罪状仍无法成立。

Qin Hui thought out all means to kill Yue Fei, and he firstly bribed Yue Fei's subordinate Wang Jun to lodge a false accusation against Yue Fei for conspiracy with his subordinates Zhang Xian and Yue Yun, but failed due to lack of evidence. Then Qin Hui framed Yue Fei for writing letter to Zhang Xian and asking him to lie about military intelligence in order to arouse fears, but also failed due to lack of evidence.

岳飞被押了两个多月以后，秦桧终于沉不住气，直接下令监狱看守秘密将岳飞在狱中杀害。

另一位抗金将领韩世忠得知岳飞被害，亲自上朝质问秦桧，岳飞到底犯了什么罪。秦桧说：“虽然没找到岳飞父子和张宪的书信，但谋反的事莫须有（意思是或许有）。”韩世忠愤怒地说：“这‘莫须有’的罪名怎么能使天下人服气呢？”大臣范如圭也上书痛责秦桧丧权辱国，说：“你若不是丧心病狂，怎么会做出如此之事呢？你必定遗臭万年！”

Two months after Yue Fei was arrested, Qin Hui couldn't retain his composure and directly offer the jail guard to kill Yue Fei in the prison.

Another General conquering Jin state named Han Shizhong, he got the news and queried Qin Hui in the imperial court, and Qin hui said, “Although we didn't find out the letter between Yue Fei's family and Zhang Xian, there is possibility for Yue Fei on conspiracy.” Han Shizhong said angrily, “How can the possible crime convince people?” The minister Fan Rugui also bitterly rebuked that, “You must be frenzied to do this! You must remain infamous in history!”

132

刻舟求剑

Making his mark

出自 《吕氏春秋·察今》。

释义 比喻不懂事物已发展变化而仍静止地看问题。

战国时期，有个楚国人，有一次乘船渡江，船驶到江心的时候，他一不小心，把随身携带的一把宝剑掉落江中。他

In the Warring States Period, a person of Chu state took a boat across the river, when the boat arrived at the center of the river, he carelessly dropped his treasured sword to the

赶紧伸手去抓，但已经来不及了。

river, he tried to grasp but it was too late.

船上的人都为他感到惋惜，但那个楚国人似乎并不在意，他马上掏出一把小刀，在船舷上刻了一个记号，跟大家说："这就是宝剑落水的地方。"

The other people on the boat all felt pitiful, but that Chu person didn't care and he immediately took out a little knife to make a mark on the rail of the boat, and he said, "This is the very place where my treasured sword fell."

大家很纳闷，不知道他为什么这样做。

People all felt puzzled without knowing the reason.

船靠岸后，楚国人立即从船上刻记号的地方下水，去捞取掉落的宝剑。捞了半天，却不见宝剑的影子。他觉得很奇怪，自言自语说："我的宝剑不就是在这里掉下去的吗，怎么会找不到呢？"

When the boat approached the land, that Chu person immediately jumped into the river for searching his treasured sword, but found nothing. He felt strange and talked to himself, "This is indeed the right place where my treasured sword fell, but why I can't find it?"

这个时候，船上的人们才明白过来，纷纷大笑起来，说："船一直在行进，而你的宝剑却不动，你怎么能找得到你的剑呢？"

Now people on the boat just came to understand and began to laugh and said, "The boat has been moving forward, but your treasured sword doesn't move, how can you find it?"

133

卧薪尝胆

Sleep on firewood and taste gall

出自 《史记·越王勾践世家》。

释义 刻苦自励，发奋图强。

春秋时期，吴国和越国爆发战争，越王勾践大败吴军，年老的吴王因伤重而

In the Spring and Autumn Period, a war broke out between Wu and Yue states, Gou Jian, who was the king of Yue completely defeated

死。吴王的儿子夫差继位，他在大臣伍子胥的帮助下，练兵强国，三年后又发兵讨伐越国，一直攻到越国都城会稽。

Wu's troops. The old king of Wu died due to heavy hurt, and his son Fu Chai succeed to his throne, by the support of the Prime Minister Wu Zixu, Fu Chai industriously trained soldiers to strengthen the power of nation. Three years later, he launched attacks to the capital Kuaiji of Yue state.

在越国面临灭亡之际，越国大夫文种买通吴国大臣伯嚭，向夫差极力求情，夫差终于答应保存越国，让越王勾践与王后和大夫范蠡一起到吴国为奴。三年后，夫差生病，勾践为夫差尝粪便以寻找病源，使夫差深受感动，便释放了勾践。

On the brink of Yue's destruction, a Yue minister Wen Zhong bribed the Wu's minister Bo Pi for beg for leniency, and finally Fu Chai agreed to conserve Yue and detained Yue's king Gou Jian and queen as well as the minister Fan Li to Wu as slaves. Three years later, Fu chai fell ill, and Gou Jian tasted his faeces for distinguishing the sources of the disease, and Fu Chai was deeply moved and thus released Gou Jian.

回到越国后，勾践放弃了舒适安逸的王宫，搬进破旧的马厩中居住。他睡在柴草上，在房梁上吊着一只奇苦无比的猪苦胆。每天醒来，他都要先尝一口苦胆，以表示不忘屈辱之意。二十年的时间，经过勾践和一干大臣的不懈努力，越国开始

When Gou Jian came back to Yue, he gave up the comfortable palace and moved into shabby stable. He slept on firewood and hang on the beam a pig gall which was extremely bitter. Everyday as he wake up, he would firstly take a bite on the gall for reminding the past humiliated times. Through unremitting endeavor of twenty years, Yue state became a strong country.

变得强大起来。

公元前473年，勾践率领三万雄兵，一举将吴国的姑苏城团团围困。夫差向越国求和，被勾践断然拒绝，最终夫差被迫自杀身亡，吴国的版图也被全部并入越国。

In 473 BC, Gou Jian led thirty thousand of troops to enclose the capital Gusu of Wu at one stroke. Fu Chai begged for leniency, but was flatly refused by Gou Jian, finally Fu Chai was compelled to commit suicide and Wu's territory was wholly incorporated into Yue state.

134

图穷匕见

When the map is unrolled, the dagger is revealed

出自 《战国策·燕策三》。

释义 比喻事情发展到最后，显露出了真相或本意。

战国末年，秦王嬴政一心想统一中原，不断向各国进攻。在灭掉韩国以

In the end of the Warring States Period, Ying Zheng as the King of Qin was bent on unifying the central plain, and continuously launched attacks

后，秦军占领了赵国都城邯郸，又一直向北进军，逼近燕国。

燕国的太子丹原来在秦国当人质，后来偷偷地逃回燕国。他一心要替燕国报仇，寻找能刺杀秦王的人。后来，他物色到了一个名叫荆轲的勇士。

荆轲向太子丹献计，准备带着原秦国逃亡将领樊於期的头颅，和燕国督亢的地图去献给秦王，以得见秦王，伺机下手行刺。太子丹又为荆轲准备了一把锋利的匕首，让工匠用毒药煮过，作为行刺的武器，还派了一个年轻的勇士秦舞阳做荆轲的副手。

荆轲到了咸阳，秦王命令在咸阳宫接见他们。荆轲捧着装有樊於期头颅的盒子，秦舞阳捧着地图，一步步走上台阶。秦舞阳因为害怕而两腿发抖，荆轲担心露

on other countries. Han state was destructed, Qin's troops occupied Zhao's capital Handan, and then moved northward to Yan state.

The Prince Dan of Yan was originally a hostage in Qin, and then furtively fled back to Yan. He was determined to revenge and had been looking for an assassin who could help him to kill the king of Qin, and finally a warrior named Jing Ke was selected.

Jing Ke offered advice to the Prince Dan that he prepared to dedicate the head of Fan Wuji, who was the former fleeing general of Qin, and a map of Dukang of Yan, in order to see the king of Qin, and watched his chance for assassination. The Prince Dan also prepared a sharp dagger boiled with poison as the weapon to assassinate the king of Qin, as well a young warrior Qin Wuyang as Jing Ke's assistant.

As Jing Ke arrived in Qin, the king of Qin granted interview at the palace of Xianyang. Jing Ke went step by step, holding the box with the head of Fan Wuji inside, and the warrior Qin Wuyang followed with Yan's map. Qin Wuyang shook his legs due to great fear, so Jing

出破绽，便从秦舞阳手里接过地图，捧着木匣上去，献给秦王。

Ke took over the map to dedicate to the king of Qin.

荆轲当着秦王的面，慢慢地打开地图，到地图全部打开时，预先卷在地图里的匕首露了出来。秦王一见，惊得跳了起来。荆轲绕着朝堂上的大铜柱子追赶，却始终无法刺中秦王。这时有个伺候秦王的医生，拿起手里的药袋对准荆轲扔了过去。荆轲刚一分神，秦王就拔出宝剑，砍断了他的左腿。荆轲受伤倒地，两旁的武士趁机一拥而上，结果了他的性命。

In front of the King of Qin, Jing Ke slowly unroll the map, and when it was fully unrolled, the prepared dagger suddenly revealed, which scare the king of Qin to jump up. Jing Ke chased around the huge copper pillar in the court, but he failed to stab at the king. At this moment, a doctor of the king threw his hand-held drug bag to Jing Ke, as Jing Ke was distracted, the King of Qin pulled out his treasured sword and cut off Jing ke’s left leg. Jing Ke fell down to the ground, and the warriors on two sides seized the chance to rush forward and killed him.

135

夜郎自大

Ludicrous conceit of the king of Yelang

出自 《史记·西南夷列传》。

释义 骄傲无知，自负自大。

汉朝的时候，在西南方有个名叫夜郎的小国，它的国王因为从未离开过自己的

During the Han Dynasty, there was a small state named Yelang in the southwest. The king of Yelang never went out to see the outside

国土，就一直以为自己统治的是全天下最大的国家。

有一天，夜郎国国王与部下去巡视国境，他指着前方的土地问："这里哪个国家最大啊？"部下为了迎合国王的心意，就说："当然是夜郎国最大了！"走着走着，国王又抬起头来，望着前面的高山问："天底下还有比这座山更高的山吗？"部下回答说："天底下没有比这座山更高的山了。"后来，他们来到河边，国王又问："我认为这应该是世界上最长的河流了。"部下仍然异口同声地回答说："大王说得一点都没错。"从此以后，国王就更加相信夜郎是天底下最大的国家了。

后来，汉武帝为寻找通往印度的通道，曾派使者到达夜郎。这个骄傲无知的国王不知道自己的国家仅和汉朝的一个县差不多大，却不

world and took for granted that Yelang was the largest country in the world.

One day, the king and his subordinates made an inspection tour, the king pointed at the forward territory and asked, "Which country is the biggest one in the world?" His subordinates flattered and said, "Yelang is certainly the biggest country in the world!" They continued to walk and the king held up his head upon the forward high mountain and asked, "Is there any mountain higher than this mountain?" His subordinates answered, "There's no other mountains higher than this one." Then he came to the riverside, the king asked again, "I think this river is the longest one in the world." His subordinates answered with one voice, "What Your Majesty said is absolutely right!" From then on, the king became more confident that Yelang was the largest country in the world.

Afterwards, the Emperor Wu of Han once dispatched envoy to Yelang for finding the pass to India. But this ignorant and arrogant king had no idea that Yelang was only as large as one of Han's counties and

知天高地厚地问使者："汉朝和我的国家哪个大？"

到西汉末期，夜郎国与南方小国发生争斗，因不服从汉朝出面调解，夜郎国王被汉朝军队斩杀。从此，史籍中就不再有关于夜郎的记载，只留下了一句"夜郎自大"的成语。

even asked the envoy, "Han and Yelang, which one is larger?"

By the end of the Western Han, a battle happened between Yelang and another small southern state, the king didn't obey the mediation plan proposed by Han, so he was killed. From then on, there 's no record of Yelang, leaving only one sentence "ludicrous conceit of the king of Yelang".

136

奇货可居

Hoard as a rare commodity

出自 《史记·卷八十五》。

释义 把稀有的货物囤积起来，等待高价出售。

吕不韦最初是卫国的一个富商，经常往来于各地做买卖。一次，他来到赵国的

Lu Buwei was a rich merchant in Wei originally, and always traveled from place to place for business trade. One time, he

都城邯郸，遇到了在赵国做人质的秦国公子异人。异人是秦国太子安国君的儿子，因为母亲夏姬不得宠，所以被送到赵国当人质。

came to Zhao's capital Handan and met Qin's Prince Yi Ren, who was the son of Qin's Prince An Guo and was sent to Zhao as a hostage due to that his mother Xia Ji lost favor.

当时赵国正与秦国交战，异人的处境非常困窘，吕不韦却以商人的独特眼光，看到了他身上的价值，说“异人就像一件奇货，可以囤积下来，以待高价售出”，认为这是一个难得的值得投资的机会。于是他告诉异人，愿意帮助他回国成为太子。异人自然非常高兴，并表示有朝一日成为国君，一定会与吕不韦共享天下。

At that time Zhao was in a battle with Qin, so Yi Ren was strained in his circumstances. Whereas Lu Buwei recognized Yi Ren's value by his unique eyesight of a merchant and took it as a precious opportunity of investment, so he said, "Yi Ren is like a rare commodity, which should be stored for a high selling price in the future". Then he expressed to Yi Ren his willingness to help him back to his country as a prince, and Yi Ren was certainly very happy and promised that if he became the king in the future, he would definitely share the country with Lu Buwei.

此后，吕不韦立即带着大量财宝去到秦国，求见深受安国君宠爱的华阳夫人，极力说服没有生过儿子的她认异人为自己的儿子，并让她请求安国君派人将异人接回秦国。

Afterwards, Lu Buwei took a lot of treasure to Qin for the concubine Hua Yang, who was deeply favored by the Prince An Guo, and he strongly convinced Hua Yang to adopt Yi Ren as her own son since she didn't have a son, and also asked her to request the Prince An Guo to take Yi Ren back.

异人回国后，安国君又答应华阳夫人的请求，立他为太子。几年后，安国君做了国君，但仅仅一年后就死去，异人如愿以偿继任国君，称为秦庄襄王。

As Yi Ren came back, the King An Guo fulfilled his promise to establish Yi Ren as the prince. Several years later, the Prince An Guo became the king, but died only one year later, so Yi Ren finally fulfilled his wishes to assume the throne as the King Zhuang Xiang of Qin.

秦庄襄王没有食言，他即位后，就任命吕不韦为丞相，封为文信侯，并赏赐给他河南洛阳的十万户，作为他的封地。

The King Zhuang Xiang of Qin didn't lose his words, after he assumed the throne, he immediately appointed Lu Buwei as the Prime Minister and ennobled him as vassal Wen Xin, awarding him the territory in Luoyang of Henan with a hundred thousand of population.

137

孤注一掷

Stake all on one cast of the dice

出自 《宋史·寇准传》。

释义 倾其所有，冒险来决一胜负。

北宋真宗年间，契丹军队大举入侵中原，他们长驱直入，一直抵达澶州

During the reign of the emperor Zhen Zong in the Northern Song Dynasty, Qidan troops made massive invasion on the central plain, and

（今河南濮阳），边境告急文书接连送到京城。当时寇准正担任宰相，他接到告急文书后，扣留下来没有上报，还像平时一样从容镇定，并没有露出半点惊慌之色。

宋真宗听说此事后，非常愤怒，责问寇准说："边关军情如此紧急，你为什么隐瞒不报？"寇准笑着回答："陛下息怒，我已经做好了打败契丹军队的谋划，请陛下御驾亲征，敌人一定会不战而逃。"

当年十二月，宋真宗亲自率领文武百官，冒着严寒来到澶州，宋军军心大振。寇准号令全军以逸待劳，等待战机。果然，几天后契丹军队前来攻城，等敌人疲惫时，寇准命令将士出击，一举打败敌兵。

they marched straight to Chanzhou which was the current Puyang of Henan, so the frontier sent emergent notice to the capital continuously. When the temporal Prime Minister Kou Zhun received the notice, he concealed instead of reporting to the emperor and acted unhurriedly and calmly as usual without any expression of fear.

When the Emperor Zhen Zong heard of it, he was very angry and scolded Kou Zhun, "Why did you conceal the emergent notice from the frontier?" Kou Zhun smiled and said, "Your Majesty, please mollify, I've already worked out the scheme to defeat Qidan, please lead the troops personally and the enemies will certainly flee without any defence."

In December of that year, the Emperor Zhen Zong personally led civil and military officials to Chanzhou in spite of bitter cold, which greatly encourage the morale of troops. Kou Zhun ordered all troops to wait at ease until the enemies were exhausted. As expected, a few days later, Qidan troops attacked Chanzhou and turned to be tired after a period of time, then Kou Zhun ordered soldiers to attack and completely defeated enemies at one stroke.

在澶州取得胜利后，宋真宗对寇准更加重用。朝中另一位大臣王钦若心生嫉妒，便在宋真宗面前说寇准的坏话："赌输的赌徒往往会把所有的钱押上，作为最后一次赌注。寇准再三要陛下亲征，是把陛下当作他的最后一个赌注，这不是拿陛下的生命冒险吗？"

宋真宗听信了谗言，不久便罢免了寇准的宰相一职。

Upon the victory in Chanzhou, the Emperor Zhen Zong put Kou Zhun in a more important position. Another minister Wang Qinruo became jealous and spoke ill of Kou Zhun to the emperor, "A gambling loser will usually stake all on one cast of the dice as the last chance to win. The reason why Kou Zhun repeatedly invited Your Majesty to lead troops personally is that he regarded Your Majesty as his last stake, that was actually risking the life of Your Majesty!"

The Emperor Zhen Zong followed the slanderous words and soon dismissed Kou Zhun from the post of the Prime Minister.

138

居安思危

Skeleton at the feast

出自 《左传·襄公十一年》。

释义 处在平安的环境里，要想到可能有的危险。

春秋时期，宋、齐、晋、卫等十二个国家，有一次联合出兵攻打郑国。郑国

In the Spring and Autumn Period, twelve countries including Song, Qi, Jin, Wei and the others jointly launched an attack on Zheng.

国君急忙向其中最大的晋国求和，晋国的国君晋悼公同意了，剩下的十一个国家也就停止了进攻。

The King of Zheng hurried to sue for peace to the biggest country Jin, and when Jin agreed to stop attacks, the other eleven countries stopped.

郑国为了表示感谢，给晋国送去了大批礼物，其中包括著名乐师三人、兵车一百辆、歌女十六人，还有许多精美乐器。

In order to express gratitned, Zheng sent lots of presents including three famous musicians, one hundred chariots, sixteen sing-song girls and many exquisite musical instruments.

晋悼公见送来这么多的礼物，非常高兴，将八个歌女赏赐给功臣魏绛，对他说："你这几年为我出谋划策，事情办得都很顺利。现在就让咱们一同来享受吧！"

The Duke Dao of Jin was very glad and awarded eight sing-song girls to the meritorious minister Wei Jiang and said, "You have been masterminding schemes for me in these several years and everything goes well, so let's indulge in joy together!"

可是，魏绛却谢绝了晋悼公的赏赐，并且劝告晋悼公说："我们国家的事情之所以办得顺利，首先应归功于您的领导才能，其次是靠各位大臣齐心协力，我个人有什么贡献可言呢？不过希望您在享受安乐的同时，能够想到国家还有许多事情要办，就像古书上所说的那样，'居安思危，思则

Whereas, Wei Jiang declined the award of the Duke Dao of Jin and persuaded, "The success should give credit to your leadership abilities and concerted efforts of all the ministers, instead of myself only. I sincerely hope you will keep in mind the important things to do when you enjoy the happiness, just as the sayings in the ancient book that we should be prepared for danger in times of safety."

有备，有备无患’。”

晋悼公听了魏绛这番话，深受感动，高兴地接受了他的意见，从此对他更加敬重。

The Duke Dao of Jin was deeply moved and gladly accepted Weijiang’s advice, showing more respect for him.

139

拔苗助长

Haste makes waste

出自 《孟子·公孙丑上》。

释义 不顾事物的发展规律，一味要求速成，结果反而把事情弄糟。

宋国有一个农夫，他担心自己田里的禾苗长不高，就天天到田边去看。

A farmer of Song was always worried that the seedlings of cereal crops couldn't grow tall, so he went to cropland for examination everyday.

可是，一天，两天，三天……几天过去了，禾苗好像一点儿也没有往上长。农夫在田边着急地转来转去，自言自语道："我得想一个办法，帮助它们快快生长。"

Whereas, several days later, the seedlings didn't seem to grow, and the farmer was anxious to walk around and said to himself that he should find a way to make them grow fast.

农夫绞尽脑汁，有一天终于想出了办法。他飞快地跑到田里，用手把禾苗一棵棵地往上拔，从早上一直忙到太阳落山，把所有的禾苗都拔了一遍。

The farmer racked his brains and found a way one day, so he run to the cropland and pulled up the seedlings one by one until sun set.

他回到家里，虽然十分疲劳，但还是很开心地跟家人说："今天可把我累坏了，力气总算没白费，我帮禾苗都长高了一大截。"

Then he came back home, in spite of great tiredness, he happily said to his family people, "Today I am really exhausted to pull up all the seedlings and make them grow much taller."

他的儿子听了，急忙跑到田里一看，禾苗已经全都枯死了。

Upon his words, his son hurriedly run to the cropland and found that all the seedlings withered.

140

明珠暗投

Cast pearls before swine

出自 《史记·鲁仲连邹阳列传》。

释义 比喻有才能的人得不到重视。

汉朝初年，汉高祖刘邦陆续消灭了割据地方的诸侯，把自己的子孙分封

At the beginning of the Han Dynasty, the Emperor Gao Zu of Han successively exterminated all the vassals and distributed

到各地，想以此来稳定国家。当时很多很有才能的人都到各地的诸侯那里，谋求出路。

有一个叫邹阳的人，他刚开始的时候投奔了吴王刘濞，后来刘濞叛乱造反，邹阳上书劝谏，吴王不听，于是邹阳离开吴王，又跟随了梁孝王刘武。

梁孝王是汉文帝的小儿子，也就是汉景帝的弟弟。他在七国之乱时支持朝廷，为平定叛乱立下了大功，被授予天子旌旗，权势几乎可以与汉朝天子相比拟，因此动了谋求皇帝继承人的野心。邹阳极力劝说梁孝王打消这个念头。而梁孝王的国相羊胜等人由于嫉妒邹阳，于是在梁孝王面前说了很多邹阳的坏话。梁孝王大怒，把邹阳关进了监狱，并想杀掉他。

his descendants to various regions for the realization of stability. At that time, many capable people came to meet the vassals for working opportunities.

A person named Zou Yang followed the King of Wu, Liu Bi. When Liu Bi launched insurgency, Zou Yang submitted a written statement for persuasion,but Liu Bi rejected, so Zou Yang left the King of Wu and followed Liu Wu as the King Xiao of Liang.

The King Xiao of Liang was the youngest son of the Emperor Wen of Han, as well as the younger brother of the Emperor Jing of Han. During the rebellion of the seven kingdoms, the King Xiao of Liang fully supported the imperial court and made great contribution to squash rebellions, so he was awarded the banner of the Emperor with almost equal political power as the Emperor of Han, thus he came up with the ambition to assume the throne. Zou Yang tried to persuad the King Xiao of Liang to give up this idea. At the same time, the Prime Minister Yang Sheng and other ministers spoke ill of Zou Yang due to jealousy, so the King Xiao of Liang was extremely angry, then he put Zou

Yang into jail and wanted to kill him.

邹阳在狱中给梁孝王写了一封信，信中除了列举前朝的例子证明能人贤人总是引起别人的嫉妒陷害之外，还做了一个比喻，说如果把珍贵的明珠暗暗投放到满是行人的路上，就会引起路人之间的警惕和愤怒。邹阳借用这样的比喻，来说明自己就如那颗明珠一样，因为自己的才能而被小人嫉妒愤恨，于是陷害自己，引来了灾祸。

In jail, Zou Yang wrote a letter to the King Xiao of Liang, listing examples of the former dynasty that those capable people are easy to arouse jealousy. He also made a metaphor that it would arouse alter and anger of the passengers by stealthily casting precious pearls on the road, in order to express that he himself was like that pearl, he was envied by villains due to his excellence, and thus leading framing and disasters to him.

梁孝王看到这封情真意切的信后，大受感动，派人从牢狱中把邹阳放出来。邹阳也从此成为梁孝王的贵宾。

The King Xiao of Liang was deeply moved by this sincere letter and released Zou Yang from the jail, and then Zou Yang became the distinguished guest of the king.

141

杯弓蛇影

An illusory snake in a goblet

出自 汉·应劭《风俗通义》。

释义 比喻因疑神疑鬼而引起恐惧。

晋朝时期，有个叫乐广的人，很喜欢结交朋友。有一天，他邀请一位朋友到家

In the Jin Dynasty, a person named Yue Guang liked to make friends. One day, he invited one friend to his home, when they were

里，两个人一边喝酒一边聊天，正喝得畅快时，这位朋友突然停下来，也没说有什么事，就马上告辞回家了。乐广心里很是纳闷。

drinking happily, his friend suddenly stopped and immediately left without saying anything, and Yue Guang felt puzzled.

过了几天，乐广听说这位朋友病得很厉害，于是亲自登门去看望。一见面，乐广便问："前几天我们在一起喝酒你还好端端的，怎么一下子就病倒了呢？"

Several days later, Yue Guang heard that friend was ill seriously, so he went to visit that friend. Yue Guang asked, "Several days before when we were drinking together, you seemed very good at that time, how did you suddenly fall ill?"

这位朋友刚开始还支支吾吾，在乐广的一再追问下，他才说出实情："那天您盛情招待我喝酒，可是我喝了几杯以后，突然间发现酒杯里有一条蛇，在杯中慢慢地蠕动，顿时感到非常恶心。回家后全身都很不舒服，总觉得肚子里有一条小蛇，就这样一病不起了。"

That friend hesitated to answer and finally spoke out the truth under the repeated questioning of Yue Guang "On that day when I was drinking, I suddenly saw a snake slowly swim in the wine cup, and then I felt sick. When I came back, I felt uncomfortable as if there was a little snake in my belly, thus I fell ill seriously."

乐广回家后，心里一直在想：酒杯里怎么会有蛇呢？于是坐到那天朋友坐过的凳子上，前面又放上酒

After Yue Guang came back home, he was wondering why a snake would be in the wine cup, thus he sat at the chair which that friend took on that day and put on a

杯，果然见到杯中有一条蛇的影子。他细心观察，终于发现了原因所在。

wine cup on the table, and then he suddenly saw a shadow of a snake and knew the real reason.

乐广立刻把朋友再次请到家中，扶他坐在上次喝酒的地方，给他斟满一杯酒，说："你看看酒杯里有什么？"

Then Yue Guang invited that friend to his home again and helped him sit at the same place, he fulfilled his wine cup and said, "Let's see what is in the wine cup."

这位朋友紧张地说："和上次一样，杯里有一条蛇。"

That friend said nervously, "The same as last time, there is a snake in the wine cup."

这时，乐广指着墙上挂着的弓，说："都是它在作怪，杯中的蛇其实是这张弓的影子！"随后，乐广把弓取了下来，杯里的小蛇果然没有了。这位朋友恍然大悟，顿时消除了恐惧和疑惑，病也就很快痊愈了。

At this moment, Yue Guang pointed at the bow on the wall and said, "The shadow of snake is actually this bow!" Then Yue Guang took down the bow, and the shadow of snake disappeared. That friend was suddenly enlightened and all his fear and doubts disappeared, and he also recovered very soon.

142

杯水车薪

A drop in the ocean

出自 《孟子·告子》。

释义 比喻力量太小，对解决问题作用不大。

从前有个樵夫，有一天在山上砍了满满的一车柴，便高高兴兴地推着车回

Once upon a time, a woodcutter chopped a full cart of firewood and happily pulled the cart back home. Halfway though, he was very

家了。走到半道，由于天气炎热，他口干舌燥，渴得很厉害。这时正好看见路边有一家茶馆，于是他便来到茶馆门前，把柴车停在外面，进到屋里要了一碗茶水。樵夫刚坐下喝了一会儿茶，就听见外面有人高喊：“不好了，救火啊！柴车着火了！”

thirst due to the hot weather. At this moment, he happened to see a tea house beside the road, he parked his cart out the tea house and went inside to ask for a bowl of tea. The woodcutter had just sat down to drink the tea for a while, when he heard someone shouting outside, “The firewood cart is on fire! Hurry to help!”

樵夫一听，立即站起身来，端着茶碗就冲了出去。只见车上的木柴已经噼噼啪啪地烧了起来，他急忙把茶杯里的水向燃烧的柴车泼去，但这点水太少了，丝毫不起作用。最后火越来越大，整个柴车都化为了灰烬。

The woodcutter immediately stood up and ran out with the bowl of tea water and splashed the tea water on the firing cart, but the tea water was too useless to take effect, and then the fire became strong and the whole cart of firewood were burnt out.

143

歧路亡羊

A lamb going astray at a fork in the road

出自 《列子·说符》。

释义 没有正确的方向就会误入歧途。

杨朱是战国初期伟大的思想家、哲学家，道家杨朱学派的创始人。

At the beginning of the Warring States Period, there was a person named Yang Zhu, who was a great ideologist, philosopher and the originator of Yang Zhu's Taoism school of thought.

有一天，杨朱的邻居家走失了一只羊。邻居很焦急，请了很多亲友去四处寻找。过了一会儿，他又来找杨朱请求说："先生，我想请您家的仆人帮助我去找羊。"杨朱觉得很奇怪，说："走失了一只羊，竟要派这么多人去寻找，真是小题大做！"邻居苦笑着解释说："村子外有好几条岔路，人少了是不行的。"

One day, the neighbor of Yang Zhu lost a goat and was very anxious to find it everywhere. After a while, he turned to Yang Zhu for help, "Your Teacher, could I ask for the help of your servants to find the goat?" Yang Zhu was strange and said, "It would make a fuss for too many people to find a goat!" The neighbor explained with a wry smile, "There are several forks outside the village, so I need a lot of people."

杨朱无奈，只好叫仆人帮他去找羊。过了一段时间，前去找羊的人都陆陆续续地回来了。杨朱问他们："羊找到了没有？"邻居垂头丧气地说："出村子上了大路后，有几条岔路，岔路中还有岔路。越往远走，岔路就越多，所以这么多人寻找，到后来也弄不清楚羊究竟是从哪条岔路上走

Yang Zhu had no choice but to ask his servants to help the neighbour finding the goat. After a while, the people who went to look for the goat came back one after another. Yang Zhu asked them, "Have you found the goat?" The neighbor said dejectedly, "There are some branches out of the village on the main road, and there are branches in the branches. The farther you go, the more forks there are, so even though so many people searched, they couldn't figure out which fork

失的。”

杨朱听后没有说话，神色变得忧伤起来。他的学生不解，问他说：“先生，一只羊不值多少钱，再说逃走的那只羊也不是先生家的，您为什么如此忧伤呢？”

杨朱仍然没有说话。后来有个学生把这件事告诉了一位叫心都子的学者，他解释说：“岔路太多了，所以羊容易走失。同样，读书人因学说不一致而找不到真理，就会误入歧路，一无收获。这大概就是你们先生忧伤的原因吧。”

the goat astray from.”

Yang Zhu didn’t speak aften hearing this, and turned to be sad. His student was puzzled and asked, “Your Teacher, a goat isn’t worth much, and it is not yours, why are you so sad?”

Yang Zhu still kept silent. And then, one student told this story to a scholar named Xin Du Zi, the scholar explained, “There are too many forks in the road, so it’s easy for the goat to go astray. Similarly, a scholar will also go astray in front of many inconsistent schools of thoughts, that maybe the reason why your teacher was said.”

144

狐假虎威

Ass in the lion's skin

出自 《战国策·楚策一》。

释义 凭借别人的威势来欺压人。

有一次，楚宣王问群臣："听说北方诸侯都害怕我国将领昭奚恤，果真是这

Once the King Xuan of Chu said to his ministers, "It is said that the northern vassals were all afraid of our General Zhao

样的吗？”有一位名叫江乙的大臣讲了如下故事作为回答。

Xixu, is it true?" One minister naked Jiang Yi answered as the following story.

老虎靠捕捉各种野兽作为食物，有一天，老虎捉到一只狐狸，正当它张开嘴巴，准备把狐狸吃进肚子的时候，狐狸突然说："您不敢吃我，上天派我做群兽的领袖，如果您吃掉我，就违背了上天的命令，会受到严厉的惩罚。"

The tiger always caught various wild animals for food. One day, the tiger caught a fox and when it opened his mouth and ready to eat, the fox suddenly said, "You dare not eat me. God has sent me to be the leader of the beasts. If you eat me, you will violate the command of the God and be seriously punished."

老虎听了狐狸的话，半信半疑。这时，狐狸更加神气十足地挺起胸膛，对老虎说："难道您不相信我说的话吗？那么您现在就跟我来，走在我的后面，看看群兽见了我，有哪一个敢不逃跑的。"

The tiger was dubious, and the fox took chance to puffed out its chest proudly and said, "Don't you believe in my words? Now you walk behind me and let's see which wild animal dares to run away at sight of me."

老虎信以为真。于是狐狸就大模大样地在前面开路，而老虎则小心翼翼地在后面跟着。森林里的许多小动物发现走在狐狸后面的老

The tiger was fully convinced, so the fox walked audaciously in the front and the tiger followed cautiously. At sight of the tiger, many small animals were frightened and all fled away.

虎时，都不禁大惊失色，纷纷逃散。

老虎不明白群兽是害怕自己才逃跑的，还以为它们是真的害怕狐狸呢。

The tiger took it for true that those animals were really afraid of the fox, without knowing that is was itself which frightened those animals.

“所以”，江乙说：“北方诸侯之所以畏惧昭奚恤，完全是因为大王的兵权都掌握在他的手里，他们畏惧的其实是大王的权势呀！”

The minister Jiang Yi continued to say “ The reason for the northern vassals’ fears towards Zhao Xuxi, is because he holds the military power, and what they are afraid is the power and influence of Your Majesty!”

145

狗尾续貂

Join a dog's tail to a marten

出自 《晋书·赵王伦传》。

释义 用不好的东西补接在好的东西后面，极不相称。

晋武帝司马炎死后，儿子晋惠帝司马衷继位。他对朝政一窍不通，大权落到了

After the Emperor Wu of Han Si-ma Yan died, his son, the Emperor Hui of Jin, Si-ma Zhong assumed the throne. Since he knew

贾后手里。赵王司马伦以此为借口，带兵冲入宫廷，杀死了贾后，自封为相国。不久，司马伦又废掉晋惠帝，自称皇帝。

nothing about the affairs of state, the real power fells into the hands of the Queen Jia. By this excuse, the Emperor Si-ma Lun of Zhao led troops to the imperial court and killed the Queen Jia, and ennobled himself as the Prime Minister. Before long, Si-ma Lun dethroned the Emperor Hui of Jin and enthroned himself.

司马伦称帝以后，为了收买人心，大肆分封官爵，甚至连他的一些家奴也得到了爵位，至于朝中的大臣，加官晋爵的就更多了。每到朝会的时候，宫殿里总是挤得满满的。

After Si-ma Lun became the emperor, for the purpose of buying popularity, he generally enhanced official posts and even his servants were ennobled, therefore, the imperial court became very crowded in morning meeting.

当时，皇帝左右的侍中、散骑常侍等一级高官，一般只设四人，司马伦竟设了九十七人之多。按照规定，这些人的帽子上都应该插有貂尾作装饰，可是因为设置的官员太多了，找不到那么多貂尾，最后只好用狗尾来代替。因此，当时的洛阳流传着“貂不足，狗尾续”的民谣。

At that time, usually there were only four posts for the first-class officials, but Si-ma Lun even set ninety-seven posts. According to the regulations, the hats of those officials were usually decorated with marten tails, but then it could only be replaced by dog tails because of too many officials. Thus a folk song went around in Luoyang as “Lacking of marten tails, supplement of dog tails”.

司马伦称帝才一个多

Only one month later, the vassals launched

月，各地的诸侯王就联合起来，发兵讨伐他。几十万人马杀奔洛阳，司马伦的军队抵抗不了，于是他被迫写下退位诏书，百官又迎接晋惠帝回来复位。司马伦前后仅仅做了一百天的皇帝，便被赶下了台。

attacks in unison, hundreds of thousands of soldiers attacked Luoyang and defeated Si-ma Lun's troops. So Si-ma Lun was forced to write a statement of abdicating the throne, and the Emperor Hui of Jin was enthroned again. Finally, Si-ma Lun was impeached only after one hundred days as the emperor.

146

玩物丧志

Be a playboy without ambitions

出自 《尚书·旅獒》。

释义 因贪玩某种事物而不求上进。

春秋时期，卫国有个鼎鼎大名的国君，即卫懿公。他自从当了国君后，就整日

In the Spring and Autumn Periods, there was a very famous emperor in Wei, who named the Duke Yi of Wei. As he became the emperor,

歌舞升平，一味玩乐。卫懿公尤其喜欢养鹤，对它们很是着迷。在得知他的这一爱好之后，很多大臣也都把正事丢到一边，而把心思全集中到了搜集仙鹤的事情上。卫懿公对于给自己进献仙鹤的人，也是非常的大方，要官给官，要钱给钱。

he indulged himself in songs and dance for fun all day. The Duke Yi of Wei was specially fascinated with raising cranes, so many ministers also concentrated on collecting cranes for the emperor. And the Duke Yi of Wei was very generous in awarding official posts and money to these ministers.

卫懿公把所有的鹤都集中起来，按成色把它们分为上、下两等，不同的等级享受的食宿条件也不一样。卫懿公还专门命人为爱鹤们用上等的木材打造了一辆大车，每次出行，这些鹤都会坐在车上随行。由于鹤走在队伍的最前面，如同护驾的将士，所以人们都戏称它们为“鹤将军”。

The Duke Yi of Wei assembled all the cranes and graded them into superior and inferior classes, with different accommodations. The duke also specially ordered to build up a huge cart with superior wood so that all the cranes could accompany him in the trip. Because the cart holding cranes went in the front just like guards, so people joked the cranes as the Crane Generals.

卫懿公为了养鹤，向百姓横征暴敛，人们怨声四起。当时卫国北部的少数民族北狄势力强大，看到卫国衰落，于是发兵来攻打。卫

In order to raise cranes, the Duke Yi of Wei extorted excessive taxes and levies on civilians and aroused general complaints. As Wei's nation power declined, the minority group in northern Wei, Bei Di, was strong and

懿公得到情报，大惊失色，马上让人通知各位将领准备迎战。可是，卫国的将士们都说："鹤享有俸禄和官职，就派鹤去打仗吧！"

卫懿公无奈之下，于是拜大夫渠孔为将，亲自随军去抵抗北狄。还没到边界，卫军就遇到了一些北狄士兵，只见他们三人一行、五人一伍，没有一点军队的阵式。渠孔不知这是北狄人的计策，轻率地就命人击鼓前进。北狄人假装失败逃跑，把卫军引入他们的埋伏中，把卫军团团包围。卫国士兵本来就无心作战，见到敌人如此凶猛，都丢盔卸甲而逃，卫懿公最后也被狄人杀死。

powerful, so they launched attacks on Wei. The Duke Yi of Wei was frightened at this news and immediately noticed generals for the battle. But the Wei's generals all said, "The cranes enjoy benefice and official posts, let the cranes resist the enemies!"

In despair, the Duke Yi of Wei ennobled the minister Qu Kong as the General to lead troops against the enemies. When they nearly arrived at the frontier, Wei's troops encountered some Bei Di soldiers in groups of three or five persons, without any formation of an army. Qu Kong didn't understand that it was stratagem of Bei Di and rashly led troops forward with beating drums. Bei Di troops pretended to flee away and drew Wei's troops into the ambush, and thus Wei's troops were enclosed. Since Wei's troops didn't have any morale, when they saw fierce enemies, they threw away their helmets and armors and all fled. Finally, the Duke Yi of Wei was killed by Bei Di.

147

画龙点睛

Making the finishing point

出自 唐·张彦远《历代名画记》。

释义 比喻在整体中突出重点。

南北朝时期的梁朝，有位著名的大画家叫张僧繇，他的绘画技术高超，当时梁

In Liang State of the Southern and Northern Period, a famous painter Zhang Sengyao was masterly at painting, and even the Emperor Wu of

武帝信奉佛教，修建了很多寺庙，都让他去作画。

Liang asked him to paint in many temples because the emperor believed in Buddhism.

有一年，梁武帝要张僧繇为金陵安乐寺的墙壁上画四条金龙。他答应了下来，仅用三天时间就画好了。很多人前去观看，都纷纷称赞这些龙画得栩栩如生，惟妙惟肖，就像真龙一样活灵活现。可是当人们走近一看，却发现这四条龙全都没有眼睛。

One year, the Emperor Wu of Liang ordered Zhang Sengyao to paint four golden dragons on the walls of the An Le Temple in Jinling. Zhang Sengyao agreed and finished the painting only in three days. Many people went to have a look and praised that these dragons were so vivid that they seemed to be living dragons. But when they got closer, they found none of these four dragons has eyes.

大家纷纷请求张僧繇，让他把龙的眼睛点上。张僧繇说："给龙点上眼睛并不难，但是点上了眼睛，它们就会破壁飞走了。"

People all asked Zhang Sengyao to add the eyes, Zhang Sengyao said, "It's easy to add eyes, but if I add the eyes, they will go through the walls and fly away."

人们都不相信，认为他在说谎。张僧繇没有办法，只好答应给其中的两条龙"点睛"。他当着众人的面，提起画笔，轻轻地给两条龙点上眼睛。这时，天空突然乌云密布，狂风四起，雷鸣电闪，被"点睛"的两

But people didn't believe in his words and thought he was lying, so Zhang Sengyao had to add eyes to two of the dragons under the witness of all the people. At this moment, the sky suddenly became cloudy and strongly windy with thunder rumbling and lighting flashing, and then the eyes-lightened dragons went through the walls and flied to the sky with

条龙冲破墙壁，张牙舞爪地飞向了天空。

threatening gestures.

过了一会儿，云散天晴，人们都已经被吓得目瞪口呆，一句话也说不出来。回头再看墙上，只剩下了没有被点上眼睛的两条龙。

After a while, the clouds disappeared and the sky cleared up, people were all stunned to be wordless, and only those two dragons without eyes on the wall.

148

画饼充饥

Draw cakes to alley hunger

出自 《三国志·魏书·卢毓传》。

释义 用空想来安慰自己或欺骗别人。

三国时期，魏国有个人名叫卢毓。他十岁的时候就成了孤儿。后来，他

In the Three Kingdoms Period, there was a person named Lu Yu, who lost parents in his ten years old. And then, his two brothers passed

的两个哥哥又先后去世，他努力奉养寡嫂和侄儿，因而颇受人们的赞扬。

away successively, so he had to work hard to nourish his widowed sister-in-law and nephew, which was greatly praised by people.

卢毓后来做了官，因为他为人忠厚，学识渊博，魏文帝把他提拔为侍中。在职三年，卢毓提出过很多好的建议，魏文帝于是又提拔他担任吏部尚书，并且要卢毓推荐一个人接替侍中的职位。卢毓推荐了郑冲。魏文帝说："这个人你不推荐我也知道，你重新推举一个我不知道的人吧。"卢毓又推举了阮武和孙邕二人，后来，魏文帝选择孙邕担任了侍中。

Then Lu Yu became an official, and the Emperor Wen of Wei promoted him to the Counselor due to his honesty and profound knowledge. During the three years of his office, Lu Yu had proposed many good suggestions, so the Emperor Wen of Wei promoted him to the Minister of Personnel and asked him to recommend a person to take over his original post of counselor. Lu Yu recommended Zheng Chong. The Emperor Wen of Wei said, "I know the person you recommended, please recommend another one I don't know." Lu Yu recommended Ruan Wu and Sun Yong, and the Emperor Wen of Wei selected Sun Yong.

有一次，魏文帝对卢毓说："国家能不能得到有才能的人，关键就在你了。选拔人才，不要只看那些有名声的，名声不过像在地上画的饼一样，是不能吃的。"卢毓回答说："靠名声不可能得到真正有才能的人，只

Once, the Emperor Wen of Wei said to Lu Yu, "You are very important in selecting talents for our country, you shouldn't promote those prestigious people only, because the reputation is just like the drawing cake and inedible." Lu Yu answered, "The reputation is not the only criterion for judging a person's talent, relying on reputation can only find ordinary talents.

能发现一般的人才。我认为最好对他们进行考核，看他们是否真有才学。现在废除了考试法，全看一个人的名声进行提拔或降职，所以真伪难辨，虚实混淆。”魏文帝采纳了卢毓的意见，下令制定考试法，用推荐和考试相结合的办法录用人才，受到了人们的称赞。

I think it is best to take exams for them. But nowadays the examination is abolished, the reputation become the only judgement for promotion or demotion, so it's difficult to distinguish." The Emperor Wen of Wei took Lu Yu's suggestions and ordered to establish examination system, and use the way of both examination and recommendation to distinguish talents, which was greatly praised by people.

149

画蛇添足

Gild the Lily

出自 《战国策·齐策二》。

释义 自作聪明，反而弄巧成拙。

楚国有一家人，在祭祀完祖先之后，把祭祀用的一壶酒，赏给手下的办事人员

There was a family in Chu State, after they finished worshiping their ancestors, they would award the wine to the servants. But only one

喝。因为参加的人很多，一壶酒让大家都喝肯定不够，但如果让一个人喝，就能喝个痛快。可是，这一壶酒到底给谁喝呢？

jug of wine was not enough for so many people, and that would be fine if only one person drink this jug of wine. So who would drink this jug of wine?

这时候，有个人建议说，咱们每个人在地上画一条蛇，谁画得又快又好，就把这壶酒归他喝。大家都认为这个办法好，都同意了。于是，就在地上画起蛇来。

At the moment, someone suggested holding a contest for drawing a snake on the ground, and the person drew best and fastest would win this jug of wine. People all agreed and began to draw.

其中有个人画得很快，没几下就最先画好了。他一边端起酒壶准备喝，一边回头看看别人，发现大家还都没有画好呢。他心里十分得意，于是又拿起一根树枝，给蛇画起脚来，并且炫耀说："你们画得好慢啊，我再给蛇画几只脚也不算晚！"

One person drew fast and was the first to finish. He took up the jug and prepared to drink, at this time, he turned back to look at other people who didn't finish yet. So he was very proud and took up the branch to draw feet for the snake, he also showed off, "You draw so slowly, it will not be late for me to add several feet for the snake."

正在他给蛇画着脚的时候，另外一个人已经画好了。那个人一把把酒壶从他的手里夺过去，说："你见过蛇吗？蛇是没有脚的，你为什么要给

When he was drawing the feet, another person finished drawing and took over the jug of wine from his hand and said, "Have you ever seen the snake? The snake has no feet, why do you add feet to it? You draw it wrongly, so I

他添上脚呢？你画错了，所以这壶酒应该归我了！”

win the jug of wine.”

那个人说完，就仰起头来，咕咚咕咚把酒喝了下去。而那个给蛇画脚的人，只能是满脸尴尬，在一旁眼巴巴地看着。

And then the second man drank the wine with his head up. That person who added feet to the snake could only stand there awkwardly, and watching eagerly.

150

空中楼阁

Castles in the air

出自 《百喻经·三重楼喻》。

释义 指脱离实际的理论、计划及空想。

从前有个愚蠢无知的富翁，有一天，他去拜访另外一位富翁。那位富翁的家是

Once upon a time, a stupid rich man went to visit another rich man who had a bright and spacious house gorgeously

一个三层楼，建造得十分华丽美观，明亮宽敞。富翁心中非常羡慕，他呆呆地望着人家的楼房，暗暗地想：我的钱财一点儿也不比他少，为什么不可以建造一座这样高大美观的楼房呢？

built with three floors. The stupid rich man admired very much and stared at the house blankly and thought, "I also have lots of money, why not build up a such a beautiful big house?"

富翁回到家里以后，马上就把当地的工匠找来，问道："那座气派非凡的高楼是你建的吗？"工匠回答说："是我建的。"富翁很高兴，对工匠说："你也照它的样子给我建一座高楼吧。"工匠答应了。

When the rich man came back home, he called in the local craftsman and asked, "Is that impressive house built by you?" The craftsman said, "Yes, it's me." The rich man was glad and said, "Please build up a same one for me." The craftsman agreed.

没过多久，工匠就动手打地基，开始建造高楼了。富翁看到后，感到奇怪，就问："你们这是干什么呢？"工匠答道："建三层楼房啊。"富翁听了，直摇脑袋，着急地说："我不要下面两层，赶快给我建造最上面的第三层。"工匠听了他的话，哭笑不得，耐着性

Before long, the craftsman began to lay the foundations, and the rich man felt strange and asked, "What are you doing?" The craftsman answered, "I'm building the three-floor house for you." The rich man was anxious to say, "I don't want the lower two floors, please hurry to build the uppermost third floor." The craftsman was at a loss whether to cry or to laugh, but he still explained patiently, "The third floor can't be built without building the first and second

子给他解释说："如果不造第一层和第二层，第三层是建不起来的。"富翁却仍然坚持他的意见："我不要下面两层，你们一定要给我建最上面的那层。"

floors." Whereas the rich man still clung to his mind, "Anyway, I don't want the lower two floors, you must only build the uppermost third floor for me."

人们听说了这件事情后，都觉得这个富翁真是太愚蠢可笑了。

People all felt that the rich man was too stupid and ridiculous.

151

金玉其外，败絮其中

A dandy but deceitful appearance

出自 明·刘基《卖柑者言》。

释义 外表很华美，里面却一团糟。

刘基字伯温，是元末明初的军事家、政治家、文学家，明朝开国元勋。他在

Liu Ji with his style name of Bowen, was a militarist, politician, litterateur and one of founding fathers of Ming Dynasty by the end

杭州的时候，有一次去买水果，遇到一个卖水果的人。这个人很会储藏柑橘，保存的柑橘经过一个冬天和一个夏天都不会腐烂，橘皮鲜红滋润，非常好看。因此他卖的柑橘的价格虽然很高，买的人却不少。

刘基向他买了一个柑橘，剥开皮以后，发现里面的果瓤干得就像棉絮一样，没法食用。刘基气愤地责问道："你为什么弄虚作假欺骗顾客？"卖柑橘的人笑了笑，说："我做这个生意已经很多年了，我愿意卖，人家愿意买，谁都没意见，只有您不满意。您可知道，当今世上欺骗人的多的是。那些腰间佩着兵符好像是保卫国家的武将，难道真有孙子、吴起的作战本领吗？那些头戴乌纱帽神气十足的人，难道真是治国的人才吗？其实他们也没多大本

of Yuan and the beginning of Ming periods. When he was in Hangzhou, he went to buy fruit and met a fruit seller who was good at storing tangerines. He could keep them fresh for a periods of winter and summer, with red and good-looking tangerine peels. So many people chose to buy his tangerines in spite of the high price.

Liu Ji bought a tangerine and opened it, but he found it was wizened as cotton fibre and uneatable at all. Liu Ji scolded angrily, "Why you practise fraud and cheat the customers?" The man smiled and said, "I've doing business for many years, I'm willing to sell and people are willing to buy without any discontent except for you! Do you know there are many people practising fraud? Do those military officers wearing commander's seals really have the capability of Sun Zi and Wu Qi? Are those people wearing official hats really the talents for governance? In fact, they are not capable at all and only concentrate on fulfilling themselves by wasting the food and money of our country, who are just like the tangerines I sell, glossy outside but rotten inside."

事，只顾自己吃饱了肚子，耗费国家的粮食和钱财。这些人和我卖的柑橘一样，看起来光鲜亮丽，但是肚子里什么能耐都没有。”

刘基听了这番话，哑口无言。回到家里后，他写了《卖柑者言》这篇文章，其中就有“金玉其外，败絮其中”之句。

Liu Ji was rendered speechless upon his wording, so he went home and wrote *The Words of Tangerines-selling Man*, with the sentence of “a dandy but deceitful appearance.

152

金石为开

Sincerity can make metal and stone crack

出自 晋·葛洪《西京杂记》。

释义 只要专心诚意去做，什么疑难问题都能解决。

西汉时期，有个著名的将领，名叫李广，被称为飞将军。李广天生口齿笨拙，

In the Western Han Dynasty, there was a famous general named Li Guang, who was praised as the Flying General. Li Guang was

不善言谈，可身材高大，臂力超人，精通射箭。

born with a clumsy tongue and not talkative, but he had a tall figure and strong arm muscle, with proficiency in archery.

有一次，他到郊外去打猎，忽然发现前面的草丛里蹲卧着一只猛虎，正在等待捕捉食物。李广立刻振作精神，瞄准老虎，拉弓搭箭，用足力气射出一箭，正中老虎。李广等了一会儿，看老虎一动不动，就大着胆子走近前去，仔细一看，原来被射中的根本不是什么老虎，而是一块形状像老虎的大石头。刚才那一箭不仅深深地射入石头当中，而且箭尾也几乎全部没入了石头。

Once he went hunting, and he suddenly found a fierce tiger crouching down on the ground and waited to catch prey. Li Guang immediately kept up his spirits, he drew the bow and fitted the arrow. After he aimed at the tiger, he used his gull strength to shot an arrow exactly at it. Li Guang waited for a moment and emboldened himself to have a look at the still tiger, but when he got closer, he found it was a tiger-shaped big stone instead of a real tiger. The arrow was deeply shot to the inside of the stone with the tail of the arrow nearly embedded completely.

李广很惊讶，他不相信自己能有这么大的力气，于是想再试一试，就往后退了几步，张弓搭箭，用力向石头射去。可是，一连几箭都没有射进去。

Li Guang was surprised at his such great strength and wanted to try again, so he took a few steps back, fitted the arrow and drew the bow at the stone with his full strength. Whereas, not a single arrow was shot into the stone.

人们听说这件事以后，感到很惊奇，疑惑不解，于

People all felt puzzled by this news and went to ask the scholar Yang Xiong. Yang

是就去请教学者扬雄。扬雄回答说：如果做事时保持专心诚意，即使像金石那样坚硬的东西也会被感动的。“精诚所至，金石为开”这一成语也就由此流传了下来。

Xiong answered, “If a person focuses all of his mind on one thing, even something as hard as stone would be moved.” Thus the idiom of “sincerity can make metal and stone crack” became popular from then on.

153

金屋藏娇

Keep a mistress in a love nest

出自 汉·班固《汉武故事》。

释义 建造华丽的房屋让所爱的妻妾居住。

中国历史上赫赫有名的汉武帝刘彻，他的原配妻子陈皇后，小名叫阿娇，

Liu Che was well-known as the Emperor Wu of Han in Chinese history, his first wife was the Queen Chen with her childhood name as

父亲是堂邑陈午，是汉朝的开国功勋；母亲是汉景帝刘启的同母姐姐馆陶长公主，也是当时朝廷中举足轻重的人物。

A Jiao. The father of the Queen was Chen Wu who was one of the founding father of Han, and the mother of the Queen was the eldest Guan Tao Princess as the biological sister of the Emperor Jing of Han, Liu Qi, She was also an important person in the current imperial court.

汉武帝刘彻是汉景帝的嫔妃王美人所生，排行第九。景帝一共有十四个儿子，其中宠妃栗姬生育了皇长子刘荣，最初被立为太子。

The Emperor Wu of Han, Liu Che, was born by the concubine of Emperor Jing, Beauty Wang, as the ninth seniority. The Emperor Jing had fourteen sons, therein, the eldest son Liu Rong was born by his beloved concubine Li Ji and primitively ennobled as the Prince.

馆陶长公主打算将女儿阿娇许配给太子刘荣，期望日后成为皇后。她派人去探询栗姬的意思，谁知栗姬怨恨长公主经常向景帝进献美女，使皇帝不能专宠自己，竟然断然拒绝。馆陶长公主非常生气，于是起了废掉太子之心。

The eldest Guan Tao Princess intended to marry her daughter A Jiao to the Prince Liu Rong, expecting her daughter to be the Queen in the future. She sent someone to inquire about Li Ji's intentions, but Li Ji hated the eldest Guan Tao Princess because she always contributed beauties to the Emperor Jing and made Li Ji unable to be specially beloved, so Li Ji flatly refused. The eldest Guan Tao was very angry and intended to dethrone the Prince.

一天，馆陶长公主抱着刘彻问：“彻儿长大了要讨媳妇吗？”刘彻说：

Once day, the eldest Guan Tao Princess hugged Liu Che and asked, “Do you want a wife when you grow up?” Liu Che answered,

“要啊。”长公主于是指着左右的侍女，问刘彻想要哪个，刘彻都说不要。最后长公主指着自己的女儿阿娇，问：“那阿娇好不好呢？”刘彻笑着说：“好啊！如果能娶阿娇做妻子，我一定会造一个金屋子给她住。”

此后，为了报复栗姬，让女儿成为一国之母，馆陶长公主不时在景帝面前说栗姬的坏话，还经常夸赞刘彻，最终使得景帝废掉太子刘荣，并把刘彻立为太子。

“Of course!” The eldest Guan Tao Princess pointed at the maidservants standing on the two sides asked which one he liked, but Liu Che said no one is what he liked. And then, the eldest Guan Tao Princess pointed at her daughter A Jiao and asked, “Do you like A Jiao?” Liu Che smiled and said, “I like A Jiao, and if I could marry her, I will build a golden house for her.”

Afterwards, in order to revenge on Li Ji and help her daughter to become the queen, the eldest Guan Tao Princess always spoke ill of Li Ji and spoke well of Liu Che. And finally, she persuaded the Emperor Jing to dethrone the Prince Liu Rong and enthrone Liu Che as the Prince.

154

鱼目混珠

Pass fish eyes for pearls

出自 汉·魏伯阳《参同契》卷上。

释义 以假乱真，以次充好。

从前，有一个叫满意的人。一次，他到南方去办事，在一家不起眼的铺子

Once upon a time, there was a person named Man Yi. Once he went southward for business and saw an impressive big pearl which

里，看到一颗以前从来没见过的大珍珠，于是用身上所有的钱和值钱的物品，把它买了下来。回到家以后，满意用上好的木材做了一个盒子，上面镶嵌了金银和其他宝物，然后把珍珠放在里面，严密地收藏起来。只有在遇到重大的节日时，才拿出来给两三个知己欣赏一番。

he had never seen before, so he spent all his money and valuable articles to buy it. When he came back home, Man Yi made a wooden box inlaid with gold, silver and other precious treasures, and then he cautiously store the pearl in the box. Only by the occasions of important festivals, he would took it out for appreciation with his bosom friends.

邻居寿量听说了这件事，非常羡慕，自己也很想拥有这么一颗大珍珠。有一次，寿量在路上发现了一颗很大的鱼眼睛，误以为是珍珠，就捡回家，然后到外面大肆宣扬。

His neighbor Shou Liang heard of it and admired so much that he also wished to have a same big pearl. Once Shou Liang found a big fish eye on the way, he mistakenly thought it as pearl, so he took it home and whooped it up everywhere.

不久，两人都得了一种奇怪的病，卧床不起。家里人为他们请了一个郎中，看过病人，郎中说这种病需要珍珠粉来和药，才能药到病除。

Before long, both Man Yi and Shou Liang got a strange disease and remained in bed. Their family invited a doctor and the doctor said, “The medicine will be effective if you blend it with pearl powder.”

两个人各自用自己的珍珠和药吃下，满意很快就好

Then Man Yi and Shou Liang individually took the medicine blended with their own pearl,

了；寿量却没有什么作用，就又去找那个郎中来看。郎中说："你把你用的珍珠给我看一下。"寿量把剩下的珍珠拿了出来。郎中一看，大笑着说："这哪是什么珍珠，它就是海洋中一种大鱼的眼睛。真是鱼目混珠啊！"

and then Man Yi recovered very soon, but Shou Liang didn't recover, so he invited the doctor again. The doctor said, "Let me have a look at the pearl you used." Shou Liang took out the remaining pearl, the doctor laughed and said, "This is not pearl at not, it is a fish eye. You're really pass fish eyes for pearls!"

155

举棋不定

Of two minds

出自 《左传·襄公二十五年》。

释义 犹豫不决，拿不定主意。

春秋时期的卫国国君卫献公骄横粗暴，大臣孙文子和宁惠子发动军事政变，把

In the Spring and Autumn Periods, because the Emperor Xian of Wei was arrogant and rude, so the ministers Sun Wen Zi and Ning Hui

他赶下了台。卫献公带着母亲和弟弟逃到齐国，过着流亡的生活。此后，孙文子和宁惠子二人就掌握了朝政大权，并拥立卫殇公为国君。

Zi launched a military coup to impeach him. The Emperor Xian of Wei fled to Qi state with his mother and younger brother, living in exile. Then Sun Wen Zi and Ning Hui Zi held the imperial power and enthroned the Duke Shang of Wei as the emperor.

当宁惠子病得快要死的时候，他开始后悔，觉得驱逐国君是一件耻辱的事，于是嘱咐他的儿子宁悼子把卫献公接回来。同时，逃亡在外的卫献公也在积极活动图谋复国，他派人与宁悼子联系，承诺回国后绝不掌管朝政，全部由宁悼子处理。于是宁悼子欣然同意。

When Ning Hui Zi was nearly ill to death, he began to regret and realized that expelling the emperor was a humiliating doing, so he dispatched his son Ning Dao Zi to take the Duke Xian of Wei back to country. At the same time, the Duke Xian of Wei in exile was positively scheming at recover his imperial power and he forwarded his promise to Ning Dao Zi that he would not take hold of the imperial power and all the affairs of state would be decided by Ning Dao Zi, thus Ning Dao Zi agreed.

但是，有不少大夫反对献公复位。大夫右宰穀见了献公以后，回来劝宁悼子说："献公虽然在外流亡十二年，但粗暴的脾气一点没有变，要让他回来，大家的死期就到了。"另一位大

Whereas, some ministers are opposed to recover the Duke Xian. After the minister You-zai Hu met the Duke Xian, he persuaded Ning Dao Zi, "Although the Duke Xian was in exile for twelve years, his rude tempers don't change at all. If you take him back, all of us will die." Another minister Da Shuyi also persuaded Ning

夫大叔仪也劝告宁悼子说："下棋的人举着棋子犹豫不决，不知所措，就不能战胜对手。对待国君这样的大事，如果摇摆不定，一定会招来灭族之祸。"

宁悼子不顾大夫们的劝告，把献公接了回来。卫献公复位后，为了报自己被宁氏驱逐之仇，最终还是杀掉了宁悼子。

Dao Zi, "If a chess player holds a chess hesitantly without any decisions, then he will not defeat the opponent. Similarly, if you are of two minds on such important matters regarding the future emperor, you will certainly bring the disaster of extermination on your entire family."

But Ning Dao Zi ignored the persuasions of the ministers and took the Duke Xian back to country. After the Duke Xian completed the restoration, for revenging on the hatred of being expelled, he finally killed Ning Dao Zi.

156

削足适履

Cut the feet to fit the shoes

出自 汉·刘安《淮南子·说林训》。

释义 不顾具体条件，生搬硬套。

刘安所著的《淮南子》中记载有这么两个故事。

第一个故事是：春秋

In Huai Nan Zi written by Liu An, there are two little stories.

The first story is as the following. In the

时期，有一次楚灵王亲自率领军队征伐蔡国，攻下蔡国后，楚灵王便让自己的弟弟弃疾留守蔡国，全权处理那里的军政要务，然后他带领大军继续推进，准备一举灭掉徐国。弃疾并不甘心仅仅当个地方首脑，常常为此而闷闷不乐。他的手下有个叫朝吴的谋士,看出他的心思，就劝他说："现在楚王率军出征在外，国内空虚，你不妨在此时引兵回国，杀掉灵王的儿子，另立新君，然后由你掌管朝政，将来当上国君还成什么问题吗！"弃疾听了朝吴的话，带兵返回楚国，杀死灵王的儿子，把灵王的另外一个儿子子比立为国君。楚灵王听说儿子被弟弟杀死，非常心寒，就上吊自杀了。弃疾得知楚灵王死了，马上逼迫子比自杀，自立为王，这就是臭名昭著的楚平王。

Spring and Autumn Periods, the Emperor Ling of Chu personally led troops to attack Cai State. When Cai State was defeated, the Emperor Ling of Chu asked his younger brother Qi Ji to stay in Cai for completely handling the military affairs, and he led troops to move forward for purpose of defeating Xu State at one stroke. Qi Ji was reluctant to be a local leader and always upset. One counsellor Zhao Wu read his minds and persuaded, "Now the Emperor of Chu personally led troops and the treasury was empty, why don't you lead troops back to kill the son of the Emperor Ling and enthrone a new emperor? If you take hold of the imperial power, you will probably become the emperor!" Qi Ji followed Zhao Wu's words and led troops back to Chu State, then he killed the son of the Emperor Ling ans enthroned another son Zi Bi as the Emperor. When the Emperor Ling of Chu heard that his son was killed by his younger brother, he was so depressed and hang himself to death. When Qi Ji heard of the death of the Emperor Ling, he immediately forced Zi Bi to suicide and enthroned himself as the emperor, which was the notorious Emperor Ping of Chu.

另一个故事是：晋献公宠爱骊姬，对她言听计从。骊姬提出要将自己所生的幼子奚齐立为太子，晋献公满口答应，并将原来的太子杀害了。因为晋献公还有重耳和夷吾两个儿子，骊姬觉得他们对奚齐将来继承王位是极大的威胁，又建议杀了重耳和夷吾，晋献公竟然也同意了。他们的密谋正巧被一位正直的大臣听到，立即转告了重耳和夷吾，二人听说后，立即分头跑到国外避难去了。

刘安评论这两件事说："听信坏人的话，使父子兄弟自相残杀，就像砍去脚趾去适应鞋的大小一样，太不明智了。"

Another story is as the following. The Emperor Xian of Jin specially beloved Li Ji and completely followed her words. Once Li Ji proposed to enthrone her biological son Xi Qi as the Prince, and the Emperor Xian of Jin agreed and killed the former prince. Because the Emperor Xian of Jin still had two sons named Chong Er and Yi Wu, and Li Ji took them as an extreme threat to the future throne, so she proposed to kill Chong Er and Yi Wu, and the Emperor Xian of Jin also agreed. One minister happened to hear about their conspiracy and noticed Chong Er and Yi Wu at once, who immediately fled to other countries.

Liu An made comments on these two stories, "Following the words of evil people and making brothers or father and sons kill each other, is just like cutting off feet to fit the shoes, which is really unwise".

157

前倨后恭

Change from arrogance to humility

出自 《史记·苏秦列传》。

释义 对人的态度前后截然不同。

苏秦是战国时期著名的外交家和谋略家，师从鬼谷子。学成后，他周游列国，

In the Warring States Period, there was a famous diplomatist and tactician named Su Qin, who learned after Gui guzi. After he completed

向各国国君阐述自己的政治主张，但没有一个国君采纳他的意见。苏秦身无分文，垂头丧气，穿着旧衣破鞋回到家乡洛阳。

his study, he traveled around various countries for propagation of his political opinions, but not a single emperor took his advice. Ad Su Qin was penniless and depressed, he went home with worn clothes and shoes.

回到家里，家人见他如此落魄，都不给他好脸色。妻子父母都不跟他说话，他的嫂子不但不给做饭，还狠狠地训斥了他一顿。

When he came back home, his family all looked down upon him due to his poverty, and even his wife and parents refused to talk with him, and his sister-in-law strictly scolded him and refused to cook for him.

苏秦心里非常难过，只怪自己学问不到家，没能取得荣华富贵。因此他立志苦读，钻研学问。一年后，他又到赵国游说，受到赵王重用，被封为武安君。苏秦接着又说服了当时的齐、楚、燕、韩、赵、魏六国联合抗秦，并兼任六国的国相。

Su Qin was very depressed and blamed himself for not gaining prosperity and wealth due to lack of knowledge. Thus he was determined to study hard. One year later, he traveled to Zhao State for propagation again, and this time he was employed in an important position and ennobled as the Duke Wu An. Afterwards, Su Qin persuaded the current six countries to attack Qin in union, including Qi, Chu, Yan, Han, Zhao and Wei, and Su Qin took the additional post of Prime Minister of the six countries.

有一次，苏秦因公事路过洛阳，前呼后拥，声势威严，老百姓都赶来迎送。他的父母拄着拐杖，在三十

Once Su Qin passed by Luoyang, many civilians came out for welcome, with a blockbuster of retinue. His parents waited on the crutch at the big crossroad thirty miles

里外的大路口等候。回到家里，妻子躲在旁边，都不敢正眼看他。而他的嫂子则慌忙趴在地下，连连磕头恕罪。苏秦笑道："嫂子，为什么从前傲慢无礼，现在这么恭敬呢？"他的嫂子说："因为您的地位尊贵，又有钱。"苏秦叹息说："唉！贫贱的时候则父母不认亲子，富贵的时候则妻嫂畏惧。人生在世，又怎么能忽视钱财地位这些身外之物呢！"

away. When he came back home, his wife hided in the side and dared not to look at him directly. His sister-in-law hurriedly kneed on the ground and constantly kowtowed for forgiveness. Su Qin smiled and said, "Sister-in-law, why are you arrogant before and so humble now?" His sister-in-law answered, "Because you are noble and rich now." Su Qin sighed, "Alas! The parents disown their son due to his poverty, and the wife and sister-in-law dread due to his richness. So a person shouldn't ignore those worldly possessions such as money and status!"

158

南辕北辙

Poles apart

出自 汉·刘向《战国策·魏策》。

释义 比喻行动和目的正好相反。

战国末期，魏国国力逐渐衰弱，可是魏王仍想出兵攻打赵国。魏国谋臣

By the end of the Warring States Period, although the national power weakened, the Emperor of Wei still wanted to attack Zhao

季梁当时正奉命出使邻邦，听到这个消息，立刻从半路上折返回来，风尘仆仆地去求见魏王，劝阻他讨伐赵国。

State. The Wei's counselor Ji Liang was going to serve as an envoy in the neighboring state by the imperial order, and when hearing of this news, he immediately went back in a hurry to dissuade the emperor for attack.

季梁对魏王说："今天我回来的时候，在大路上遇见一个人赶着车，正在朝着北面前行。他告诉我，说他想到楚国去。我问他，楚国在南边，你为什么反而往北走呢。他说，不要紧，我的马好，跑得快。我提醒他，马虽然不错，但是这也不是去楚国的路啊。那人指着车上的口袋说，不要紧，我带的路费多。我告诉他，即使路费很多，但这样也去不了楚国啊。他又说，不要紧，我的车夫特别擅长赶车。这个人真是太糊涂了，他的方向不对，即使马跑得特别快，路费带得特别多，马夫特别会赶车，却只能使他离目的地越远。"

Ji Liang said to the Emperor of Wei, "Today when I'm back on the way, I saw a person was driving his cart northwards. He told me he would go to Chu State. I asked him why he took the opposite direction because Chu State was in the south. But that person told me it didn't matter because his horse could run very fast. I reminded him no matter how fast the horse could run, it was the wrong direction. That person pointed at the bag on the cart and told me it didn't matter because he took lots of money. I told him it was the wrong direction to Chu State in spite of enough money. That person told me his driver was very good at driving cart. That person was really very stupid, he took the wrong direction, so even if his horse could run very fast, he took enough money and his driver was good at driving cart, he would not arrive at his destination."

说到这里，季梁话锋一转，说："如今，大王要成就霸业，一举一动都要取信于天下，才能树立权威，使得众望所归。如果仗着国家强大，军队精良，动不动就进攻其他国家，就不能建立威信，正像那个要去南方的人反而朝北走一样，只能离成就霸业的目标越来越远了。"

At this moment, Ji Liang turned the subject and said, " Nowadays, if Your Majesty wants to be the king of the world, it is necessary to be cautious about your each and every move, in order to convince people, establish your prestige and gain popular confidence. If you frequently launch attacks on other countries just counting upon our strong national power and picked troops, you will not establish your prestige, just like that person took a northward way opposite to his southward destination, it will be more and more difficult for you to become the king of the world."

魏王听了季梁的一席话，恍然大悟，便停止了伐赵的打算。

The Emperor of Wei was suddenly enlightened and stopped the plan of attacking Zhao State.

159

拾人牙慧

Follow suit

出自 《世说新语·文学》。

释义 拾取别人的只言片语当作自己的话。

殷浩是晋朝人，很有学问，尤其喜好《老子》和《易经》，并能引经据典

In the Jin Dynasty, there was a person named Yin Hao who was learned, as he specially liked to read *Lao Zi and the Book*

谈得头头是道，因此受到那些风流辩士们的推崇。曾经有人问殷浩："将要做官而梦见棺材，将要发财而梦见大粪，这是为什么呢？"殷浩回答说："官本是腐臭之物，所以将要做官而梦见死尸；钱本是粪土，所以将要发财而梦见粪便。"当时的人都认为这是至理名言。

of Changes and could even cite the classic chapters clearly and logically, so he was admired by those talented and romantic debaters. Someone once asked Yin Hao, "A person will secure official position if he dreams of coffin, and a person will make a fortune if he dreams of faeces, what's the reason?" Yin Hao answered, "The official position is originally putrid, so a person will secure official position if he dreams of dead bodies, and the money is originally faeces, so a person will make a fortune if he dreams of faeces." People of the time all thought it as words of wisdom.

殷浩曾被任命为建武将军，统领扬州、豫州、徐州、兖州、青州的兵马，后来因为作战失败被罢免官职，并流放到信安（今浙江省境内）。

Yin Hao was once appointed as the Genenal of Jian Wu, leading troops in Yangzhou, Yuzhou, Xuzhou, Yanzhou and Qingzhou. Afterwards, he was removed from his post due to failure in a battle and exiled to Xin'an, which is the current Zhejiang Province.

殷浩有个外甥名叫韩康伯，非常聪明，也善于谈吐。殷浩很喜欢他，但对他的要求却十分严格。殷浩被流放的时候，韩康伯也随同前往。有一次，殷浩看到

Yin Hao had a nephew named Han Kangbo who was very smart and eloquent. Yin Hao liked him very much and was strict with him. When Yin Hao was in exile, Han Kangbo also accompanied. Once Yin Hao saw his nephew was making comments by mechanically

他正在对别人发表言论，仔细一听，他所讲的完全是抄袭自己的片言只语，套用自己说过的话，没有他个人的创见，却还露出一副洋洋得意的样子。殷浩很不高兴，说：“康伯连我咀嚼后剩下的渣滓都没得到，就自以为了不起，真不应该啊。”

copying his words without any his individual opinions with a jaunty looking. Yin Hao was unhappy and said, “Kangbo should not have be like that because he even doesn’t get the left scum after my chewing.”

160

指鹿为马

Call white black

出自 《史记·秦始皇本纪》

释义 故意颠倒黑白，混淆是非。

秦始皇死后，赵高和李斯为了保住自己的权势，假传圣旨，命令本应继承皇位

Upon the death of the First Emperor of Qin, in order to keep their own power, Zhao Gao and Li Si issued a false decree and ordered

的秦始皇大儿子扶苏自杀身亡，立次子胡亥即位，也就是秦二世。赵高自己担任宰相，处在一人之下，万人之上的位置。但他仍不满足，日夜盘算着要篡夺皇位，可是又不清楚朝中大臣有多少人能听从他，有多少人反对他，于是心生一计，准备试一试自己的威信。

the emperor's oldest son Fu Su to suicide and enthrone the second son Hu Hai as the Second Emperor of Qin. Zhao Gao was the Prime Minister who was second only to the emperor, but he was still unsatisfied and schemed at usurping the throne day and night. He was wondering how many people would submit to him and how many people would oppose him, so he hit upon an idea to sound out his own prestige.

一天上朝时，赵高让人牵来一只鹿，对秦二世说："陛下，我献给您一匹好马。"秦二世一看，笑着对赵高说："丞相搞错了，这是一只鹿，你怎么说是马呢？"赵高却坚持说："请陛下看清楚，这的确是一匹千里马。"秦二世又仔细看了看，问道："马的头上怎么会长角呢？"赵高转身指着众大臣，大声说："陛下如果不信我的话，可以问问众位大臣啊。"

One day in the imperial court, Zhao Gao led a deer in the court and said to the Second Emperor of Qin, "Your Majesty, I will contribute you a good horse." The Second Emperor of Qin had a look and smiled, "You Prime Minister must mistake, it is a deer, why do you call it a horse?" Zhao Gao insisted, "Your Majesty, please take a look carefully, it is really a swift horse." The Second Emperor of Qin took a closer look and asked, "Why does a horse have a horn on its head?" Zhao Gao turned around and said loudly, "If Your Majesty don't believe me, you could ask those ministers."

朝堂上站着的大臣们顿

All the ministers in the court were

时都不知所措，那些胆小又有点正义感的人都低下头，不敢说话。而那些平时就巴结赵高的小人，都纷纷跳出来赞成赵高的说法，对皇上说："这确是一匹千里马！"而只有不多的几个胆大正直的人，坚持认为是鹿而不是马。

suddenly at a loss and those timid ministers even lower their heads without any words. But those vile people usually flattering Zhao Gao all agreed Zhao Gao's opinion and said to the emperor, "It is indeed a swift horse!" Only few bold and upright ministers insisted that it was a deer instead of a horse.

后来，赵高通过各种手段，把那些不顺从自己的正直大臣都治了罪，有的甚至满门抄斩。

Then by various means, Zhao Gao finally convicted those upright and insubordinate ministers of crimes and some ministers were even executed family extermination.

161

按图索骥

By following up a clue

出自 《汉书·梅福传》。

释义 比喻办事机械死板。

春秋时期，有个秦国人叫孙阳，是个非常有名的相马专家，他一眼就能看出一

In the Spring and Autumn Periods, there was a person named Sun Yang in Qin State, who was a famous horse expert and able to

匹马的好坏。因为传说中负责管理天上马匹的神仙叫伯乐，所以人们都把孙阳称作伯乐。

distinguish good and bad horses only at one glance. According to the legends, there was an immortal named Bo Le who was responsive to supervise heaven horses, so people all name Sun Yang as Bo Le.

伯乐曾经把自己鉴别马匹的知识和经验写成了一本书，叫《相马经》，书里写了各种各样的千里马的特征，并画了不少插图，供人们作为识马的参考。

Bo Le once wrote a book named *On Distinguishing Horses* on the basis of his own knowledge and experiences, describing the characteristics of various swift horses with many pictures for people's reference.

伯乐有个儿子，资质很差，他读了这本书以后，自以为学到了父亲的本领，便照着书上说的到处去找寻千里马。有一次他见到一只癞蛤蟆，赶忙抓了回去，告诉他父亲说："《相马经》上说千里马的主要特征是高脑门，大眼睛，蹄子像摞起来的酒曲块。我找到的这匹马，和你说的差不多，只是蹄子不像摞起来的酒曲块！"

The son of Bo Le was poor in his qualification, and after he finished reading this book, he thought he had grasped the skills of his father, so he began to find swift horses according to the book. Once he saw a toad, he hurried to seize it and told his father, "According to *On Distinguishing Horses*, the main characteristics of swift horses are high forehead, big eyes and feet like piled blocks of yeast. This horse I seized is similar to what you said, merely the feet are not so like piled blocks of yeast!"

伯乐看着儿子逮回来

Bo Le looked at the toad seized by his

的癞蛤蟆，又好笑又好气地说：“这匹马爱跳，没办法骑啊！”

son, he felt angry and funny, “But you can’t ride on this so-called horse because it likes to jump!”

162

狡兔三窟

A wily hare has three burrows

出自 《战国策·齐策四》。

释义 比喻藏身的地方特别多。

战国时期，齐国的孟尝君门下养了三千宾客，其中有一个叫冯谖，是个很有才能的人，但一直没有受到孟尝君的重视。

In the Warring States Period, the Lord Meng Chang provided for three thousand guests, therein, a person named Feng Xuan was very capable, but was not paid important attention by the Lord Meng Chang.

一天，孟尝君对各位宾

One day, the lord said to his guests, "I lent

客说："我在薛地放了不少债，谁能为我去收取本利？"冯谖抢着说："我愿意去。"孟尝君点头同意。冯谖又问道："我收完了债，要给您买些什么回来？"孟尝君随口说："先生看我家里缺什么，就买什么吧。"

lots of money in the place of Xue, who can go to collect the principal and interest for me?" Feng Xuan rushed to say, "I'd like to go." The lord nodded for agreement. Feng Xuan asked again, "After finishing the collection, what do you need me to buy?" The Lord Meng Chang randomly said, "You can buy something which I don't have."

冯谖来到薛地，召集老百姓核对完债券，然后一把火将它们都烧掉了。他对老百姓说："孟尝君体谅大家的苦处，命令我将所有的债券一概免除！"借债的百姓们无不感动流泪。

Feng Xuan came to the place of Xue and called in the civilians for checking the debt voucher, and then set all the debt vouchers on fire. He said to the civilians, "The Lord Meng Chang understood and sympathized with your sufferings and ordered me to exempt all of your debts!" All the civilians were moved to tears.

冯谖回去向孟尝君汇报以后，孟尝君很不高兴。一年后，齐王罢免了孟尝君，宾客们也散去了。冯谖劝他去薛地居住，孟尝君的车走到离薛地还有一百里的地方，薛地的老百姓就前来迎接。孟尝君感叹说："先生为我买了'义'，我今天才算真正见到了。"冯谖说：

When Feng Xuan came back and reported to the Lord Meng Chang, the Lord Meng Chang was greatly unhappy. One year later, when the Lord Meng Chang was removed from his office by the Emperor of Qi, all of his guests dispersed. Feng Xuan persuaded him to stay in the place of Xue, when the cart went to nearly one hundred miles away from the place of Xue, the civilians of Xue all came out for welcome. The Lord Meng Chang sighed, "Today I really

"狡兔三窟，才能免除一死，如今只有一窟，还不能高枕而卧，让我再为您凿两个窟吧。"

understand that you had bought benevolence for me." Feng Xuan said, "A wily hare will escape death if it has three burrows. Now there's only one burrow and we can not live lightheartedly, let me build another two burrows."

冯谖去到魏国游说，魏王派人带着一百辆马车和一千两黄金，去薛地邀请孟尝君到魏国做相国。冯谖又劝孟尝君拒绝他们的聘请。魏国的使者往返了三次，孟尝君还是没有同意。

Feng Xuan went to Wei State for propagation, and the Emperor of Wei dispatched people to bring one hundred horse carts and one thousand bars of gold for inviting the Lord Meng Chang as the Prime Minister of Wei. Feng Xuan persuaded the Lord Meng Chang to refuse, and the Lord Meng Chang refused for three times in spite of three round trips of the Wei's envoys.

齐王知道后，担心孟尝君为别国卖力，忙派大臣到薛地去向孟尝君谢罪，恢复了他相国的职务。

Upon this news, the emperor of Qi worried that the Lord Meng Chang would work for other country, so he hurried to appointed ministers to apologize and also recovered Meng chang's post of the Prime Minister.

随后，冯谖又劝孟尝君向齐王请赐先王的祭器，在薛地建造宗庙供奉起来。宗庙建成后，冯谖对孟尝君说："三窟已成，您可以高枕无忧了。"

Afterwards, Feng Xuan persuaded Lord Meng Chang to beg for the sacrifice utensils of the late emperor and enshrined it in the temple of Xue. When the temple was build up, Feng Xuan said to the Lord Meng Chang, "Now three burrows are ready, you can live without any worries."

163

背水一战

Fight to win or die

出自 《史记·淮阴侯列传》。

释义 不留后路，决一死战。

楚汉战争期间，韩信为汉王刘邦出谋划策，先攻取了关中，然后东渡黄河，打

During the wars between Chu and Han, Han Xin masterminded a scheme for Liu Bang, the Emperor of Han, and they firstly seized the

败并俘虏魏王豹，接着向东攻打赵王歇。

Guanzhong Region and then crossed the Yellow River eastward, and finally defeated and captured the Emperor Bao of Wei, and then they went eastward to attack the Emperor Xie of Zhao.

当时，韩信大军正准备通过一道极为狭窄的山口，叫井陉口。赵王手下的谋士李左军主张一面堵住井陉口，一面派兵抄小路切断汉军的运粮通道，韩信的部队没有后援，就一定会败走；但大将陈余不听，仗着兵力优势，坚持要与汉军正面作战。

At that time, the troops led by Han Xin tried to go through a extremely narrow mountain pass named Jingxing Pass. A counselor of Zhao,Li Zuojun, proposed to block off Jingxing Pass on the one hand and cut off the food transportation pass by taking a little path on the other hand, and he believed that the troops of Han Xin would definitely defeated because they didn't have any back-up. Whereas, the big general Chen Yu didn't take his advice and insisted on a face-to-face battle due to the military advantages.

韩信了解到这一情况后，下令部队在离井陉三十里的地方安营，随后，他派出两千名骑兵从小路隐蔽前进，要他们在赵军离开营地后迅速冲入赵军营地，换上汉军旗号；又派一万军队故意背靠河水排列阵势来引诱赵军。

Upon this news, Han Xin ordered the troops to pitch camps thirty miles away from Jingxing Pass, and then he dispatched two thousand cavalrymen to move forward in a little path stealthily. He also ordered that when Zhao's troops left their camps, the cavalrymen should rush into the camp and replaced the Zhao's flag with Han flag. And at the same, he dispatched ten thousand troops to seduce Zhao's troops by a battle array back to the riverside.

天亮以后，韩信率军发

In the daylight, Han Xin led troops to launch

动进攻，双方展开激战。不一会儿，汉军假装败回水边阵地，赵军全部离开营地前来追击。这时，韩信命令主力部队出击，背水结阵的士兵因为没有退路，也回身猛扑敌军。赵军无法取胜，正要回营，忽然看到营中已插遍了汉军旗帜，于是四散奔逃。汉军乘胜追击，打了一个大胜仗。

attack and they were in fierce battle. After a moment, Han's troops pretended to withdraw to the riverside due to failure, and Zhao's troops all left their camps to pursue. Then Han Xin ordered the main force to attack, and the Han's troops at the riverside also fiercely attack the enemies due to that no route of retreat behind. When Zhao's troops were defeated and prepared to go back to their camps, they suddenly saw many Han's flags in the camps, so they dispersed everywhere. Han's troops took the chance to pursue and won the battle finally.

事后，有的将领问韩信："兵法上说，列阵要背靠着山，现在您让我们背靠水排阵，竟然取胜了，这是一种什么策略呢？"

Afterwards, someone asked Han Xin, "According to the military books, the troops should in array with mountains behind, but you ordered us to make array with river behind and we even won the battle, what is the strategy?"

韩信笑着说："兵法上不是还说'置之死地而后生'吗？如果有退路，士兵都逃散了，怎么能让他们拼命呢！"

Han Xin smiled and said, "There's also a saying that the soldiers will fight for their lives out of desperation and eventually win the battle. If a route of retreat is available, the soldiers will disperse, and how can they fight desperately?"

164

草菅人命

Look upon human lives as they are grass

出自 《汉书·贾谊传》。

释义 看待杀人像割草一样。

贾谊是汉文帝时的一个著名文人，他从小聪慧好学，很有才华，因此被文帝

In the reign of the Emperor Wen of Han, there was a person named Jia Yi, who was smart and studious as a child, thus he was appointed

召为博士，后又担任过太中大夫的官职。因为招人嫉妒陷害，被贬为长沙王太傅。

as Learned Scholar by the emperor and as the Minister. Because he was envied and framed, so he was degraded to the master of the King of Chang Sha.

后来，汉文帝又把他召回宫中，让他担任梁王刘揖的太傅。梁王是汉文帝最宠爱的儿子，文帝原本打算让他将来继承皇位，所以希望贾谊好好教导他。贾谊就此发表了一通议论，他说："辅导皇子，教他读书固然重要，但更重要的是教他怎样做一个正直的人。假如像秦朝末年赵高教导秦二世胡亥那样，传授给胡亥的是严刑酷法，不是杀头割鼻子，就是满门抄斩。结果胡亥一当上皇帝，就胡乱杀人，看待杀人就像割草一样，不当一回事。这难道是胡亥的本性生来就坏吗？他所以这样，是辅导他的人没有引导他走上正道啊。"

Afterwards, the Emperor Wen of Han called him back to the imperial court and appointed him as the master of Liu Yi, the King of Liang. The King of Liang was the most beloved son of the emperor, and the emperor intended to enthrone him in the future and wished Jia Yi to teach him well. Thus Jia Yi made some comments, "It is indeed important to teach the prince to read, but it is much more important to teach him to be an upright man. For example, by the end of Qin dynasty, Zhao Gao taught the Second Emperor Hu Hai lots of brutal punishments such as cutting head or nose and family extermination. Therefore, as Hu Hai became the emperor, he began to kill people recklessly and regard killing people as mowing grass. Is Hu Hai a bad person by nature? The reason is his master didn't teach him the right things."

后来，梁怀王不慎骑马

Afterwards, the Emperor Huai of Liang

摔死，贾谊自责没有尽到太傅的责任，因此整天郁郁不乐，常常哭泣，一年多后就死了，当时才33岁。

accidentally fell off the horse and died, and Jia Yi blamed himself for not fulfilling his responsibility as a master, so he was upset everyday and always cried. And finally, after more than one year, he died at his thirty-three years old.

165

退避三舍

Retreat about thirty miles as a condition for peace

出自 《左传·僖公二十二年》。

释义 比喻不与人相争或主动让步。

春秋时期，晋献公听信谗言，杀了太子申生，又派人捉拿申生的异母哥哥重

In the Spring and Autumn Periods, the Emperor Xian of Jin believed in slanderous words and killed the Prince Shen Sheng, and

耳。重耳被迫逃出晋国，在外流亡十九年。

also ordered to capture Chong Er, the elder half-brother of Shen Sheng. Thus Chong Er was forced to flee out of Jin for exile for nineteen years.

后来，重耳来到楚国，楚王认为重耳日后一定会有大的作为，就用国君的礼节迎接他，把他作为贵宾相待。

Afterwards, Chong Er went to Chu State, and the King of Chu believed that Chong Er would make great achievements in the future, so the emperor welcomed Chong Er in the etiquette of an emperor and treated him as an distinguished guest.

一天，楚王设宴招待重耳，两人一边饮酒一边谈话，中间楚王问重耳说："你如果有一天回晋国当上国君，该怎么报答我呢？"重耳回答说："要是托您的福，果真能回国当政的话，我愿与贵国结成友好关系。假如有一天晋楚之间发生战争，我一定命令军队先退避三舍（一舍等于三十里），如果还不能得到您的原谅，我再与您交战。"

One day, the Emperor of Chu held a banquet for Chong Er. They talked with each other when drinking, the Emperor of Chu asked Chong Er, " If one day you become the Emperor of Jin State, what will you return to me?" Chong Er answered, "If thanks to your kind support and I become the emperor, I promise to establish friendly relations with your country. If one day a battle happens between Chu and Jin, I promise to order my troops to withdraw for ninety miles. If I still can't get your forgiveness, then I will fight with you."

四年后，重耳真的回到晋国当了国君，就是历史

Four years later, Chong Er came back to Jin and became the emperor as the famous

上有名的晋文公。晋国在他的治理下日益强大。公元前633年，楚国和晋国的军队发生战争，晋文公为了实现他许下的诺言，下令军队后退九十里，驻扎在城濮。楚军见晋军后退，以为对方害怕了，马上追击。晋军利用楚军骄傲轻敌的弱点，集中兵力，大破楚军，取得了城濮之战的胜利。

Emperor Wen of Jin, and Jin became more and more strong under his governance. In BC 633, a battle broke out between Chu and Jin, and the Emperor Wen of Jin kept his promise and ordered his troops to withdraw for ninety miles to Chengpu. Upon Jin's withdrawa, Chu's troops thought Jin was afraid and immediately pursued to attack. Jin's troops utilized the weakness of undermining the enemies, so they concentrated all the forces and greatly defeated Chu's troops, and finally won the battle of Chengpu.

166

首鼠两端

Have two minds

出自 《史记·魏其武安侯列传》。

释义 在两者之间动摇不定。

西汉时期，汉武帝的母亲王太后有个同母异父的弟弟叫田蚡，他靠着太

In the Western Han Period, the Empress Dowager Wang was the mother of the Emperor Wu of Han, who had a half-brother named Tian

后的势力做了丞相。田蚡掌握大权后，开始营私舞弊，任意诬陷自己不喜欢的人。有一次，田蚡向功臣窦婴索要城南的田地，窦婴不给；田蚡又听说另一位功臣灌夫也替窦婴抱打不平，因此跟灌夫和窦婴结下了仇。

后来，田蚡结婚，王太后吩咐诸侯、宗室和大臣们都到丞相府去祝贺。窦婴和灌夫也去了。酒席上，灌夫因为受到田蚡等人轻视，气得破口大骂起来。为此，田蚡拘捕了灌夫。这件事闹到了武帝那里，武帝便召集大臣们来研究如何处理。窦婴坚决反对对灌夫治罪，也有一些大臣惧怕田蚡的权势，极力赞成治罪。御史大夫韩安国说："灌夫在平定七国之乱的时候立有大功，虽说酒后闹事，但没有死罪。可是丞相说他不对，也有道

Fen. Tian Fen was appointed as the Prime Minister by the power of the Empress Dowager Wang. As Tian Fen was in big power, he began to do various malpractices and arbitrarily framed up those people he didn't like. Once Tian Fen asked for the farmlands in the south of city to the meritorious minister Dou Ying, but was refused. And Tian Fen also heard that another meritorious minister Guan Fu was in defence of Dou Ying, so he also bred enmity with Guan Fu.

Afterwards, Tian Fen got married, and the Empress Dowager Wang asked all the vassals, imperial clans and ministers to congratulate, Dou Ying and Guan Fu also joined. In the banquet, Guan Fu swore with anger due to the despise of Tian Fen and his followers, thus Tian Fen arrested Guan Fu. As this event was escalated to the Emperor Wu, the emperor called in ministers for solutions. Dou Ying firmly opposed to declare Guan Fu guilty, but some ministers were afraid of Tian Fen's power and strongly approved of guilty declaration. The Royal Doctor Han Anguo said, "Guan Fu made great contributions in pacifying the rebellions of the seven kingdoms. Although he made some troubles when drunken, it should not be capital crime to death. But the Prime Minister

理，究竟如何处置，请皇上定夺吧！”

罢朝以后，在皇宫门外，田蚡招呼韩安国坐上他的车子，生气地说：“我本来是和你一起对付窦婴，你为何首鼠两端，迟疑不决呢？”

最后，田蚡还是想方设法害死了窦婴和灌夫。不久，他自己也因为内心恐惧惊吓而死。

must have some reasons to think him wrong, so let the emperor make final decisions!”

When the morning court finished, Tian Fen met Han Anguo outside the gate of the imperial palace and asked him to get on the cart, he said angrily, “Originally I intended to cooperate with you to be against with Dou Ying, but why are you so shilly-shally?”

Finally, Tian Fen tried all means to kill Dou Ying and Guan Fu, but before long he died due to inner fear and scare.

167

倾国倾城

Drop-head Gorgeousness

出自 《汉书·外戚传下》。

释义 多形容妇女容貌极美。

汉武帝时期，宫廷乐师李延年有一个妹妹，是个歌女，生得婀娜多姿，楚

In the period of the Emperor Wu of Han, the court musician Li Yannian had a younger sister, who was a sing-song girl with charming

楚动人，尤其擅长歌舞。李延年想把她进献给汉武帝为妃，便请平阳公主帮忙引荐。

一天，汉武帝在宫中饮酒，平阳公主也在座。饮到中间，乐师开始奏乐助兴，李延年唱起了自己新写的一首歌："北方有佳人，绝世而独立。一顾倾人城，再顾倾人国。宁不知倾城与倾国，佳人难再得。"汉武帝听完，不禁叹息说："世间哪有你所唱的那种佳人啊！"平阳公主于是趁机说："陛下有所不知，延年的小妹就是一位倾国倾城的绝世佳人。"武帝立刻下令召李氏入宫，见她果然是姿容出众，体态轻盈，于是便把她纳为妃子，称为李夫人。

appearance and specially good at singing and danceing. Li Yannian intended to contribute her to the Emperor Wu of Han as a concubine, so he asked the Princess Ping Yang to help recommend.

One day, the Emperor Wu of Han was drinking in the imperial palace, and the Princess was also in presence. As the court musician began to play music for entertainment, Li Yannian began to sing a song newly written by himself, "There is a beauty in the north, and you can find no match to her in the world. I would like to pay the price of a city or even a state just to win her heart. It's worth it because this is a once-in-a-lifetime opportunity. Lose her and you will never find another." The Emperor Wu of Han couldn't help to sigh, "It is impossible for such a gorgeous beauty existing in the world!" The Princess Ping Yang took the chance and said, "Don't Your Majesty know that the younger sister of Li Yannian was just such a gorgeous beauty." The Emperor Wu of Han immediately called in Li Yannian's younger sister to imperial court, and ennobled her as Concubine Li because she really had an outstanding appearance and well-rounded figure.

李夫人入宫只有短短几年，就不幸染病在身，卧床不起。武帝亲自去看望她，李夫人一见武帝到来，急忙用被子盖住脸，不让武帝看到她的容颜。任凭武帝再三呼唤，李夫人只是独自哭泣。武帝一怒之下拂袖而去。

But only few years later, the Concubine Li unfortunately illed and completely bedridden. The Emperor Wu came to see her, but she hurried to cover her face with quilt, unwilling to let the emperor see her sick looks in spite of repeated calls of the emperor, the Concubine Li was weeping alone, then the emperor went off in a huff.

等武帝走后，李夫人的姐妹们都为这事责备她。李夫人叹气说："我本来出身微贱，皇上之所以眷恋我，只是因为平时的容貌而已。现在我病已将死，他如果见到我的容颜与以前大不相同，必然心生厌恶，又怎么会在我死去后照顾我的兄弟呢？"

Then many sisters of the Concubine Li all blamed her, and the Concubine Li sighed, "I'm originally born in humility, and the emperor loves me only because of my beautiful appearance, now I'm ill and dying, if the emperor see my face, he will certainly disgust me, and thus how will he care for my brothers after my death?"

几天后，李夫人去世。武帝因为最后没能得见李夫人一面，反而更加怀念她，于是将李夫人用皇后的礼仪安葬，并把李延年和弟弟李广利都予以封官加爵。

Several days later, the Concubine Li died. Because the Emperor Wu didn't have the chance to see her for the last time and he missed her very much, so he buried the Concubine Li in the etiquette of the queen and ennobled Li Yannian and his younger brother Li Guangli with official and vassal.

168

唇亡齿寒

The teeth can't live without lips

出自 《左传·僖公五年》。

释义 比喻两者关系密切，相互依存。

春秋时期，晋献公将要出兵攻打虢国。但是因为中间必须要经过虞国，

In the Spring and Autumn Periods, the Emperor Xian of Jin planned to lead troops for attacking Guo State. Because they must pass through

他担心虞国不肯答应借路。大臣荀息出主意，让他把自己的名贵玉石与良马送给虞国的国君，然后再向他借路。晋献公有些舍不得，荀息劝他说："这两件宝贝只不过是暂时寄存在那里罢了，迟早还是要归还给您的。"

Yu State, so the emperor worried that Yu State wouldn't agree to let them pass. The Minister Xun Xi came out an idea and asked the emperor to firstly contribute a precious jade and swift horse to the Emperor of Yu State and then ask for the permit of the pass. Whereas the Emperor Xian of Jin was reluctant, the Minister Xun Xi persuaded, "These two things are just temporarily stored there and will be turned to you sooner or later."

晋献公于是决定按荀息的计策行事。虞国的国君见到这两件稀世宝物后，非常喜欢，打算给晋国借路。虞国大夫宫之奇劝阻说："虢国是我们的邻国，他们和我们的国家就是一种唇齿相依的关系，如果嘴唇没有了，牙齿就会挨冻。您同意给晋国借路，让他们攻打虢国。如果晋国今天消灭了虢国，我们明天就会被晋国吞掉，太危险了。"

Thus the Emperor Xian of Jin decided to follow Xun Xi's advice. As the Emperor of Yu State saw these two rare and precious treasures, he liked them very much and agreed to lend the pass to Jin State. The Minister Gong Zhiqi persuaded, "Guo State is our neighboring country just as the relationship between teeth and lips, and the teeth will feel cold without lips. It is very dangerous for you to lend pass to Jin State for attacking Guo State, because once Jin wipes out Guo State, we will also be wiped out in the future."

可是，虞国国君由于贪恋晋国的宝玉和良马，一意孤行，听不进宫之奇的

But the Emperor of Guo State strongly clung to the precious jade and swift horse, so he insisted on his own ideas without taking the advice of

劝阻，给晋国军队让出了一条攻打虢国的必经之路。晋国兵强马壮，很快就消灭了弱小的虢国。在班师回朝途中，又顺便消灭了毫无准备的虞国。

Gong Zhiqi and lent a necessary pass for Jin's troops to attack Guo State. Since Jin State had strong soldiers and sturdy horses, the weak Guo State was soon wiped out. On the way back to Jin State, Jin's troops took the convenient chance to wipe out the unprepared Yu State.

晋献公看着失而复得的宝玉和良马，得意地说："宝玉还是我原来的那一块，没有变样；只是这匹马又多长了一颗牙齿，比去年大一岁了。"

The Emperor Xian of Jin looked at the regained precious jade and swift horse and said proudly, "The jade is still that one without any changes, but the swift horse grows up one year with a newly-grown tush."

169

害群之马

A black sheep

出自 《庄子·杂篇·徐无鬼》。

释义 比喻危害集体的人。

黄帝是中华民族的始祖之一。

The Yellow Emperor is one of the earliest ancestors of Chinese nation.

有一次，黄帝到具茨山

Once, the Yellow Emperor went to Juci

去拜见大隗，在襄城的旷野迷了路。这时，他正巧遇到了一位放马的少年，便向他问路，说："你知道具茨山在什么地方吗？"少年回答说："知道。"黄帝又问："你知道大隗居住在什么地方吗？"少年也回答说知道。

Mountain to visit Da Wei and got lost in the wild field of Xiang City. At the moment, he happened to meet a young horse grazer and asked the way, "Do you know where is Juci Mountain?" The young man said, "Of course I know." The Yellow Emperor asked again, "Do you know where Da Wei lives?" The young man also said yes.

黄帝听后，心里很高兴，说："这位少年真是特别啊，不仅知道具茨山，而且还知道大隗居住的地方。那我再问你，你知道如何治理天下吗？"少年不慌不忙地回答说："治理天下也没有什么大不了的。前几年我在外面游历，生了一种头眼眩晕的病，有位长者对我说，'你还是乘坐太阳车去襄城的旷野里游玩吧。'我现在身体好多了，又打算去更多的地方。所谓治理天下，也不过如此罢了。"

The Yellow Emperor was happy to hear that and said, "You are really a special young man, not only you know the location of Juci Mountain, but you also know the living place of Da Wei. Then let me ask you again, do you know how to govern a country?" The young man answered unhurriedly, "It is not difficult to govern a country. A few years ago when I travelled outside, I got a disease of dizziness, and an old man told me that I should take the sun cart to the wild field of Xiang City for travelling. And now I am much better and have plans for travelling to more places. It is the same for governing a country."

黄帝便再次询问少年究竟如何治理天下。少年只

The Yellow Emperor asked the young man again for how to govern a country, the young

得说："治理天下，其实与放马没什么两样，也就是要将危害马群的坏马驱逐出去而已！"

man could only say, "Governing a country is the same as grazing horses, you just need to expel the black sheep out of the herd!"

黄帝听了，恭恭敬敬地称呼少年为"天师"，并对他拜了几拜，然后才离开。

As the Yellow Emperor heard the answer, he respectfully address the young man as the Celestial Master and made several bows to him, and then left.

170

捉襟见肘

Out at the elbows

出自 《庄子·让王》。

释义 顾此失彼，穷于应付。

曾参是孔子的弟子之一，他曾经居住在卫国，过着非常艰苦的生活，经常一

Zeng Shen was one of the disciples of Confucius and once lived a very poor life in Wei State. He always had no rice to eat for three

连三天不生火做饭，十年没换过一件新衣服，穿着用乱麻絮做的袍子，破烂不堪，分不清表里。他戴的帽子也很破旧了，以至于正一正帽子，系帽的绳带就断了；一拉衣襟，就露出了胳膊肘；一穿鞋，鞋后跟就会裂开。由于吃得很差，他的脸上出现了浮肿，手掌脚底都长满了老茧。

days continuously, didn't change clothes for ten years. He wore a torn gown made of tattered oakum which couldn't be distinguished the inside and outside layer. His hat was so worn-out that its strings would be immediately broken as he straightened his hat. As soon as he pulled his clothes, his elbows came out; as soon as he put on shoes, the heel piece ripped off. Because he couldn't eat well, so he got the disease of edema. Because he always worn torn shoes, there were lots of callus on his palms and frame feet.

虽然如此穷困，但是曾参并不因此而忧愁，他经常拖着破鞋，高唱着《商颂》之歌，歌声洪亮，充满天地，好像是金石制作的乐器发出的声音一样。曾参就这样自由自在地过着自己的生活，天子不能召他为臣，诸侯不能攀他为友。

Although he was so poor, he didn't feel worried at all. On the contrary, he always wore his torn shoes and loudly sang the song of *Ode to Shang*, with resonant voice full of heaven and earth just like the sound made by golden-stoned musical instruments. Thus Zeng Shen lived a life lightheartedly, refusing to be submitted to the imperial court and make friends with vassals.

鲁国国君曾经派使者去给他赠送采邑，对他说："请用采邑的收入做件衣服吧。"曾参不接受。使者说："这不是您向国君要

The emperor of Lu State once dispatched envoy to give fief to him and said, "Please use the earning of the fief to make clothes." But Zeng Shen refused. And the envoy said, "This is not what you asked for, this is what

求的，而是国君要奉送您的，为什么不接受呢？”曾参说：“接受的人往往会在心里害怕赠送的人，赠送的人往往对接受的人表现出骄纵，能不能使国君赠给我采邑而对我不骄纵，我很担心这一点啊！

the emperor give you, why don't you accept?" Zeng Shen said, "The receiver will always be afraid of the giver, and the giver always show arrogance to the receiver, so I'm really worried wether the emperor give me fief but will not show arrogance to me!"

171

捕风捉影

Catch at the shadow

出自 《汉书·郊祀志下》。

释义 说话做事没有确切的事实根据。

谷永是西汉成帝时候的人，担任过光禄大夫、大司农等职。

There was a person named Gu Yong, who once took the official posts as Imperial Minister and Grand Minister of Agriculture.

汉成帝二十岁做皇帝，到四十多岁还没有孩子。他听信方士的话，在长安郊外的上林苑大搞祭祀活动，祈求上天赐福，花了很多钱财，但并没有什么效果。

谷永向汉成帝上书说：“现在有些人大谈神仙鬼怪，宣扬祭祀的方法，听他们说话，满耳都是美好的景象，就像马上能遇见神仙一样；可是你要寻找它，却虚无缥缈，好像要捕捉住风和影子一样，不可能得到。所以古代贤明的君王绝对不会听信这些话。周代史官苌弘想要用祭祀鬼神的办法帮助周灵王，让天下诸侯来朝会，可是周王室更加衰败，诸侯反叛的更多；楚怀王隆重祭祀鬼神，祈求神灵保佑打退秦国军队，结果却一败涂地，不仅土地被秦国夺取，自己也做了俘虏；秦始

The Emperor Cheng of Han assumed the throne at his twenties and didn't have children until his forties. Thus he followed the warlock's advice and grandly present sacrifice activities in the ShangLin Imperial park in the suburb of Chang'an, for the purpose of pleading the Heaven to bless, but it wasn't effective in spite of spending lots of money.

Gu Yong submitted a written statement to the Emperor Cheng of Han, "Nowadays some people eloquently talk about celestial spirits and preaching methods of sacrifice. As you're listening to their description of beautiful scenes, it is just as if you will meet the celestial immediately. But if you want to find it, it is just like catching the wind and shadow which are all illusory. Therefore, the wise emperors in the ancient times would not believe in those words at all. In Zhou dynasty, the official historian Chang Hong intended to help the Emperor Ling of Zhou by means of worshiping celestial spirits in order to make all vassals submit, but Zhou State declined and the vassals rebelled more fiercely. The Emperor Huai of Chu ceremoniously worshiped celestial spirits for pleading to beat back Qin's troops, but Chu suffered a crushing defeat with the lands seized by Qin State and the emperor captured. After the First Emperor of

皇统一天下后，派徐福率领童男童女下海求仙采药，结果一去不回，遭到天下人的怨恨。从古到今，这些帝王们凭着尊贵的地位、众多的财物，寻遍天下去访求神灵、仙人，经过了多少岁月，却没有丝毫应验。希望您不要再让那些行为不正的人干预朝廷的事。”

Qin completed the unification of the world, he asked Xu Fu to make virgin boys and girls go down the sea for fairly herbal medicine, but the virgin boys and girls didn't come back, so he was hated by people. From ancient times to the present, upon their exalted status and numerous possessions, many emperors tries all means to find celestials and immortals for many years, but without any achievement. Hope Your Majesty forbid those malfeasant people to interfere in the imperial affairs."

汉成帝认为谷永说得很有道理，便听从了他的意见。

The Emperor Cheng of Han thought it reasonable and followed his advice.

172

桃李不言，下自成蹊

A man of true worth attracts admiration

出自 《史记·李将军列传》。

释义 为人正直诚实，用不着到处宣扬，就能受到别人的敬仰。

西汉时期，有一位勇猛善战的将军，名叫李广。他一生跟匈奴打过七十多次

In the Western Han Period, there was a brave and skillful general Li Guang, who fought with Xiongnu for over seventy times and made

仗，立下无数战功，但他一点也不居功自傲。不仅在平时待人和气，而且能够与部下同甘共苦，每次朝廷给他的赏赐，他都会统统分给官兵们；而打起仗来，他也总是身先士卒，奋勇杀敌。

numerous contributions, but he never claimed credit for himself. Li Guang was not only kind to his subordinates, but also willing to share weal and woe with them. Each time when the imperial court granted rewards to him, he would distribute to the soldiers. He would always took the lead in battles to kill the enemies bravely.

公元前119年，卫青、霍去病远征匈奴，李广担任前将军随同前往。大军出塞后，卫青命令李广所部从东边出发。李广不想放弃与匈奴首领面对面交战的机会，便向卫青请求打先锋，但卫青没有答应。

In 119 BC, Wei Qing and Huo Qubing made expedition to conquer Xiongnu, with the accompany of Li Guang. When the troops went outside of the frontier, Wei Qing ordered Li Guang to depart from the east. Li Guang didn't want to give up the fighting chance with the Xiongnu chief, so he asked for permit to be a pioneer, but Wei Qing refused.

从东边走，不仅绕道而且路远，加上没有向导，李广的部队迷失了方向，没能赶上与匈奴作战。卫青大军与匈奴主力交战，虽然打了胜仗，但是却让匈奴首领逃掉了。他们在回师途中遇上李广，卫青手下的长史责问他为什么迟到，李广没有回答，长史就让李广派他的部

Because the troops departed from the east and made a detour for a long way without any guidance, so Li Guang's troops got lost and missed the fighting chance with Xiongnu. Although Wei Qing won the battle with Xiongnu, the Xiongnu chief run away. On the way back to the imperial court, Wei Qing's subordinate Chang Shi scolded why they were late, Li Guang didn't answer, so Chang Shi asked Li Guang to let his subordinates be

属去大将军府接受审讯。

interrogated in the Big General court.

回到军营后，李广越想越不是滋味，悲愤之下，于是就拔刀自刎了。

When Li Guang came back to camp, he felt grief and indignation, so he took out the sword and committed suicide.

消息传出后，李广军中的将士都为之痛哭。百姓听到这个消息，不论认识不认识李广的人，都为之落泪，纷纷悼念他。

As the news spread, soldiers all bitterly cried for Li Guang, and the civilians also shed tears for mourning Li Guang no matter they knew him or not.

司马迁在《史记》中为李广立传时，称赞道："桃李不言，下自成蹊。"意思是说，桃李虽然不会说话，但仍然会吸引人们来赏花尝果，以至树下都走出一条小路。而李广就是以他的谦虚和正直的品质，赢得了人们的崇敬。

When Si-ma Qian was writing biography for Li Guang in the *Historical Records*, he praised, "Though peach and pulm trees do not speak, a path is worn beneath them." That means peaches and plums can't speak, but they still attract people to taste fruits and appreciate flowers, so that even a new path built up under the trees. Li Guang won the admiration of people just by his humility and uprightness.

173

爱屋及乌

Love me love my dog

出自 《尚书大传》卷三。

释义 由于喜爱某人，也连带喜爱与他有关系的人或物。

商朝末年，商纣王残暴无道，失去民心，周武王趁机起兵灭掉商朝，建立了

By the end of Shang Dynasty, the Emperor Zhou of Shang was brutal and lost civilian's popularity. The Emperor Wu of Zhou took

周朝。但周武王对如何处理商朝留下的官员很伤脑筋，于是问姜太公：“周朝建立了，对商朝的这些官员到底应该怎样处置呢？”姜太公说：“我听说，如果喜爱一个人，就连他家屋上的乌鸦都不以为不祥，不觉得讨厌了；如果憎恨一个人，就会连带着厌恶他的家人下属。所以应该把这些昔日的敌对者都杀了，一个也不留，您看怎么样？”

the chance to lead troops to wipe of Shang Dynasty and established Zhou Dynasty. The Emperor Wu of Zhou was nerve-racking about the arrangement of the previous officials, so he consulted the Master Jiang, “How should I arrange those officials of Shang Dynasty?” The Master Jiang said, “If you like a person, you will even like the crow on the roof of his house; and if you hate a person, you will even hate his family and subordinates. I think we should kill those old-time opponents, what do you think?”

周武王不同意姜太公的意见，于是，他又召见召公，问了同样的问题。召公回答说：“那些跟商纣王一起压榨老百姓的贪官污吏，一定要把他们处死；而那些爱护老百姓的公正廉洁的好官员，就应该让他们活着。我们必须把有罪的和无罪的、好的和坏的区分开来。坏的处以死刑，一个也不留。”

The Emperor Wu of Zhou didn’t agree with the Master Jiang, so he called in the Duke Zhao and asked the same question, and the Duke Zhao answered, “We must kill those malfeasant oppressing civilians, and let live those impartial and honest officials. We must distinguish the guilty and the innocent, as well as good and bad, and thus the bad should be eliminated.”

周武王听了，还是不满意，于是又向周公询问。周公说："我认为应当让这些人全部回到自己的家里，各自耕种自己的田地，自食其力。然后，再通过施行仁政来感化全国的老百姓，这样天下必然太平。"

The Emperor Wu of Zhou was still not satisfied with the answer, so he turned to the Duke Zhou. And the Duke Zhou answered, "I think we should let all those people go back home to do farming for self-sufficiency. Then we will implement benevolence policy to influence civilians for the purpose of universal peace and stability."

武王听后十分高兴，就遵照周公所说的办法去治理国家，结果天下很快就安定了下来。

The Emperor Wu was very glad at the answer and followed the advice of the Duke Zhou, and finally the country became stable very soon.

174

狼狈为奸

Act in collusion with each other

出自 唐·段成式《酉阳杂俎》。

释义 比喻互相勾结干坏事。

据唐代段成式所著的《酉阳杂俎》记载，狼和狈，是两种长相十分相似的

According to *The Miscellaneous Essays of Youyang* by Duan Chengshi in the Tang Dynasty, the wolves and the jackals have

动物，都喜欢偷吃猪羊等家畜。它们唯一不同的是，狼的两条前腿长，两条后腿短；而狈则正好相反，它们的两条前腿短，两条后腿长。正是由于这一点不同，让狼和狈能够优势互补，从而结成了亲密的伙伴关系。它们每次出去偷食，一般都会相互配合，通力合作。

similar appearance and they all like to steal livestock such as sheep or pigs. The only difference between them is that the wolves have long front legs and short rear legs, but the jackals are just opposite and they have short front legs and long rear legs. Therefore, they can complement each other advantages and form into close relationship as partners. So they usually make concerted efforts in cooperation for stealing food each time.

有一次，一只狼和一只狈结伴同行，来到一户人家的羊圈外面。羊圈里面养着很多肥羊，可是羊圈又高又坚固，狼和狈都不能爬上去。于是它们想出了一个主意：先让狼骑在狈的脖子上，然后狈把自己的两条后腿直立起来，它的长腿把狼抬得很高，接下来，狼就用它两条长长的前腿攀住羊圈，慢慢伸直身体后，再把两条前腿探进羊圈里面，把圈里的羊叼出来。

Once a wolf and a jackal went out together and came to a sheepfold with lots of fat sheep inside. But the fence was so high and firm that both the wolf and the jackal couldn't climb up. So they came up with an idea. Firstly, the wolf rode on the neck of the jackal and next the jackal stood up his rear legs, so the long legs of the jackal lifted up the wolf, and then the wolf hang his long front legs on the fence and slowly straighten its body to put front legs inside the sheepfold, and finally the wolf used its mouth to pick the sheep out of the sheepfold.

狼和狈经常采取这种合

Since the wolves and the jackals usually

作方式来偷羊，所以人们也经常可以看到这两种野兽会走在一起，显得非常亲密。

cooperate in this way to steal sheep, people can always see the two kinds of wild beasts walking together with close relationship.

175

班门弄斧

Teach fish to swim

出自 唐·柳宗元《王氏伯仲唱和诗序》。

释义 比喻在行家面前卖弄本领，不自量力。

鲁班，姓公输，名般，是春秋时期的鲁国人。他聪明灵巧，善于制作各种精巧

In the Spring and Autumn Periods, there was a person lived in Lu State, whose surname was Gong Shu and family name was Ban. He

器具，留下了很多发明创造，民间历来把他奉为木匠的始祖，他的名字也就成了内行人的代称。

was smart and good at making various exquisite wares. Since he had made many inventions and creations, people always worshiped him as the earliest ancestor of carpenter, so his name also became the synonymous of the professionals.

唐代文学家柳宗元在他《为王氏伯仲唱和诗》所作的序中说："操斧于班郢之门，斯强颜耳。"意思是说，在鲁班和郢这样使用斧子的大行家面前，显示自己的本事，是一种太不谦虚的可笑行为。这也是"班门弄斧"一词的最早来源。而俗语所说的"鲁班门前弄大斧"则出自另一首诗：

采石江边一堆土，
李白之名垂千古。
来来往往一首诗，
鲁班门前弄大斧。

According to *the Preface of Antiphon Poetry by Wang Bozhong* by the litterateur Liu Zongyuan in the Tang Dynasty, there is one sentence "It is ridiculous to hold an axe in front of the house of Lu Ban", which means that it is an immodest behavior to show off one's skills in front of a famous expert. This is also the source of the idiom "teach fish to swim". And the folk adage "flourish an axe in the front of Lu Ban's house" originates from another poem, "There is a pile of soil, and Li Bai was popular for thousands of years. People are all familiar with one poem which describes to flourish an axe in the front of Lu Ban's house."

这是明朝梅之涣写的《题李白墓诗》。李白是唐代的大诗人，传说他在采石江边的小船中对月畅饮，喝得大醉，看见水中

This is *The Poem on Tomb of Li Bai* written by Mei Zhihuan in the Ming Dynasty. Li Bai was a great poet in the Tang Dynasty, and it is said that once Li Bai drank in a small boat besides the river under the moonlight.

月影，竟然探出身子去捕捉，掉入江中而死。因此在这个地方后来出现了不少名胜，不但有李白墓，还有谪仙楼、捉月亭等。有些冒充风雅的游人在李白墓上胡乱题写，十分可笑。梅之涣写这首诗的用意，就是讥讽这些人在诗人面前炫耀自己，就跟在鲁班的门前要弄斧头一样可笑。

He was heavily drunken and even went out to catch the shadow of the moon in the river, and thus fell into the river and died. Because there were many scenic spots such as Li Bai Tomb, Banished Immortals Tower and Catching Moon Pavilion and etc., so many artificially elegant travelers always randomly wrote on the tomb of Li Bai, which was a ridiculous behavior. The purpose of this poem by Mei Zhihuan is to satirize those people for their behavior of showing off in front of poets, just like flourish an axe in the front of Lu Ban's house.

176

病入膏肓

Beyond cure

出自 《左传·成公十年》。

释义 比喻事情到了无法挽救的地步。

春秋时期，晋景公得了重病，他听说秦国有一个医术高明的医生缓，便专程派人去请。在医生来之前，晋景公做了个梦，梦见他的

In the Spring and Autumn Periods, the Emperor Jing of Jin got serious disease and ordered to pick up the doctor Huan, who was very famous for his excellent medical skills in Qin State. Before the doctor arrived, the

病变成了两个童子，正悄悄地在他身旁说话。其中一个童子说："那个医术高明的缓马上就要来了，恐怕会伤害到我们，我们该怎么逃避呢？"另一个童子说："我们躲在肓（心脏和膈膜之间）的上边、膏（心尖脂肪）的下边，他就拿我们没办法了。"

Emperor Jing of Jin had a dream that his disease turned to be two virgin boys stealthily talking beside him. One virgin boy said, "That excellent doctor is coming and will probably hurt us, how can we escape?" The other one said, "Let us hide in the place which is above the heart and its membrane and under the fat of the heart tip, then he can't do anything to hurt us."

不久，医生缓到了，立刻被请进晋景公的卧室。他为晋景公诊断后，说："这个病的病灶位于肓的上边、膏的下边，艾灸和针刺、药物都发挥不了作用，没办法治了！"

Soon after the doctor arrived and was immediately invited into the bedroom of the Emperor Jing of Jin. After he made diagnosis on the emperor, he said, "The focus of this disease locates in the place which is above the heart and its membrane and under the fat of the heart tip, so moxibustion, acupuncture and drugs can't work at all. The disease is cureless!"

晋景公一听，医生所说的和他梦到的两个童子的对话一样，非常佩服，连连点头称赞说："你的医术真高明啊！"于是让人送了一份厚礼给医生，让他回秦国去了。

Since what the doctor said was just the same as what the emperor heard in his dream, the emperor admired the doctor very much and continuously praised, "You are really an excellent doctor!" Thus the emperor granted generous gifts and sent him back to Qin State.

177

破釜沉舟

Last resort

出自 《史记·项羽本纪》。

释义 下决心不顾一切地干到底。

秦朝末年，各地人民纷纷举行起义，反抗秦朝的残暴统治。原楚国名将

By the end of Qin Dynasty, civilians held uprisings everywhere to resist the brutal governance of Qin. The uncle and nephew

项燕的后代项梁、项羽叔侄，也在楚地起兵，拥立楚王的孙子熊心为王，号称楚怀王。

Xiang Liang and Xiang Yu were both the descendants of Xiang Yan, who was a famous general in the former Chu State, they also held uprisings in the place of Chu, intending to enthrone Xiong Xin as the Emperor Huai of Chu, who was the grandson of the former Chu emperor.

有一年，秦国的三十万人马包围了赵国的巨鹿，赵王连夜向楚怀王求救。楚怀王任命宋义为上将军，项羽为次将，让他们带领二十万人马去援救赵国。宋义听说秦军兵强马壮，心里害怕，走到半路就停了下来，不再前进。军队中没有粮食，士兵用蔬菜和杂豆煮了当饭吃，宋义也不管不顾，自己照样举办宴会，大吃大喝。项羽大怒，杀了宋义，自己带着部队赶去救赵国。

One year, three hundred thousand of Qin's troops enclosed Julu of Zhao State, so the Emperor of Zhao turned to the Emperor Huai of Chu for help that very night. The Emperor Huai of Chu appointed Song Yi as the Top General and Xiang Yu as the Assistant General and ordered them to lead two hundred thousand of soldiers to rescue. As Song Yi heard that Qin State had picked soldiers and strong horses, he was afraid and stopped to move forward in the halfway. Due to lack of rice, the soldiers took vegetables and mixed beans as food, but Song Yi didn't care and still held banquet with extravagant wine and dine. Xiang Yu was greatly angry and killed Song Yi, and then led the troops to rescue Zhao State.

项羽先是派出一支部队，切断了秦军运粮的道

Firstly, Xiang Yu dispatched a troop to cut off the pass of transporting food of Qin's troops,

路，然后亲自率领主力渡过漳河，解救巨鹿。等到楚军全部渡过漳河以后，项羽让士兵们饱饱地吃了一顿饭，每人再随身携带三天干粮，然后传下命令：把渡河的船凿穿沉入河里，把做饭用的锅（古代称釜）砸碎，附近的房屋也一把火统统烧毁。以此来表示他有进无退，一定要夺取胜利的决心。

and then personally led the main force to cross Zhang River to rescue Julu. As all of Chu's troops crossed Zhang River, Xiang Yu asked the soldiers to have a good dinner and granted each soldier for three days of solid food, and then he ordered to chisel the boat down into the river and smash the cooking wares as well as burned out the nearby houses, for the purpose of showing his determination to win the battle without any retreat.

在项羽的亲自指挥下，楚军将士以一当十，奋勇杀敌，把秦军打得大败，解了巨鹿之围。

By the command of Xiang Yu in person, the Chu's soldiers were so brave that each one could be worth ten, and finally they completely defeated Qin's troops and successfully rescued the enclosure of Julu.

178

破镜重圆

A broken mirror joined together

出自 宋·李致远《碧牡丹》。

释义 夫妻分开后重又团圆。

南朝后主陈叔宝的妹妹乐昌公主，不但容貌秀美，而且很有文学才华。

In the Southern Dynasty, the later emperor Chen Shubao had a younger sister named the Princess Le Chang, who was not only beautiful,

成年后，她自己作主，下嫁给江南才子徐德言为妻，夫妇二人互敬互爱，夫唱妇随，成了一对人人羡慕的佳偶。

后来，北方的隋朝军队入侵陈国，陈国灭亡。陈后主及皇族被俘虏，一同送往隋国国都长安。乐昌公主与徐德言眼看要被活活拆散，临行前，她把一面铜镜摔成两半，一半留给夫君，一半自己收在怀中。两个人相约以后每年的正月十五日，在长安街市上沿街叫卖铜镜，直至找到对方的下落。

乐昌公主到长安后，被赐给丞相杨素，成了他的小妾。在第二年的元宵节上，乐昌公主让仆人带着她的半边铜镜，到集市上以高价叫卖。正遇上千辛万苦来到长安的徐德言，他马上认出了这半面镜子，于是向那名仆人打听妻子的下落。得知妻

but also talented in literature. As she grew up, she made her own decision to condescended to marry with the Jiangnan Talent Xu Deyan. The couples loved and respected each other in great harmony, and were greatly admired by everyone.

Afterwards, as Sui's troops invaded and wiped out Chen State, the Later Emperor Chen and his queen were captured and sent to the capital Chang'an of Sui. Before the Princess Le Chang and Xu Deyan were to be bluntly broken up, she threw a copper mirror to the ground in two parts, with one given to her husband and another one held by herself. The couples made an appointment for peddling the copper mirror on the fifth day of the first month of every year, until they found each other.

After arrived in Chang'an, the Princess Le Chang was granted to the Prime Minister Yang Su as his concubine. On the lantern festival of the second year, the Princess Le Chang asked her servant to bring the half piece of copper mirror to peddle at a high price in the fair. Just at that time, Xu Deyan also arrived in Chang'an by enduring various hardships and he immediately recognized the half piece of copper mirror, so he asked for the whereabouts of

子的遭遇后，他不禁泪流满面，在那半面铜镜上题了首诗："镜与人俱去，镜归人不归。无复嫦娥影，空留明月辉。"

his wife. As he heard of the sufferings of his wife, he couldn't help to cry and wrote a poem on that copper mirror, "Gone as the mirrors and you, and returned the mirrors but not you. No shadow of Chang'e, only the moon shines lonely in the sky."

那个仆人把题了诗的铜镜带回来，交给了乐昌公主，一连几天，她都整日以泪洗面。杨素知道这件事后，被两人的真情打动，于是让人叫来徐德言，把乐昌公主送还给他。一对恩爱夫妻最终得以破镜重圆。

The servant took back the copper mirror with that poem and handed it over to the Princess Le Chang, who was crying for some days continuously. As Yang Su heard of this, he was deeply moved by the true love of the couples, so he called in Xu Deyan and returned the Princess Le Chang to him. Therefore, a devoted couple are in union eventually.

179

胸有成竹

Have an ace up one's sleeve

出自 宋·苏轼《文与可画筼筜谷偃竹记》。

释义 比喻做事之前早有通盘的谋划。

文同，字与可，是北宋时期的著名画家，尤其擅长于画竹子。

In the Northern Song Dynasty, there was a famous painter Wen Tong, with the style name as Yuke, who was very good at painting bamboo.

文同担任洋州（今陕西洋县）太守时，别人都觉得那里是穷乡僻壤，但文同却十分开心，因为这里的满山满谷都是竹林。他一有空闲的时候，就会来到竹林之地观竹、画竹。

As Wen Tong was the prefecture chief of Yangzhou, everyone took that place as a remote and backward place, but he was very happy because there were lots of bamboo in the valley, and he always went to appreciate and paint the bamboo at leisure.

为了画好竹子，文同经常在竹林里钻来钻去。遇上三伏天气，日头像一团火烤得地面发烫，可是他照样站在阳光底下，全神贯注地观察竹子的变化。有时天降大雨，别人都忙着躲避，他却跑到竹林，顾不上抹一下脸上的雨水，就两眼一眨不眨地观察起竹子，细心地把竹子经受风雨吹打的姿态记下来。

In order to paint bamboo well, he always went through the bamboo grove. And even in dog days with roasted-like hot ground, he still stood in the sunlight and absorbedly observed the bamboo. Sometimes in heavy rain, people all hurried to find shelter, in order to remember the posture of bamboos in rains and winds, he still run into the bamboo grove and stared at the bamboo without a single blink in spite of rain water on his face.

多年细致入微的观察，使文同终于悟出了画竹的真谛。他告诉表兄苏轼说：“很多画竹的人都是一节节地画它，一叶叶地堆积它，

After many years of careful observation, Wen Tong finally understood the true essence of painting the bamboo. He told his elder cousin Su Shi, “People usually paint the bamboo by the joints one by one or by the leaves one by

这样哪里还会有完整的、活生生的竹子呢？所以画竹的时候，必定要在心里先有完整的竹子形象，拿起笔来仔细看去，就看到了他所想画的竹子，急速起身跟住它，动手作画，一气呵成。”

文同画竹的至理名言，经过苏轼《文与可画篔筜谷偃竹记》一文的转述而广为流传，后来被衍化为大家所知道的“胸有成竹”这一成语。

one, how can they paint complete and vivid bamboo? So before painting the bamboo, you must have a complete image of the complete bamboo, and then when you take up the brush, you will see the bamboo you want to paint. What you need to do is to rapidly follow it and finish the painting at one stroke.”

The famous dictum on painting the bamboo by Wen Tong was forwarded by Su Shi in *the Notes of Painting Bamboo in Yundang Valley* by Wen Yuke and became widely popular, and from which derived the popular idiom “have an ace up one’s sleeve”.

180

脍炙人口

Pleasant to everybody's taste

出自 《孟子·尽心下》。

释义 好的诗文或事物，人人称赞。

孔子的弟子中，有一对曾氏父子。父亲叫曾点，字皙；儿子曾参，字子舆。这

Among all the disciples of Confucius, there were a father and son with surname as Zeng. The father was Zeng Dian with the style

父子俩都是孔子弟子里面的佼佼者。

name as Xi and the son was Zeng Shen with the style name as Ziyu, they were both very excellent among the disciples of Confucius.

曾皙在饮食上有一个嗜好，就是特别喜欢吃果实小而圆、色泽紫黑的羊枣。他的这一嗜好给儿子曾参留下了深刻的印象。在曾皙去世后，曾参悲痛万分，怀念不已，甚至连曾皙生前爱吃的羊枣，曾参也不忍心吃一口。这件事在当时被儒家弟子争相传颂，大家都称赞曾参为孝子的典范。

Zeng Xi was very fond of eating goat jujube which was small, round and purple-black, and this left a deep impression on his son. After Zeng Xi died, Zeng Shen was so deeply grieved that he even did not eat the goat jujube which was the favorite food of Zeng Xi. And this story was positively forwarded by Confucian disciples and people all praised Zeng Shen as the example of a dutiful son.

到了战国时期，孟子的弟子公孙丑对这件事很不理解，于是就向自己的老师孟子请教。公孙丑问道："先生，您觉得烤肉和羊枣，哪一样更好吃呢？"孟子脱口而出："当然是烤肉好吃，没有哪个人不爱吃烤肉的！"

In the Warring States Period, one disciple of Mencius named Gong Sunchou could not understand and turned to Mencius for consultation. Gong Sunchou asked, "Your Master, in comparison of roasted meet and goat jujube, which one is more delicious?" Mencius blurt out "Of course the roasted meet is more precious, no one will not dislike roasted meet!"

公孙丑又问："既然如此，那么曾参和他的父亲也

Gong Sunchou asked again, "If such being the case, then both Zeng Shen and his father

一定爱吃烤肉，可是为什么曾参不戒吃烤肉，只戒吃羊枣呢，这能说明他是有孝心的人吗？”

will also like to eat roasted meet, but why did Zeng Shen only abstain from goat jujube instead of roasted meet? How can it prove that he is a dutiful son?”

孟子解释说：“美味的烤肉是大家都爱吃的食物，但是羊枣却是曾皙尤其爱吃的食物，所以曾参只戒吃羊枣，这是怕引起对故父的痛思之情啊！就好比对长辈只忌讳叫名字，不忌讳称姓一样。人的姓氏会有相同的，但名字却是自己所独有的。”

Mencius explained, “Certainly the delicious roasted meet is the favorite food of people, but Zeng Xi especially liked to eat goat jujube, thus Zeng Shen only abstained from goat jujube because he was afraid of missing his father! Just like it is a taboo to address the given names of the elders and not a taboo to address the surnames, because the surnames of people maybe the same, but the given names are unique.”

公孙丑听完孟子的一番话，终于明白了曾参追思故父的一片孝心。

As Gong Sunchou heard of the words of Mencius, he eventually understood the filial piety of Zeng Shen towards his father.

181

唱筹量沙

Sing tallies and weigh the sand

出自 《南史·檀道济传》。

释义 为了安定军心，制造假象来迷惑敌人。

南北朝时期，宋武帝的儿子宋文帝即位以后，北魏大军渡过黄河，进攻宋朝，

In the Southern and Northern Dynasty, as the son of the Emperor Wu of Song assumed the throne and became the Emperor Wen of

在黄河以南占领了大片土地。宋文帝派檀道济率领大军抵抗。

Song, the North Wei State grandly crossed the Yellow River to attack Song and occupied huge territories, so the Emperor Wen of Song dispatched Tan Daoji to lead troops for resistance.

檀道济率领将士来到济水边，在二十多天里，跟魏军打了三十多仗。宋军节节胜利，一直追到历城（在今山东省）。这时候，魏军趁着宋军防备有些松懈，派两支轻骑兵向宋军前后两翼发起突然袭击，把宋军的辎重粮草放火全部烧掉。宋军断了粮草，没法维持下去，准备从历城退兵。北魏将领得到这一消息后，就派出大军追赶檀道济，想把宋军围困起来。

Tan Daoji led troops to the side of the Ji River and was in more than thirty battles with Wei's troops during over twenty days. As Song's troops won the battles successively and pursued the enemies until Li City which in the current Shandong Province. At this time, as the military defence was slightly slackened, Wei's troops took the chance to dispatch two teams of light cavalry for suddenly attacking the front and rear of Song's troops, and the supplies and food of Song's troops were all burned out. Song's troops could not maintain due to a lack of food and had to withdraw from Li City. As the general of the North Wei got the news, he dispatched huge army to pursue Tan Daoji in order to enclose Song's troops.

宋军将士看到大批魏军前来，都有点害怕。檀道济却不慌不忙地命令将士就地扎营休息。当天晚上，宋军军营里灯火通明，檀道济亲

Upon the arrival of many Wei's troops, the soldiers of Song were afraid, but Tan Daoji unhurriedly ordered the soldiers to encamp for rest. At that very night, the camps of Song were full of lights and Tan Daoji

自带人在营寨里查点粮食，只见一只只米袋里面全是雪白的大米，一些士兵用斗量米，另一些士兵手里拿着竹筹唱着计数。

was personally checking food inside camps. Wei's troops saw that there was all white rice in rice bags, and some soldiers used pipes for measurement and other soldiers used bamboo tallies for counting.

这个消息马上被魏兵的探子听到了，赶快去告诉魏将，说宋军军营里的粮食还绰绰有余。魏将信以为真，不敢再步步紧逼。其实，檀道济在军营里量的并不是白米，而是一斗斗的沙土，只是在沙土上覆盖着少量白米罢了。

Upon this news, the scout of Wei immediately went to told the general and said there was sufficient rice in camps of Song. The general of Wei believed and dared not to pursue tightly. Actually, Tan Daoji was measuring pipes of sand instead of rice, he only put a few rice onside the sand.

天亮以后，檀道济命令将士披盔戴甲，自己穿着便服，乘着一辆马车，大模大样地沿着大路向南转移。魏将本来就对宋军有点害怕，再看到他们从容不迫地撤退，生怕中了埋伏，不敢追赶。

As the day broke, Tan Daoji wore a casual gown sitting in a cart and ordered soldiers to wear helmet and armour and pompously move southward along the way. The general of Wei was originglly afraid of Song's troops, now upon viewing that Song's troops were withdrawing unhurriedly, he was afraid of being ambushed and dared not to pursue.

就这样，檀道济凭借他的镇静和智谋，使宋军得以安全回师。

Therefore, Tan Daoji led troops to safely withdraw by his composure and resourcefulness.

182

唾面自干

Pocket an insult

出自 《新唐书·娄师德传》。

释义 指受了污辱，极度容忍，不加反抗。

娄师德是唐朝的大臣，为人大度，在他当上宰相以后，对人更加谦让有加。

In the Tang Dynasty, there was a minister named Lou Shide, who was very generous and treated people more humbly after he became the Prime Minister.

一次，娄师德和李昭德同行，因为体胖走得很慢，李昭德责怪他说:“真让人不耐烦，这个乡下种田汉!”娄师德笑着说:“我不算乡下种田汉，还能算到谁的头上？”还有一次，娄师德坐在光政门外的横木上等待马匹，有个县令也来与他并肩坐下。旁边有个差人看见了，忙对县令说:“这是宰相啊!”县令连忙起身说:“死罪死罪!”娄师德说:“人都有不认识的人，法律条文上哪有因此判死罪的？”

Once, Lou Shide walked with Li Zhaode, and Lou Shide was too fat to walk quickly, so Li Zhaode scolded, “It is really annoying, you peasant!” Lou Shide smiled and said, “If I'm not a peasant, then who will be a peasant?” One more time, Lou Shide was sitting on the ledger outside the Gate Guangzheng for waiting horses, at the moment, a county magistrate came to sit with him, a servant beside saw and hurried to say, “This is the Prime Minister!” The county magistrate immediately stood up and said, “Please forgive my death penalty!” Lou Shide said, “We can not know everybody, which is the rules for death penalty in the articles of law?”

当初，狄仁杰做宰相就是娄师德暗中推荐的，但是狄仁杰并不知情，反而对他有些轻视，多次排挤他。武则天觉察到这一情况，便问狄仁杰：“娄师德知人吗？”狄仁杰回答说：“臣与他同列为官，没有听说他知人。”武则天于是说：

Di Renjie was originally recommended to be the Prime Minister by Lou Shide in secret, but Di Renjie knew nothing about it, so Di Renjie even despised and squeezed out Lou Shide. The Empress Wu Zetian was aware of this and asked Di Renjie, “Does Lou Shide distinguish the talents?” Di Renjie answered, “He and I were both imperial officials, and I never heard that he was good at distinguishing talents.” The Empress Wu

"我之所以重用你，就是他推荐的，这应该可以称作知人了吧。"狄仁杰非常惭愧，由衷地感叹娄师德的胸怀竟能如此宽大。

Zetian said, "I appoint you to the important post because Lou Shide recommended you, thus I think he is good at distinguishing talents." Di Renjie was very ashamed and admired the generousness of Lou Shide.

后来，娄师德的弟弟被提升为代州都督，出发前，娄师德嘱咐他说："我从小就没有什么才能，却已经位居宰相。你现在又担任一州长官，侥幸占据高位，会招来别人的嫉妒。这如何是好啊？"弟弟说："从今以后，即使有人把唾沫吐到我脸上，我也不去争吵，只能自己擦掉它，这样就不会为兄长添忧了吧？"娄师德说："这正是我担忧的。有人向你吐唾沫，是因为对你发火，你擦了它，就会使他更加恼火。唾液不去擦自己也会干掉，不如笑着来承受它。"弟弟大为折服，连忙说："我一定记在心里。"

Afterwards, the younger brother of Lou Shide was promoted to be the prefecture chief, before departure, Lou Shide enjoined him, "Although I was very ordinary when I am a child, I become the Prime Minister nowadays. Moreover, you are so lucky to become the prefecture chief, which will easily attract jealousness of others. What should we do?" His younger brother said, "From now on, even if someone spit on my face, I will not quarrel with him and only wipe it by myself, then you will not be worried, is it right?" Lou Shide said, "That is exactly what I am worried. Someone spit on you, that is certainly because he is angry with you, but if you wipe it, that will inflame his anger. The spit would be dry even if you don't wipe it, so you should endure it happily." His younger brother was completely convinced and hurried to say, "I will keep it in mind."

183

弹冠相庆

Congratulate each other

出自 《汉书·王吉传》。

释义 一个人做了官，其他人也互相庆贺将有官可做。

王吉，字子阳，是西汉昭帝时期的人，为人十分正直。他的邻居家有一株高大

In the Western Han Dynasty reigned by the Emperor Zhao, there was a person named Wang Ji with the style name as Ziyang, who was very

的枣树，结满果实的树枝伸进了他家的院子里。王吉的妻子随意摘了几颗枣子给他吃，事后，王吉得知枣子是偷摘邻居家的，便将妻子赶走。邻家听说后，执意要把枣树砍掉，后经再三劝说，王吉才将妻子召回。

upright. His neighbor planted a tall jujube tree and the fruit-bearing branches reached out into his yard. His wife randomly picked up several jujubes and gave him to eat, and when he knew they were picked up stealthily, he drove his wife away. Upon the news, the neighbor insisted on cutting down the jujube tree. Finally, Wang Ji called back his wife by repeated persuasion.

王吉因为品德高尚，声名远播，所以被朝廷选拔为官，后来又调到昌邑王府担任中尉。昭帝死后，大将军霍光迎昌邑王为帝。王吉立即写信告诫昌邑王，让他改掉过去任性的毛病，要千万小心谨慎。但是昌邑王根本没有把王吉的话当回事，称帝不到一个月，就因为胡作非为而被废黜了。

Thanks to his noble character, Wang Ji became popular and was appointed as an imperial official, and then transferred to be the lieutenant in the Palace of Chang Yi. As the Emperor Zhao passed away, the Big General Huo Guang intended to enthrone Chang Yi. Wang Ji immediately wrote a letter and persuaded the King Chang Yi to get rid of willfulness and take full cautiousness. Whereas, the King Chang Yi did not take it seriously and was impeached only after one month due to his malfeasance.

霍光认为昌邑王犯下的过失，是由于府中的官员们没有尽职尽责地劝谏，于是下令将昌邑王府的大小官员全部下狱。经过审理，霍光了解到王吉曾不止一次地劝

Huo Guang believed that the reason that King Chang Yi made serious mistakes was because the officials of the Palace Chang Yi did not dutifully persuade the King Chang Yi, so Huo Guang ordered to arrest all the officials of the Palace Chang Yi in the prison. After interrogation, Huo Guang got to know

谏过昌邑王，于是从轻处分了他。

王吉在宣帝时重新被起用担任官职。当时，有个叫贡禹的人，与王吉是同乡，两人情意相投，交往很深。贡禹以前因为在工作上与上司持不同看法，受到上司指责，便辞官而去。这时候听说王吉复出做官，贡禹高兴得弹掉帽子的灰尘，表示庆贺。所以后来有“王阳在位，贡公弹冠”的说法，这也就是成语“弹冠相庆”的来由。

that Wang Ji had persuaded the King Chang Yi many times, so he gave Wang Ji a lesser punishment.

During the reign of the Emperor Xuan, Wang Ji was reappointed as the imperial official. At that time, Wang Ji had a close friendship with his fellow townsman named Gong Yu. In the past, due to different opinions with his supervisor, he was blamed and then quitted his post. Now as he heard Wang Ji was reappointed again, Gong Yu was very happy and flipped off the dust on his hat for congratulation. Afterwards, there was a saying of “Wang Ji in power and Gong Yu congratulates”, which is origin of the idiom “congratulate each other”.

184

得陇望蜀

The more one gets, the more one wants

出自 《后汉书·岑彭传》。

释义 比喻贪得无厌。

东汉初年，刘秀称帝以后，招降了赤眉军，收复关东地区，又开始把军事锋芒

As Liu Xiu assumed the throne at the beginning of the eastern Han, he summoned the red-brow peasants to surrender and recovered the

直指盘踞在陇西的隗嚣和蜀地的公孙述。

east of the Hangu Pass, and then he set his aims directly at Wei Xiao occupied in Longxi of Gansu and Gong Sunshu occupied in the place of Shu.

刘秀亲自率领大军来到陇西，与隗嚣展开激战，双方互有胜负。隗嚣由于自己势单力孤，就与蜀地的公孙述联合起来，共同抵抗刘秀。

Liu Xiu personally led troops to Longxi and launched fierce attacks with Wei Xiao and they both did not defeat the other. Due to lack of military strength, Wei Xiao united with Gong Sunshu to commonly attack Liu Xiu.

为了一举攻克陇西，刘秀指挥手下名将吴汉、岑彭、耿彝等人，兵分九路而进，大败隗嚣军队，接连夺取十六个县。隗嚣逃进了西城，被吴汉、岑彭等部重重包围起来。刘秀向隗嚣下诏，让他投降，但遭到了拒绝。

In order to conquer Longxi at one stroke, Liu Xiu ordered his subordinates Wu Han, Cen Peng and Geng Yi to move forward in nine branches. Liuxiu completely defeated troops of Wei Xiao and seized sixteen counties continuously. Wei Xiao fled to the West City which is the current southwest of Tianshui in Gansu province and was fully enclosed by troops of Wu Han and Cen Peng. Liu Xiu issued a statement to Wei Xiao and asked him to surrender, but was refused.

正在这时，京师传来河东官兵叛乱的消息，刘秀认为陇西的战局已稳操胜券，便决定回京镇压叛乱。临走以前，刘秀给大将岑彭留下一封信，信中写道：“西城

At this time, the capital troops delivered the news about the rebellion of the soldiers in the east of the Yellow River. Liu Xiu was sure of success on the war situation in Longxi, so he decided to go back to the capital for suppressing the rebellions. Before departure, Liu Xiu left

攻克后，你便可带兵去攻打蜀地。人都是不知足的，才平定陇右（即陇西），又想着蜀地。每一次出兵征战，头发胡须都要变白一些啊！”

后来，人们就由此概括出了“得陇望蜀”这一成语，来比喻人心不知足。

a letter to Cen Peng, “After the west city is defeated, you can lead troops to attack the place of Shu. People are all so insatiable that even just have conquered Longxi and still want to suppress the place of Shu. My hair and beard would become whiter after each expedition!”

Afterwards, people summarized an idiom of “the more one gets, the more one wants” for describing insatiable desires.

185

惊弓之鸟

Bird on a wire

出自 《战国策·楚策四》。

释义 经过惊吓的人，碰到一点动静，就非常害怕。

战国时期，魏国有一个名叫更羸的射箭高手。

有一天，更羸陪同魏

In the Warring States Period, there was an expert in archery named Geng Lei in Wei State.

One day, Geng Lei accompanied the King

王出去散步，看见有一只大雁从远处飞来。更羸便对魏王说：“大王，我可以不用箭，只要拉一下弓，这只大雁就能掉下来。”

of Wei for walking and saw a wild goose flying from a distance. So Geng Lei said to the King of Wei, “Your Majesty, I can only draw my bow without any arrow, the wild goose will fall down.”

魏王惊奇地问：“你的射箭技术竟然能达到这样的程度？”

The King of Wei was surprised and asked, “Is your skill in archery so exquisite now?”

更羸自信地说：“能。”

Geng Lei said confidently, “Of course I can.”

说话间，那只大雁已经飞到了他们的头顶上空。更羸于是立即拉弓扣弦，随着嘣的一声弦响，只见大雁先是向高处猛地一窜，随后在空中无力地扑打了几下，便一头栽落下来。

As they chatted, that wild goose flew in the sky on top of them, so Geng Lei immediately drew his bow, and upon a sound of ‘bang’, that wild goose suddenly rushed upward firstly and then flapped several times powerlessly, and finally fell headlong down to the ground.

魏王看到后，半天合不拢嘴，连声大叫道：“啊呀，箭术竟能高超到这等地步，真是意想不到！”便问更羸是怎么将空中飞着的雁射下来的。

As the King of Wei saw, he was too surprised to close his mouth and cried loudly again and again, “Alas! It is unbelievable that your skill in archery is so exquisite!” Then the king asked Geng Lei how to make the wild goose fall down.

更羸对魏王解释说：“其实没什么，这是一只受

Geng Lei explained, “It is nothing, actually that is a wild goose once hurt by the arrow.”

过箭伤的大雁。”

魏王更加奇怪了，问道：“你怎么知道这只大雁受过箭伤呢?”

The King of Wei was more curious and asked, “How do you know that?”

更羸接着解释说：“这只大雁飞得很慢，叫声凄凉。根据我的经验，飞得慢，是因为它体内有伤；叫声凄凉，是因为它长久失群。这只大雁伤口在作痛，还没有好，心里又孤单害怕，所以当听到弓弦声响后，害怕再次被箭射中，就会拼命地往高处飞。它一使劲，本来没有愈合的伤口又裂开了，疼痛难忍，再也飞不动了，就从空中掉了下来。”

Geng Lei continued to explain, “This wild goose flew slowly and yelled miserably. According to my experience, flying slowly is because it has hurts inside its body, and yelling miserably is because it was lost for a long time. As its wound is still aching and it feels lonely and scared, as it hears the sound of bow, it was afraid to be shot again, so it struggled to fly upward. But as it exerted its strength, its unhealed wound split open and it was too painful to fly anymore, so it fell down.”

186

掩耳盗铃

Play the ostrich

出自 《吕氏春秋·自知》。

释义 自己欺骗自己，明明掩盖不住的事情偏要想法掩盖。

春秋时期，晋景公设立了六卿制度，这六卿包括范氏、中行氏、智氏、韩氏、

In the Spring and Autumn Period, the Emperor Jing of Jin established the Six Lord System which included six hereditary peers

赵氏、魏氏六个世袭贵族。后来六卿之间发生冲突，赵、魏、韩三家灭掉了范氏和中行氏。

such as Fan Clan, Zhong Xing Clan, Zhi Clan, Han Clan, Zhao Clan and Wei Clan. Afterwards, clashes broke out between the six clans, and Fan Clan and Zhong Xing Clan were exterminated by Zhao Clan, Wei Clan and Han Clan.

范氏被灭掉以后，有个人趁机溜到他们的家里想偷点值钱的东西。他看见院子里吊着一口大钟，钟用上等青铜铸成，上面的造型和图案十分精美，非常高兴，想把这口大钟背回自己家去。可是钟又大又重，他一个人根本无法搬动。他想出了一个办法，就是把钟敲碎，然后分批搬回家。

After Fan Clan was exterminated, a person took the chance and stealthily intruded into their houses for stealing valuable things. There was a big clock which was made of first-class bronze with exquisite shape and pattern, and this person was very happy and wanted to carry it back, but the clock was too heavy for him to move, so he had an idea and knocked it into small pieces for carrying back in batches.

他找来一把大锤，用力朝着大钟砸去，只听一声巨响，把他吓了一大跳。这个人心里很害怕，声音这么大，如果让人听到就糟了！他又转念一想，把自己的耳朵捂住不就听不到钟声了吗！于是他立刻找来两个布

He found a big hammer and exerted his full strength to knock the big clock, but he was terribly frightened by the blare. He was afraid that other people would hear of the sound, but on second thought, he thought that he would not hear the sound if he covered his ears. Then he found two cloth wads to plug his ears and began to knock the clock relievedly.

团，把耳朵塞住，然后放心地开始砸起钟来。

附近的人听到钟声，都纷纷赶过来，抓住了这个偷钟的人。

The nearby people heard of the blare of the bell and hurried to have a look, and then the clock stealer was seized.

这则故事出自《吕氏春秋·自知》，原文为掩耳盗钟，后来钟演变为铃，成为“掩耳盗铃”这一成语。

This story originates from *the Self-knowledge in the Lu's Spring and Autumn Annals*, and the clock in the original text was changed to bell afterwards and developed into the current idiom.

187

望洋兴叹

Lament one's littleness before the vast ocean

出自 庄子《外篇·秋水》。

释义 比喻做事力量不够或条件不充分而感到无可奈何。

很久以前，黄河里有一位河神，人们都叫他河伯。有一次，河伯站在黄河岸

Once upon a time, there was a River God in the Yellow River, and people all addressed him as He Bo. Once, He Bo stood beside the

上，望着滚滚的河水由西而来，又向东奔腾而去，兴奋地说："黄河真大呀，世上没有哪条河能和它相比。我就是最大的水神！"有人告诉他："你的话不对，在黄河的东面有个地方叫北海，那才真叫大呢。"河伯坚持说："我没见过北海，我不相信。"那个人告诉他："有机会你去看看北海，就明白我的话了。"

Yellow River and stared at the rolling water coming from the west and rushing to the east, so he said excitedly, "The Yellow River is the biggest river which unparalleled, and I'm the most superior River God!" Someone told him, "You are wrong, because there is a place named the North Sea in the east of the Yellow River." He Bo insisted on his idea and said, "I don't believe because I never see the North Sea." That person told him, "If there is a chance, I will bring you to the North Sea, then you will believe me."

秋天到了，连日的暴雨使大量支流的水都汇集到黄河里，黄河的水面更加宽阔，隔岸望去，都分不清对岸的是牛还是马。河伯更加得意，以为天下最壮观的景象都集中在了自己这里。他在自得之余，想起了有人跟他提起的北海，于是决定去那里看看。

As in autumn, the rainstorms for running days flew into the Yellow River and widened its surface. It would be impossible to distinguish the bulls and horses by looking across the river, so He Bo was further proud and believed that the grand and gorgeous views all concentrated in the Yellow River. And then he remembered the North Sea mentioned by that person, so he decided to have a look.

河伯顺着水势向东前行，到了北海，抬眼望去，只见一片汪洋，无边无际。

He Bo went eastward along the water, and as he arrived in the North Sea, he looked up and saw a boundless and endless world of

河伯不由得对着北海感叹说："俗话说，'有的人懂得了一点道理，便以为没有谁能比得上自己。'这正是批评我这种人的啊。如果不是亲自到你这里来，那我将永远被有学问的人所耻笑了。"

waters. He Bo could not help to sign in front of the North Sea, "As the saying goes that someone knows little but think himself to be unparalleled, which is exactly criticizing people such as me. If I have not come to see by myself, then I would be laughed at by knowledgeable people."

188

望梅止渴

Feed on fancies

出自 《世说新语·假谲》。

释义 用空想安慰自己或他人。

东汉末年，曹操带兵去攻打张绣，时值盛夏，一路上又都是荒山野岭，部队在

By the end of the Eastern Han, Cao Cao led troops to attack Zhang Xiu. As the soldiers walked on the winding paths in the barren

弯弯曲曲的山道上行走，头顶烈日，将士们一个个被晒得头昏眼花，大汗淋漓，可是又找不到水喝。大家都口干舌燥，每走几里路，就有人中暑倒下死去。

wastelands in the midsummer, they all felt faint and blurred with profuse sweat, but they could not find any water, thus they were so thirst that some soldiers would fall to die due to sunstroke every a few miles.

曹操看到行军的速度越来越慢，担心贻误战机，心里很是着急。他立刻叫来向导，悄悄地问他："这附近可有水源？"向导摇摇头说："泉水在山谷的那一边，要绕道过去还有很远的路程。"曹操沉思了一会儿，对向导说："你什么也不要说，我来想办法。"

As the troops moved more and more slowly, Cao Cao began to worry about delaying the chance of winning the battle, so he immediately called in the guide and asked him quietly, "Is there any source of water nearby?" The guide shook his head and said, "The spring is on the other side of the valley, and it will be a very long way to go by a roundabout route." Cao Cao contemplated for a moment and said to the guide, "Don't speak anything, I have an idea."

他一夹马肚子，快速赶到队伍前面，用马鞭指着前方说："各位将士，我知道前面有一大片梅树林，那里的梅子又大又好吃，我们快点赶路，绕过这个山丘就到梅树林了！"士兵们一听，想起梅子的酸味，就好像真

Cao Cao pressed his knees to the horse and went to the front of the troops, he pointed at the place ahead with horsewhip and said, "My soldiers, I know there is a huge forest of plum trees with lots of big and delicious plums, let us hurry up and we will arrive at the forest of plum trees by the roundabout route!" At the moment, soldiers began to think of the sour taste of

的吃到梅子一样，口里顿时生出了不少口水，精神也振作起来，鼓足力气加紧向前赶去。就这样，曹操终于率领军队走到了有水的地方。

plums just like they really tasted the plums, and a lot of saliva immediately developed, so they exerted full strength to move forward with high spirits. Finally, Cao Cao led the troops to the place with water successfully.

189

欲加之罪，何患无辞

Give a dog a bad name and hang him

出自 《左传·僖公十年》。

释义 想要给人强加罪名，不愁找不到借口。

春秋时期，晋献公有一个非常宠爱的妃子，名叫骊姬。当时，晋献公已经立儿

In the Spring and Autumn Period, Li Ji was the beloved concubine of the Emperor Xian of Jin. At that time, the Emperor Xian of

子申生为太子，准备让他继位。可是骊姬想让自己的儿子奚齐当国君，于是她千方百计地陷害申生，最终申生自杀身亡，他的两个哥哥重耳和夷吾也被迫逃亡国外。

Jin already set his son Shen Sheng as the future prince, but Li Ji wished her son Xi Qi to assume the throne, so she framed Shen Sheng by all means and finally made Shen Sheng commit suicide and his two brothers Chong Er and Yi Wu flee in exile.

后来，晋献公病重，他把自己最信任的大夫荀息叫到床前，嘱咐他好好辅佐奚齐当国君。荀息答应了。可是，等晋献公一死，晋国立刻陷入一片混乱之中。有一个名叫里克的大夫，原来是太子申生的副将，他觉得申生死得冤枉，一心想为申生报仇。奚齐当上国君不久，里克就找了个机会把奚齐给杀了。荀息只好又立奚齐的弟弟卓子做了国君，不久，里克又把卓子杀掉了，荀息也在悲愤中自杀。

Afterwards, the Emperor Xian of Jin fell in ill seriously, he called in the most reliable minister Xun Xi to his bed and asked him to support Xi Qi to be the emperor, and Xun Xi agreed. But as the Emperor Xian of Jin died, Jin State was immediately in a chaos. There was a minister named Li Ke, who was formerly the vice general of Shen Sheng. He thought the death of Shen Sheng as undeserved and was bent on revenge for Shen Sheng. Before long as Xi Qi became the emperor, Li Ke took a chance to kill Xi Qi, then Xun Xi had to enthrone Xi Qi's younger brother Zhuo Zi who was also killed by Li Ke soon, therefore, Xun Xi committed suicide in extreme grief and indignation.

后来，秦国帮助夷吾回国即位，这就是晋惠公。晋惠公担心自己像奚齐、卓子一样被弑，就想杀掉里克，

Afterwards, Qin State helped Yi Wu go back to Jin to assume the throne as the Emperor Hui of Jin. The Emperor Hui of Jin was afraid that he would be killed just like Xi Qi and Zhuo

于是派兵包围了里克家，并让人向里克喊话说："你杀掉了两个国君和一个大夫，我如果不杀你，别人就不会服我。"里克仰天长叹，说："如果我不杀他们，能轮到你来当这个国君吗？你既然已经打定主意把罪名加到我头上，还怕找不到借口吗？"于是拔剑自杀。

Zi, so he decided to kill Li Ke. He ordered to enclose the house of Li Ke and shout at him, "You killed two emperors and one minister, people will not be convinced if I don't kill you." Li Ke looked up to the sky and said, "If I did not kill them, how could you become the emperor? Now that you decide to condemn me, of course you can trump up a charge." Then Li Ke took out his sword and killed himself.

190

骑虎难下

Have a wolf by the ears

出自 南朝宋·何法盛《晋中兴书》。

释义 进退两退。

东晋时期，叛将苏峻和祖约率军攻入都城，挟持晋成帝，掌握了朝政大权。

In the Eastern Jin Dynasty, there were two traitorous generals named Su Jun and Zu Yue, they led troops to attack the capital. Then

江州刺史温峤组织了以征西将军陶侃为盟主的联军征讨叛军。在战争的初期，由于叛军兵力强盛，而联军却缺兵少粮，几次战斗都打了败仗。

they enthroned the Emperor Cheng of Jin and held the imperial power. Wen Qiao was the prefectural governor of Jiangzhou, and he organized allied forces with Tao Kan as the leader in order to subjugate the rebel forces. At the beginning of the battle, the allied forces failed due to lack of soldiers and food, in contrast with the strong military power of the rebel forces.

陶侃眼看着军心开始浮动，心中着急，就对温峤说："你鼓动我来的时候，说一切都已安排妥当，现在军中缺兵少将，粮食也所剩无几，如果不能马上添兵增粮，我只有下令撤军，等条件具备再起兵吧！"

As the military morale was affected, Tao Kan was anxious and said to Wen Qiao, "You promised everything was well prepared and persuaded me to launch the battle, but now we are in short supply of soldiers and food. If we could not improve the current situation, I have to issue an order for retreat. We would launch attacks again until we are well prepared then!"

温峤耐心地劝说道："现在皇上有难，国家处在危急关头，我们起兵讨伐叛贼，乃正义之师。现在叛军势力强盛，我军又遇到许多困难，可如果马上撤军，不仅会让人耻笑我们，而且也会使叛军更加嚣张。自古以

Wen Qiao persuaded patiently, "Nowadays our emperor is in danger and our country is in a chaos, and now we launch attacks on rebel forces, we are the troops of justice. In front of the difficulties currently, we would be laughed at and the rebel forces would become more rampant. Since ancient times, if troops want to win the battle, they should be united firstly. Our

来，要想打胜仗，首先得内部团结。我们目前的处境，就像骑在猛兽的身上，不把猛兽打死，怎么能够下来呢？只有一鼓作气坚持到底，才有出路！”

陶侃接受了温峤的劝说，激励众将士，齐心协力，克服重重困难，一举平定了叛乱。

current situation is just like riding on a wild beast, and we would not get off unless we kill it. Similarly, there would be chances of winning the battle only when we held on straight to the end at one fling!”

Tao Kan took the advice of Wen Qiao and encouraged soldiers to make concerted efforts to overcome numerous difficulties and suppressed the rebellion at one fling.

191

强弩之末

A spent bullet

出自 《史记·韩安国列传》。

释义 比喻原本强大，现已衰竭无力。

汉武帝时期，匈奴与汉朝之间经常发生战争。有一次，北方的匈奴派人来汉

During the reign of the Emperor Wu of Han, wars always broke out between Xiongnu and Han Dynasty. Once the north Xiongnu

朝要求和好，武帝一时拿不定主意，就召集大臣来商议对策。

dispatched envoys to plea for peace, the Emperor Wu couldn't make up his mind and called in ministers for discussion.

有一个名叫王恢的人，多次出任边防官吏，熟悉匈奴的情况。他建议说，匈奴反复无常，汉朝和匈奴和亲，一般过不了几年匈奴就会背弃盟约。不如不答应，而发兵攻打，把它彻底征服。

There was a person named Wang Hui, who was appointed as the border official for several times and very familiar with the situation of Xiongnu. So he advised, "Xiongnu is capricious and usually broke the covenant few years after the political marriage between Han and them. We'd better refuse their plea for peace and launch attacks to completely suppress them."

御史大夫韩安国却坚决不同意发兵，他说："派大军到千里之外作战，一定不会有好的结果。现在匈奴军马充足，行动起来迅疾如飞，我们很难在短时间内征服他们。而且我们即使得到匈奴的土地，也不能扩大多少疆土；得到匈奴的百姓，也不能增强我们的力量。这就好像强弓射出的箭，到最远处的时候，力量已经尽失，甚至连非常薄的丝绸都穿透不了。这不是说它本身

The Royal Doctor Han Guoan disagreed to attack and said, "Dispatching troops to fight in thousands of miles away will probably fail. Now Xiongnu was sufficient in soldiers and horses with advantages of swift action, it would be impossible for us to suppress them during a short period of time. Even if we won the territory of Xiongnu, it will not add too large territory for us. Even if we conquered the their civilians, it will not add too much power for us. This is just like an arrow from a strong bow, as it reaches to the farthest distance, its strength almost exhausts and can not shoot through the very thin silk cloth. This isn't to say that it has no strength itself, but because its

没有力量，而是因为到最后力量衰竭了。所以，明智之举是与匈奴和亲，安定双方的人心，加强睦邻友好关系，互不侵扰。”

strength exhausts to the end. Therefore, it is wise to make peace with Xiongnu by marriage in order to reassure the civilians and reinforce a friendly neighborhood relationship without disturbing each other.”

大臣们都认为韩安国说得有理，汉武帝也表示同意，于是接受了匈奴的和亲。在以后很长一段时间里，汉朝与匈奴都保持着相对和睦的关系。

All the ministers and the Emperor Wu of Han all agreed with Han Guoan and accepted Xiongnu's plea for marriage, and Han Dynasty and Xiongnu kept a relatively harmonious-neighborly relationship for a rather long time.

192

黄粱美梦

Fond dream

出自 唐·李泌《枕中记》。

释义 比喻人生虚幻，或比喻不能实现的梦想。

唐朝时，有一位姓卢的书生，到京城长安赶考。他路过邯郸的时候，天色已

In the Tang Dynasty, a scholar with the surname as Lu went to the capital for examination, when he passed by Han Dan,

晚，于是就找了一家便宜的旅馆住下来。

since it was getting dark, he stayed in a hotel with cheap price.

和卢生住在一个屋里的，还有一位老道士。两人便请店主为他们蒸一锅小米饭，再随便备上点小菜作为晚餐。在等待饭熟的时间里，卢生便向老道士诉说起自己的穷困生活，盼望这次进京赶考能够金榜题名，光宗耀祖，并再三恳求老道士能为他指点迷津。

An old Taoist shared the same room with the scholar Lu, and they asked the boss to prepare a pot of steamed millet and some ordinary dish as their dinner. During their waiting time, scholar Lu began to talk about his poor life with the old Taoist and expressed his wish to succeed in the imperial examinations and bring glories to his ancestors, and he also turned to the old Taoist for directions.

老道士从自己的行装中取出一个枕头，让卢生躺下来睡一觉，对他说："这样你很快就能称心如意了。"

The old Taoist took out a pillow from his luggage and asked scholar Lu to lie down for a sleep, and said, "By this way, you can realize your dream soon."

卢生奔波数日，身体非常疲惫，头一挨枕头，便很快进入了梦乡。在梦中，卢生果然金榜题名，考中头名状元，皇上将皇女许配给他为妻。在宫廷宴会上，吃的是山珍海味，奇食异果；回老家报喜的路上，他身穿红袍，骑着高头大马，众多

Since scholar Lu had traveled for many days and was very tired, so as his head touched the pillow, he fell asleep very soon. In his dream, he passed the imperial examinations as the Number One Scholar, and the emperor married his daughter to him. In the imperial banquet, he ate lots of delicacies as well as rare and precious fruits. On his way back home to announce the good news, he wore a

差人鸣锣开道，好不威风。后来他又做了大官，立下战功，当上了丞相，而且儿孙满堂，个个功成名就……

red gown and rode on a tall horse, and many servants beat the gongs to clear the way for him in an imposing momentum. Afterwards, he became a dignitary official and made prominent military achievement. Then afterwards, he was promoted to be the Prime Minister and had lots of off-springs with successful achievement and recognition.

这时候，他一觉醒来，梦中的情景已经无影无踪。他还穿着自己的那身破烂衣衫，老道士仍然坐在他的身旁，店里煮的小米饭还没有熟呢。

At this time, he woke up and all the illusions in the dream vanished. He still wore the torn clothes, the old Taoist was still sitting beside him, and the millet in the pot was not ready yet.

193

朝三暮四

Chop and change

出自 《庄子·齐物论》。

释义 比喻常常变卦，反复无常。

战国时期，宋国有一个老人，他很喜欢猕猴，因此在家里养了成群的猕猴。跟

In the Warring States Period, there was an old man who liked monkeys very much and he raised herds of monkeys in his house, so he

猕猴待的时间长了，老人对它们的性情了如指掌，而猴子们也好像懂得主人的心意似的，经常做一些奇怪的动作来逗老人开心。于是老人对这些猕猴就更加喜欢了，宁可让家里人减少口粮，也要让那些猴子顿顿吃饱。

knew about the temperament of monkeys very well. And those monkeys seemed to understand their master and always made some strange movement to amuse the old man. Therefore, the old man loved the monkeys more and more, and even if his family people did not have enough to eat, he would well feed the monkeys up.

不久，老人家里的粮食越来越缺乏，他想要限制猕猴们的食物，但又怕它们生气不听自己的话。怎么办呢？老人想来想去，终于有了一个办法。

Before long, the remaining food in his house became lesser and lesser, and the old man decided to limit their appetite, but he was afraid that those monkeys would be angry and insubordinate. The old man thought it over, and finally he came out an idea.

第二天一大早，老头就起了床，走到猴群面前，对它们说："从今天起，给你们吃的橡子，每天早上三升，晚上四升，你们看这样够不够？"猕猴们一听，都乱蹦乱跳，龇牙咧嘴地表示不满。

On the early morning next day, the old man got up and walked to the front of those monkeys, he said, "From today, I will give you three measures of acorns in the morning and four measures in the evening, do you think it enough?" The monkeys jumped up and bared their fangs to express dissatisfaction.

老人连忙说："那就改成早上四升，晚上三升，这样你们总该满意了吧？"

The old man hurried to say, "Four measures in the morning and three measures in the evening, in this way, you must be satisfied, right?"

猴子们听了，都摇头摆尾地趴在地上，表示非常满意。

The monkeys all lied on their stomach with heads nodding and tails wagging to express their satisfaction.

194

缘木求鱼

Catch fish in a tree

出自 《孟子·梁惠王上》。

释义 方向、办法不对，一定达不到目的。

孟子周游列国，来到齐国。当时，齐宣王为了扩张自己的领土，正准备去攻打邻国。孟子一贯宣扬仁治，反对

During the period when Mencius travelled around various countries, as he arrived in Qi State, the Emperor Xuan of Qi was just preparing to attack neighboring countries

战争，为了说服齐宣王，他与齐宣王进行了一段有趣的对话。

in order to enlarge his territory. As Mencius always propagated benevolent administration against wars, in order to persuade the emperor, he had an interesting talk with the emperor.

孟子问："大王心中最大的愿望是什么，可以讲给我听听吗？"齐宣王笑了笑，没有回答。

Mencius asked, "Your Majesty, may I know the biggest wish in your heart?" The Emperor Xuan of Qi smiled and said nothing.

孟子接着问："是为了肥美的食物不够吃，轻暖的衣服不够穿，还是为了艳丽的色彩不够看，美妙的音乐不够听，身边伺候的人不够使唤呢？这些，臣子们都全部能给您提供，难道您真是为了这些吗？"

Mencius continued to ask, "Are you for more delicious food? Are you for more warm clothes? Are you for more gorgeous colors? Are you for more splendid music? Are you for more servants? The ministers can provide you all of these, are you really for those things?"

齐宣王说："不，我不是为了这些。"

The Emperor Xuan of Qi said, "No, I'm not for those things".

孟子说："那您最想要的，一定就是扩张国土，收服秦国、楚国这些大国，统治中原，安抚四方民族了。不过，以您现在的做法，想实现您的这个愿望，就像爬到树上去捉鱼一样。"

Mencius said, "Then you must be for enlarging your territory, conquering large countries such as Qin and Chu states, governing the Central Plains and pacifying civilians in the world. But what you are doing now is just like catching fish in a tree and can't make you realize your wishes."

齐宣王忙问："有这么

The Emperor Xuan of Qi hurried to ask, "Is

严重吗？”

it really so serious?”

孟子说：“恐怕比这还要严重。爬上树去捉鱼，虽然徒劳无功，却也没什么后患。以您现在的做法，日后一定会有灾祸。”

Mencius said, I’m afraid it is rather more serious. Although catching fish in a tree is fruitless, it will not cause any future troubles. But what you are doing will probably cause future disasters.”

宣王问道：“为什么呢？”

孟子说：“假如邹国和楚国打仗，您认为哪一国会打胜呢？”

The emperor asked why, and Mencius said, “If Zou and Chu are in a battle, do you think which one will win?”

宣王说：“当然是楚国。”

The emperor said, “Chu State, of course.”

孟子说：“很显然，小国不可以与大国为敌，弱国不可以与强国为敌。您想征服其他几个大国，一统天下，是以弱击强，只会给自己带来灾祸。现在您如果能施行仁政，使天下做官的人都想到您的朝廷里来做官，天下的农民都想到您的国家来种地，天下做生意的人都想到您的国家来做生意，这样，天下还有谁能够与您为敌呢？”

Mencius said, “Obviously, small and weak countries can’t win against big and strong countries. You want to subdue other big countries and unite the world, that is actually the weak beating the strong, which will certainly bring disasters. If you can implement benevolent administration, then all the officials will wish to work in your imperial court, all the farmers will wish to plant in your lands, and all the merchants will wish to do business in your country. Therefore, is there anyone against you anymore?”

195

道听途说

The hearsay

出自 《论语·阳货》。

释义 泛指没有根据的传闻。

战国时期，艾子从楚国回到齐国，刚进都城就遇到了爱讲大话的毛空。毛空神

In the Warring States Period, as Ai Zi came back to Qi from Chu State, he happened to meet Mao Kong who was good at boasting.

神秘秘地告诉艾子，说有个人家的一只鸭子，一次生了一百只蛋。

Mao Kong told Ai Zi mysteriously that a person had a duck which could lay one hundred eggs.

艾子不信，说："不会有这样的事吧？"

Ai Zi disbelieved and said, "It is impossible."

毛空说："那可能是两只鸭子生的。"

Mao Kong said, "Then that one hundred eggs were laid by two ducks."

艾子摇摇头说："这也不可能。"

Ai Zi shook his head and said, "It is impossible, neither."

毛空又改口说："那大概是三只鸭子生的。"艾子还是不信。

Then Mao Kong corrected himself, "Then maybe three ducks." Ai Zi still disbelieved.

"也可能是四只、八只、十只。"艾子当然还是不相信。

Mao Kong said, "Then maybe four, eight or ten ducks." Ai Zi still disbelieved.

过了一会儿，毛空又对艾子说："上个月，天上掉下一块肉来，有三十丈长，十丈宽。"

After a while, Mao Kong said to Ai Zi, "Last month, a piece of meat dropped from the sky, which is three hundred feet in length and one hundred feet in width."

艾子不信，毛空急忙改口说："那么是二十丈长。"

Ai Zi disbelieved. Mao Kong hurried to correct himself, "Then two hundred feet in length."

艾子仍然不信。毛空又说："那就算十丈吧！"

Ai Zi still disbelieved. Mao Kong said, "Then one hundred feet in length!"

艾子实在忍不住了，反

Ai Zi could not help asking, "There will

问道：“世上哪有十丈长、十丈宽的肉，而且还会从天上掉下来，你是亲眼看见的吗？刚才你说的鸭子是哪一家的，大肉又掉在了什么地方？”

not be a piece of meat dropping form the sky, which is one hundred feet in both length and width, did you see that by yourself? Whose duck is that you mentioned? Where did that big piece of meat drop?”

毛空答不出话来，只好支支吾吾地说：“那都是我在路上听人家说的。”

Mao Kong could not answer and stammered, “It was heard from others on the way.”

艾子听了以后，回头对身后的学生们说：“你们可不要像他那样‘道听途说’啊！”

Then Ai Zi turned back to his students and said, “You should not take hearsay as true like Mao Kong!”

196

数典忘祖

Forget one's origins

出自 《左传·昭公十五年》。

释义 忘掉自己本来的情况或事物的本源。

春秋时期，晋国派荀跞和籍谈去周天子那里参加穆后的葬礼。葬礼结束后，

In the Spring and Autumn Period, the emperor of Jin dispatched Xun Li and Ji Tan to Zhou State for attending the funeral ceremony

周天子设宴招待诸侯国的使者，把鲁国进贡的壶作为酒杯。他对荀跞说：“诸侯每年都会进贡一些物品给王室，为什么唯独晋国什么都没有呢？”

荀跞拱手示意，请籍谈来回答。籍谈于是站起来，说：“早年诸侯受封的时候，大多接受过王室的宝器，但是我们晋国却没有受到赏赐，所以晋国也就不用进献宝物给王室了。”

周天子听了非常不满，就说：“你怎么忘了呢？晋国的始祖唐叔是周成王的同胞兄弟，怎么可能没分到王室的宝器呢？我记得唐叔接受了文王的鼓和车，武王的皮甲，还有斧钺、香酒、红色的弓以及很多勇士，这些难道不是王室对晋国的赏赐吗？”

接着他又责问籍谈：“我记得你的祖先是负责掌

of the Queen Mu. After the funeral ceremony, the emperor of Zhou held a banquet for envoys of vassals and used the tributary kettles from Lu States as the wine cups, and he said to Xun Li, “The vassals will pay tribute to our imperial court, but why Jin State did not?”

Xun Li cupped his hands and hinted Ji Tan to answer. Then Ji Tan stood up and said, “In the early years of ennobling vassals, most of countries received treasures from the imperial court except for Jin State, so we don’t have to pay tribute to the imperial court.”

The emperor of Zhou was very unsatisfied and said, “How could you forget? Tang Shu was the ancestor of Jin as well the full brother of the Emperor Cheng of Zhou, how could he not receive treasures from the imperial court? I remember Tang Shu received drums and carts of the Duke Wen, the leather armour of the Duke Wu as well axe-shaped weapons, aromatic wine, red bows and many warriors, aren’t those rewards from the imperial courts?”

Then he blamed Ji Tan, “I remember your ancestor was the official responsible for

管国家典籍的官员，你身为他的后人，怎么能忘记这些史事呢？”

籍谈无言以对。等他们离开后，周天子对大臣说：“这个人只会列举一堆典故来说事，反而将自己祖先掌管的典籍中记载的事情给忘了，他的子孙一定不会有出息！”

governing historical records, as his descendant, how could you forget the historical events?”

Ji Tan had nothing to say. As they left, the emperor of Zhou said to the ministers, “That person can only listed lots of historical stories but forgot the things in the historical records which wer managed by his ancestors, and his off-springs will not have good prospects!”

197

滥竽充数

Pretend to be an expert

出自 《韩非子·内储说上》。

释义 指没有真才实学的人混在行家里充数。

战国时期，齐宣王非常喜欢听人吹竽，他到处搜

In the Warring States Period, the Emperor Xuan of Qi extremely liked to

罗擅长吹竽的乐手，组成了一支三百人的吹竽乐队。其中有一个南郭先生，他本来不会吹竽，但是听说齐宣王有这种嗜好，就一心想混进乐队，便设法求见齐宣王，吹嘘自己是一名了不起的乐师，宣王一高兴，就把他编入了吹竽的乐师班里。于是，每当乐队给齐宣王吹奏的时候，这位南郭先生就混在队伍里，学着别人的样子，摇头晃脑，装模做样地在那儿凑数。由于是几百人在一起合奏，齐宣王也听不出来什么。就这样，南郭先生混了好几年，没有露出一丝破绽，和别的乐工一样享受着优厚的待遇。

hear people playing the Yu, which is a wind instrument. He gathered musicians good at playing the Yu and made up a Yu band of three hundred people. There was a person named Nan Guo, who could not play the Yu at all, but as he heard of the hobby of the emperor, he intended to sneak into the Yu band. Then he begged for an interview with the emperor and boasted that he was an excellent musician, the emperor was very happy and allow him to join in the Yu band. Therefore, each time when the Yu band played for the emperor, Nan Guo wagged his head like other musicians and pretended to play the Yu. Because three hundred musicians played the Yu together, the emperor could not find anything strange. Thus, Nan Guo enjoyed the generous treatment as the other musicians for several years without any flaws.

后来，齐宣王死了，他的儿子齐湣王继位。齐湣王同样爱听吹竽，不过他不喜欢听合奏，而是让乐师们一个个地单独吹给他听。

Afterwards, the Emperor Xuan of Qi passed away. And his son, the Emperor Min of Qi assumed the throne. The Emperor Min of Qi also liked to hear people play the Yu, but he liked solo instead of ensemble.

南郭先生听到这个消息后，吓得浑身冒汗，趁着齐湣王还没叫他演奏，就赶紧溜走了。

After hearing this news, Nan Guo was frightened to sweat all over the body, so before the Emperor Min of Qi asked him to play, he hurried to flee away.

198

墨守成规

Stick in the mud

出自 明·黄宗羲《钱退山诗文序》。

释义 思想保守，守着老规矩不肯改变。

战国时期，有一次楚国要攻打宋国，于是特地请工匠鲁班帮着设计制造了一种

In the Warring States Period, once Chu State decided to attack Song State, so the emperor asked carpenter Lu Ban to design

云梯，准备攻城之用。当时墨子正在齐国，得到这个消息，急忙赶到楚国去劝阻。他一直走了十天十夜，一到楚国的郢都，立刻找到鲁班一同去见楚王。

scaling ladders for the battle. At that time, Mo Zi was in Qi State and hurried to Chu State for persuasion upon this news. He continuously walked for ten days and ten nights to the capital Ying of Chu State and immediately asked Lu Ban to meet the emperor of Chu together.

墨子竭力劝说楚王，希望他不要攻打宋国。楚王舍不得放弃新造的攻城器械，就提出来让墨子与鲁班做一个攻防演习，想试试它在实战中的威力。

Mo Zi strongly persuaded the emperor of Chu not to attack Song State. The emperor of Chu did not want to give up the newly-deigned attacking appliance, so he asked Mo Zi and Lu Ban to prepare a war game to test the effects in the battle.

墨子说："好，咱们就当场试试吧。"说完，他解下衣带，围作城墙，用木片作为武器，和鲁班分别代表攻守两方进行演示。鲁班多次使用不同的方法攻城，都被墨子挡住了。鲁班攻城的方法已经使完了，而墨子守城的计策还绰绰有余。

Mo Zi agreed and said, "Let us try now." He loosened clothes belt and used it as walls, and he used wood pieces as weapons, then began to play a war game with Lu Ban. Lu Ban tried many methods, but was blocked by Mo Zi. As Lu Ban used up attacking methods, Mo Zi still had enough means for defence.

鲁班还不肯认输，说："我有办法对付你，但是我不说。"

Lu Ban was not willing to acknowledge defeat and said, "I have means to deal with you, but I don't say."

墨子说："我知道你

Mo Zi said, "I know your means towards

要怎样对付我，但是我也不说。”

me, but I don’t say, neither.”

楚王听不懂，问墨子是什么意思。墨子说：“鲁班是想杀害我。他以为杀了我，就没有人帮宋国守城了。可是他哪里知道，我早已经让三百名门徒守在那里等着你们去进攻了。”

The Emperor of Chu did not understand and asked Mo Zi the meaning, and Mo Zi said, “Lu Ban wanted to kill me, because he thought there would be no defence if I died. But he didn’t know I have arranged three hundred disciples to wait for his attack already.”

楚王眼看没有办法取胜，便说：“好，我决定不攻打宋国了。”

The Emperor of Chu found it impossible to win and said, “I decide to give up attacking Song State.”

因为墨子善守，后来人们就把墨子守城的规则称为“墨守成规”。

Because Mo Zi was good at defending, people addressed the defending means of Mo Zi as “stick in the mud”.

199

蝗臂当车

A mantis trying to stop a chariot

出自 《庄子·人间世》。

释义 做力量达不到的事情，必然失败。

春秋时期，鲁国有个贤人名叫颜阖，被卫灵公请去当太子蒯聩的老师。颜阖

In the Spring and Autumn Period, there was a person named Yan He, who was appointed to be the master of the Prince Kuai

听说蒯聩仗着父亲是一国之君，整天作威作福，蛮不讲理，感到教育这样一个学生十分困难，不知如何是好。

Kui. Yan He heard that Kuai Gui behaved as a tyrant in arrogance by the power of his emperor father, so he felt difficult to teach such a student and didn't know how to do.

于是，颜阖一到卫国，就先去拜访卫国的大夫蘧伯玉，向他请教如何才能教好蒯聩。蘧伯玉也是当时有名的贤人，从小就聪明过人，饱读经书，能言善辩。他与孔子是一生的挚友，在孔子周游列国的十四年里，有十年在卫国，其中两次住在蘧伯玉家，前后达九年。

Therefore, Yan He went to visit the minister Qu Boyu of Wei and consulted him how to teach Kuai Kui. Qu Boyu was a famous wise person at that time, and he was excellent, well-read and eloquent since young. Qu Boyu was also the life-time bosom friend of Confucius. During the fourteen years of Confucius travelling to various countries, he stayed in Wei for ten years and in the home of Qu Boyu twice and nine years totally.

针对颜阖的疑惑，伯玉这样回答说："颜阖先生，您先来询问情况是对的，您想教好太子确实很难办到啊。"

Upon the questions of Yan He, Qu Boyu answered, "It is right for you to consult, because it is really difficult to teach the prince well."

接下来，他进一步分析说："我举一个例子说吧！螳螂自不量力，自己跑到马路上来，举起双臂来阻挡前进的车轮，结果是可想而知的。尽管它自己认为这种举

Afterwards, Qu Boyu analyzed "Let us take an example. A mantis overestimated its strength and rushed to the road, then he lifted his front legs to block ongoing wheels, it is easy to know the result. Although the mantis thought itself as brave, it was really meaningless. You

动很勇敢，但是确实没有意义啊。颜阖先生，您的心意是好的，但您这样做就像螳臂当车一样，必须要小心慎重。有些事情不是您一个人能解决的，您还是好自为之吧！”

have good intentions, but what you do is just a mantis holding front legs to block wheels, you must be extremely cautious and care about yourself!”

200

覆水难收

Cry over spilt milk

出自 宋·王桃《野客丛书》。

释义 事情已成定局，无法挽回。

姜尚，字子牙，人称姜太公，曾在商朝当过官，因为不满纣王的残暴统治，

Jiang Shang with the style name as Ziya, and people address him as Master Jiang, who was an official in Shang Dynasty and quit

弃官而去。后来他宰过牛，卖过酒，但都因为不会做买卖，亏了本，于是来到陕西渭水边一个比较偏僻的地方隐居了起来。从此，他每天都会到水边来钓鱼，以等待贤明的君主来寻访。

his post due to dissatisfaction on the cruel governance of the Emperor Zhou. Afterwards, he did some jobs such as slaughtering bulls and selling wine, but suffered a deficit because he was not good at business. Therefore, Master Jiang went to a desolate place beside the River Wei of Shaan Xi and lived in seclusion. Then he went to the riverside for fishing, in order to wait for the visit of a wise emperor.

由于姜尚整天钓鱼，没有收入，家里的生计成了问题。妻子马氏嫌他穷，没有出息，不愿意再和他共同生活，要离开他。姜尚一再劝说她不要离开，并且说有朝一日他一定会得到富贵。但马氏认为他是在说空话，无论如何也不相信。姜尚无可奈何，只好由她离去。

Because Master Jiang was fishing all day without any income, he led a poor life, and his wife Ma disliked him and intended to leave him. Master Jiang repeatedly persuaded his wife that he would be rich and honorable one day, but his wife Ma thought he was boasting, and finally she left.

后来，周文王到渭水北岸去打猎，见到正在钓鱼的姜尚，经过一番谈话，了解到他是一个精通兵法的能人，就请姜尚一起回宫，让他做了自己的国相。

Afterwards, the Emperor Wen of Zhou went to the north shore of the River Wei for hunting and saw Master Jiang was fishing. After communication, the Emperor Wen of Zhou understood Master Jiang was a capable person with excellence in military strategy, so he invited Master Jiang to the imperial court and appointed him as the Prime Minister.

后来，姜尚帮助周武王联合诸侯消灭商朝，建立了西周王朝。这时，马氏见他又富贵又有地位，很后悔当初离开了他，便找到姜尚请求与他恢复夫妻关系。

Afterwards, Master Jiang helped the Emperor Wu of Zhou to exterminate Shang Dynasty in union with vassals, and finally established the Western Zhou Dynasty. At this time, his wife Ma knew Master Jiang was rich and honorable, so she regretted to leave and requested Master Jiang to recover their spousal relationship.

姜尚没有吭声，只是取来一壶水，倒在地上，让马氏把水收起来。马氏赶紧趴在地上去取水，但只能收到一些泥浆。于是姜尚对她说："你已离我而去，我们已经不可能复合了。这就好比倒在地上的水，难以再收回来了！"

Master Jiang said nothing and only took a kettle of water and spilt it on the ground, and he asked his wife Ma to collect the water. Ma immediately lied on the ground to collect the water, but only some mud was collected. Then Master Jiang said to her, "Since you have left me, we can not be together again, just like it is impossible to collect the spilt water!"